Dark Dimensions

Dark Dimensions

A Celebration of the Occult

EDITED BY *Colin Wilson*

WITH *Christmas Humphreys, Kit Pedler, Oliver Marlow Wilkinson, Pat Silver and Jesse Lasky Jr., Peter Tompkins*

Everest House Publishers   New York

Contents

Introduction

On a February morning in 1967, a Cambridge architect named Derek Manning came down to breakfast and found a silver tankard on the living-room floor; it had fallen from a shelf. His first thought was that a burglar had broken in, but a check of the house revealed that nothing was missing. He questioned the three children—eight-year-old Rosalind, eleven-year-old Matthew and seven-year-old Andrew: none of them knew anything about it. Four days later, the tankard was again found on the floor; this time, Derek Manning suspected some kind of practical joke. He decided to try to catch the culprit by surrounding the tankard with a ring of talcum powder, which would retain fingermarks of anyone who tried to move it in the dark; the next day the tankard was again on the floor, and the powder was undisturbed. Furthermore, various other items of crockery had been moved around in the night. The only explanation that seemed to fit was that the culprit was a ghost. Reluctantly, but feeling it was worth trying, Mr. Manning contacted a Cambridge don, Dr. A. R. G. Owen, who had investigated such matters. Owen studied the evidence, and came to the conclusion that Derek Manning had feared. The disturbances showed all the signs of "poltergeist" activity. A poltergeist is a "noisy ghost" that enjoys creating disturbances—like ringing bells and moving furniture. Modern psychical research has reached the conclusion that the "ghost" is not really a disembodied spirit, but some kind of strange subconscious energy, usually emanating from a disturbed child or adolescent. In such cases, the culprit is usually unaware that he or she is to blame.

By a process of elimination, Dr. Owen concluded that Matthew was the unconscious force behind the poltergeist. Fortunately the manifestations were fairly harmless. And in a few months, they ceased—as poltergeist activities usually do. But in this case they resumed again, four years later, on a larger scale. Matthew's bed would rise into the air and shake; heavy furniture was moved around. The house shuddered with bangs and thumps. Matthew was sent away to school as a boarder; there the disturbances continued so that the headmaster twice requested his removal—although he relented on both occasions.

And at this point, Matthew stumbled on the trick of controlling these strange forces. He tried sitting with a pencil resting gently on a sheet of paper. His hand began to move of its own accord, writing out a message which professed to be from a man who lived in the eighteenth century. After this bout of automatic writing, no poltergeist disturbances occurred for a couple of days. Henceforth, Matthew discovered that the simplest way of controlling the nuisance was to allow his hand to write as it felt inclined. Soon it was not only writing but drawing. Moreover, these drawings were of extraordinary talent, some in the style of Picasso, Dürer, Aubrey Beardsley, even Beatrix Potter. And sometimes there were strange inscriptions in foreign languages—Latin, Saxon, French and Arabic.

Matthew Manning has become one of the most talented

and extraordinary of modern psychics. After watching Uri Geller on television, he discovered that he could instantly duplicate the Israeli's spoon-bending feats; in fact, Matthew even caused spoons to bend without touching them. One of the "entities" who communicates through the medium of automatic script is a doctor, who seems to be able to make startlingly accurate medical diagnoses of visitors at a glance, and to prescribe remedies. My own first sight of Matthew was when he appeared on a television program, and accurately diagnosed ailments of various members of the audience— writing out prescriptions in a hand unlike his own.

Matthew Manning is an example of a type of psychic whose gifts seem to be completely spontaneous. He is a "man of mystery" in the sense that neither he nor anyone else has any idea of the nature of the forces at work in him. No one can even say with any confidence whether various "spirits" really make contact through him, or whether they are some dream-like manifestation of his own subconscious mind. The only thing of which I—and the many scientists who have studied him—can be certain is that he is quite genuine.

In the long and extraordinary history of psychical phenomena, there have been many individuals like Matthew Manning. In the days before recorded history, they were *shamans* or witch doctors. They were chosen because of their ability to communicate with spirits, and their powers were carefully nurtured; it was their task to diagnose and prescribe for sickness, and to foretell where the hunters of the tribe would find game. In the days when Britain still had an empire, it was her custom to scoff at the superstition of primitive tribes who believed in the powers of their witch doctor. Modern students of psychical research are less complacent. One day in 1934, a gambler walked into the office of a young university instructor named Rhine and explained that he could *make* the dice fall as he wanted. All gamblers knew, he said, that when they were in the right mood, they couldn't lose. And his demonstrations were so convincing that Rhine used the technique as the basis of a famous series of experiments at Duke University which made the word *parapsychology* respectable. The amusing thing is that parapsychology is another name for what the ancients called magic. In fact, our ancestors of a few centuries ago would have classified the gambler's knack with the dice as black magic or witchcraft.

Still, it would be an oversimplification to assume that all the great magicians of the past were simply natural psychics, like Matthew Manning and Uri Geller. Some of them were sadly deficient in psychic or magical ability, like the Elizabethan magician John Dee, or the Elizabethan astrologer Simon Forman. (It could even be true of one of the most famous names in the history of magic, Cornelius Agrippa, whose ability to conjure up demons sounds so nonsensical that it is probably pure invention.) Such men were basically scientists born into a pre-scientific age, men possessed of the same thirst for knowledge that drove Leonardo and Einstein and H. G. Wells.

Now this sounds, admittedly, like an admission that most of them were wasting their time. This is not so, and it is important to understand why it is not so. Albertus Magnus, Agrippa, Paracelsus, Dee and the rest, were fundamentally interested in the secrets of life. They took it for granted that man had once been a far more god-like being, and that he had reached his present lowly estate as a result of a fall. Yet in the midst of his suffering and self-disgust, he dreams of a golden age, a time when man will have mastered the secret of triumph over pain and death. Paracelsus found himself surrounded by disease and poverty; therefore it was self-evident that what mankind really needed was the Elixir of Life—for securing immortality—and the Philosopher's Stone—for turning base metals into gold. Modern students of alchemy insist that a few alchemists *did* succeed in turning lead into gold, but they are willing to concede that nobody discovered the Elixir of Life. So skeptics may feel justified in regarding the magicians as dupes or ignoramuses. They forget that modern science is no nearer solving that basic question: how can man become a little more god-like? That, on the contrary, by concentrating on purely physical questions, science has degraded man and brought him closer to self-destruction.

It is worth getting this matter clear before proceeding.

Discouragement is one of the commonest and deadliest ailments in human life. Everybody has experienced this—waking up on a rainy Monday morning, confronting the prospect of a week of unrelieved drudgery. And everyone knows that a boring job ceases to be boring if you have something exciting to look forward to. Human beings are at their best when galvanized by a sense of meaning. On the other hand, when people are deprived of meaning for long periods, subjected to lives in which there is nothing to look forward to—for example, in prisons—they seem to lose the will to live. Prison can make a man look ten years older in a couple of years. The sense of meaninglessness causes a leakage of inner pressure, like a tire with a flat, and he slowly deflates. The result is exactly like driving a tire when it is flat: it wears out far more quickly. (All tire manufacturers advise: "Keep inflated hard for minimum wear and tear.") Clearly, a sense of purpose, of something to look forward to, is of vital importance for human beings.

Yet here we are, stuck in an existence that seems to be a slow, perpetual drift towards death. We all have to confront a great many rainy Monday mornings. And even in the affluent societies of the West, millions of men stand at machines for eight hours a day, virtually wasting a third of their adult lives. There was a time when men were comforted every Sunday by the prospect of an eternity of bliss; but I doubt whether this incentive counts for much among modern factory workers. There must be countless millions of middle aged men and women who feel that life is really something of a damp squib:

> Birth, copulation and death
> Birth, copulation and death
> That's all the facts when you get to brass tacks
> Birth, copulation and death.

The modern world has improved the condition of the worker with television sets and second-hand cars. But the scientists who provided these comforts are also responsible for the overall feeling of futility. Biologists explain that the universe knows nothing of purpose; everything has come about by chance. Physicists tell us that the universe is exploding, and that the world will eventually freeze to death unless it falls down a Black Hole first. Zoologists declare that a man is a born killer who will end by wrecking the civilization he spent so long in building.

Now the great magicians were aware of the misery of human existence. But they were also inspired by a strange hope. Perhaps man really possesses powers of which he is unaware? Perhaps he might not be so far from discovering the Elixir of Life and the Philosopher's Stone? Perhaps there are even human beings who have discovered these secrets, and who have deliberately segregated themselves from this race of madmen and egoists? Men have always been fascinated by such legends. Shelley wrote in *Hellas* about an old Jewish caballist who lives "in a sea cavern 'mid the Demonesi."

> The sage, in truth, by dreadful abstinence,
> And conquering penance of the mutinous flesh,
> Deep contemplation and unwearied study,
> In years outstreched beyond the date of man,
> May have attained to sovereignty and science
> Over those strong and secret things and thoughts
> Which others fear and know not . . .

And W. B. Yeats, quoting these lines, adds that when in Dublin, he had been attracted to the Theosophists—the followers of Madame Blavatsky—because they had insisted on the real existence of the old Jew and his like. He was talking about Madame Blavatsky's secret Tibetan Masters.

Obviously, Shelley's Ahasuerus is a myth; so, probably, are Madame Blavatsky's Masters (although Christmas Humphreys would not agree). Yet the basic idea they represent is of inestimable importance. It is the notion that human beings need not be permanent losers. In its magical sense, the Philosopher's Stone and the Elixir of Life may be a myth. Yet how can science be confident that such ancient symbols have no meaning for modern man? We know, beyond all shadow of doubt, that hopelessness and discouragement make human beings accident-prone and illness-prone. We know that longevity is often related to a strong sense of purpose—Winston Churchill lived to be ninety in spite of drinking brandy for breakfast and smoking endless cigars. Bernard Shaw may have been unduly optimistic when he suggested that human life could easily be lengthened to three hundred years, but his general principle is obviously correct. In *Men of Mathematics*, E. T. Bell points out that mathematicians, as a species, are exceptionally long-lived; many of them reach their mid-eighties with no trouble at all. A recent survey revealed that among scientists listed in *Who's Who*, Nobel Prize winners tend to live longer than others—although scientists as a group are longer-lived than most. Of course, it may be that the qualities of vitality that make a nobel Prize winner predispose him to live longer. It is equally possible that the fact of being a famous scientist—having a public sense of purpose, as it were—makes men live longer, just as you tend to stay awake later when you are absorbed in an interesting book. The same survey made the remarkable discovery that job satisfaction was an important element in health. Overworked doctors tended to be healthier than underworked men in less interesting professions—say a car worker whose job is to tighten ten thousand nuts a day. Kamiya's discovery of bio-feedback emphasizes the same point. Men who could study their brain waves on a television screen quickly learned to control their blood pressure and heartbeat.

You may reply that there is all the difference in the world between controlling your own heartbeat by some form of self-hypnosis and controlling the natural world around us by means of magic. Which seems unanswerable—until you remember the poltergeist. In hundreds of recorded cases, doors have opened and closed, bells have rung, objects have flown through the air. Just to demonstrate their versatility, poltergeists have even caused objects to penetrate solid matter. Dr. Hans Bender mentions a case in which water somehow escaped from pipes—where there was no possibility of a leak—to form pools on the floor. In a case in Croydon in England, a picture fell from its frame—without breaking the glass at the front of the picture or the sealed cardboard at the back.

Unless hundreds of well-authenticated cases are frauds, there can be only one possible conclusion: that the human mind is capable of directing some unknown form of energy, which can act in an apparently purposive manner. Electro-encephalograph tests on Matthew Manning have shown that he produces a high level of a brainwave called theta rhythms when he is bending a spoon or deflecting a compass needle without touching it. Significantly enough, theta rhythms are also associated with epilepsy and with criminals. People with criminal tendencies display sharp bursts of theta rhythms when they are frustrated or angry. And in most cases of spon-taneous poltergeist activity, a frustrated or disturbed adoles-cent has been found to be at the back of the manifestations. Psychics like Matthew Manning and Uri Geller have appar-ently learned to control these strange, violent energies, to some extent.

Then there is the curious activity known as dowsing. Just over a year ago, someone placed a V-shaped whalebone rod in my hands, and as I walked between two standing stones, it twisted violently upwards; after an afternoon of repeating the experiment, I was finally convinced that I could actually dowse. (I have no idea of what force the rod is responding to—presumably some kind of magnetic force in the stones or in the ground.) Since then I have persuaded at least a dozen skeptical friends to hold the rod and try it near standing stones, or simply over a hidden waterpipe in our kitchen; 90 percent of them were able to do it.

Odder still, if you take a short pendulum—a wooden bead on a short piece of cotton—and hold it above your hand, it will soon begin to make a circular motion; for most people, it revolves clockwise over the right hand and anticlockwise over the left. I have no great ability with the pendulum, but I know dowsers who find it far more sensitive than the divining rod. The strangest thing about it is that the pendulum seems to be able to answer questions. You start off by asking: "What is your sign for yes?," then "What is your sign for no?" It may revolve or oscillate in various ways in answer to the questions. And you can then ask it any question that can be answered by yes or no—"Will Aunt Florence come to dinner next Wednesday?" Mr. Leonard Locker, a chief electrical engineer for south-western England, found that his pendulum, suspended over a map showing the route of an underground cable, could pinpoint faults in the cable. Stranger still, it could *predict* when a fault would occur. (Pendulums can also answer "number" questions; the user makes an arbitrary decision of how many days—or weeks or whatever—are represented by a single revolution, then simply counts the revolutions.)

All of which, of course, sounds patently absurd. Yet dowsers all over the world not only take it for granted that it works, but make practical use of it every day of their lives. I do not know why it works. But then, neither do I understand why so many astrologers can tell a man's date of birth merely by looking at him. They insist that, to a trained eye, a Cancer is as different from an Aquarius as an Australian aborigine is from a Chinaman. I am also basically skeptical enough to be convinced that much of this is probably self-deception and auto-suggestion. Yet since I have been looking at the evidence for such matters, I have come to the conclusion that there are simply many laws of the universe that science does not even suspect. And there are certain energies that science does not yet understand. After reading Paracelsus and Cornelius Agrippa, I am not sure how far they understood them either. But at least, they took it for granted that they existed, and *tried* to understand.

Let me, without apology, offer an outline of my own theory of "strange powers."

Man, as an individual species, is about three million years old, and his remoter ancestors are hundreds of millions of years older still. Animals seem to be much more in tune with nature than we are. I am not now referring to their "sixth sense," but simply to their instinctive knowledge of the seasons, and their instinct for survival. Robert Ardrey has written about a species of finch that has been on the Galapagos Islands for hundreds of generations—enough to sub-divide into fourteen species. On the Galapagos, there are no predatory hawks. Yet when a naturalist brought a few of the finches to California, the baby fledglings instantly reacted with alarm to the sight of hawks. Such is the memory of that vast computer we call instinct.

Civilization is a fairly recent acquisition. If you think of man's three-million-year evolution as a single day, then he has only been living in cities since three minutes to midnight. (If you take into account man's ape-like forebears, it is more like three seconds to midnight.) Like the finches, we must possess vast stores of instinctive knowledge that we have never had to use.

On the other hand, man is tied hand and foot by habit. An enormous part of our living is automatic. I breathe automatically, digest automatically, sleep automatically; I have even taught myself to read automatically and drive a car automatically. The possession of these habits certainly simplifies my existence. But they also narrow it. Take a simple example: when I have finished my day's writing—around five in the afternoon—I often soak in a hot bath, then pour myself a glass of wine and watch the news on TV. If something interrupts that routine and prevents me from taking a bath, then I have to wait until the next day. I say "have to"; by this I mean that if I watch the news and *then* take a bath, I feel uncomfortable, for this is the time when I usually switch off the news and play some records. When I first came to live in this house, nearly twenty years ago, I felt more free; I would cheerfully take a bath at midnight and listen to music at ten in the morning. Now this would strike me as a kind of debauchery. Habit has not only narrowed my freedom of choice; it has narrowed my consciousness.

The same thing has happened to the race in general since we became city-dwellers. We have become far more efficient at doing the things we want to do—"getting and spending," as Wordsworth says—but we have forgotten the strange, fluid freedom of our uncivilized past. We have forgotten all kinds of things that we knew instinctively in those days. For example, there seems to be a reasonable certainty that the homing instinct of birds and animals is based—at least in part—on some kind of sensitivity to the magnetic fields of the earth. There is a modern school of thought that certain old straight tracks across country—they call them "leys"—follow these lines of force, and that our ancestors erected ancient stones to mark these lines and the places where they crossed or converged. If they are right, then I suspect that my dowsing rod was responding to this magnetic force in the earth near the standing stones. In short, although my conscious self has long forgotten about the earth force, some unconscious part of me still knows all about it, like the finch's response to a hawk.

Moreover, there are other parts of me that know about other forces. Most ancient peoples are firmly convinced of the reality of the "evil eye"—of the power of ill-disposed persons to direct a beam of malevolent force towards people they dislike. Again, we dismiss this as nonsense. Yet it fits in with what we have been saying about the theta rhythms that seem to be common to violent criminals and to poltergeist activity. If someone can unconsciously cause objects to fly through the air, then it seems to me likely that they could, if they tried, "put the hex" on someone they hated. Of course, this could also be unconscious. The writer John Cowper Powys noticed that whenever he felt furious with someone, misfortune usually befell the object of his irritation; being basically a gentle man, he was horrified, and ended in a state of "neurotic benevolence." He could be compared to a very strong man who smashes things and hurts people unless he takes great care to control his strength. I suspect that this kind of power is probably common to writers and poets—to anyone who is accustomed to using the imagination and controlling creative energies. And there are probably many people who are born with such power. I spoke of it once to a girl I knew, and she told me seriously that she had always possessed it; on one occasion, she said, she had cursed a boyfriend who left her for another woman, and within a week or two he had been found hanged. The girl in question was not particularly creative, as far as I know, but she was a rather unhappy, tense girl, who struck me as being full of great nervous force. In fact, come to think of it, I suppose she was the type we traditionally think of as a witch. Of course, it is just as likely that she was indulging in a kind of vengeful wishful thinking. Yet I am inclined to believe her.

"Magical thinking" seems to be natural to human beings. At least, it was until about two hundred years ago. We think of Isaac Newton as a scientist; yet his notebooks reveal that he spent an enormous amount of time conducting experiments in alchemy, and almost as much in writing an immense commentary on the Book of Daniel, which he accepted as literally true.

In the nineteenth century, it became a point of honor for scientists to be tough minded, and to reject anything that looked like superstition. Understandably, for they were really fighting a battle against organized religion. We find this hard to understand, for we think of clergymen as harmless characters who run charity bazaars and complain about the emptiness of the churches on television. Yet even today, there are still parts of the world where the priest's word is law, and where a dominant and bad-tempered priest can behave like a combination of Hitler and Stalin without exciting comment or provoking rebellion. A century ago, the church had real power—the same kind of power as the army or the government. And this power was based on the fact that 99 percent of the population implicitly believed every word in the Bible, and spent much of their time listening to solemn pronouncements from bishops and priests. Anthropologists were already writing about the bizarre customs and beliefs of primitive tribes; no intelligent person could have any difficulty recognizing the parallel with modern Christianity. So understandably, it irked scientists like T. H. Huxley to see feebleminded idiots in clerical collars rising up in public and accusing Darwin of infidelism. It would only have shocked and alienated the public to declare frankly that Christianity has no more claim to ultimate truth than the religions of ancient Egypt or Greece or Rome—or modern Zululand, for that matter. The scientists played their cards far more subtly, emphasizing again and again that no sensible man should believe anything unless it strikes him as logical and rational. They appeared to be explaining the rules of scientific thought; in fact, they were planting mines under the walls of the churches.

Science won the battle, but it paid a huge price. It committed itself to opposing everything the church stood for: not just superstition and sloppy thinking, but the belief in purpose, meaning and spiritual evolution. And, most disastrous of all, optimism.

And this, I think, explains the occult revival that began in the early 1960s. Scientists are inclined to dismiss it as an outburst of hysteria and irrationalism; they classify occultists with the Jesus freaks of California, and—even less flatteringly—with the Nazis. Yet no one who has actually tried reading the Kabbalah, or the original alchemical texts, or even modern studies of extra-sensory perception, can accept this for a moment. They require very nearly as much intellectual effort as a book on quantum mechanics. It is true that there is a great mass of popular occult literature, mostly in paperback, that is aimed at a semi-literate public; but then, there is also a flourishing literature on popular science. It only testifies to a widespread interest in the subject. On a deeper level, the occult revival is a reaction against the worst absurdities of modern science, its insistence that the universe is meaningless and purposeless, that evolution is a matter of chance, that man must be judged purely as an animal—or, worse still, as a bundle of mechanical reflexes. For the flat truth is that science has no right whatever to pronounce on such matters; it knows no more about them than any clergyman does. The objective truth is that no one knows. Einstein believed the universe to be purposeful; Professor Jacques Monod is equally convinced that it is purposeless. You may take either side with the certainty that neither has had the last word.

On the other hand, *if* paranormal research can prove the existence of telepathy, extrasensory perception, precognition, poltergeists and out-of-the-body experiences, it will have taken a long step towards proving some of the basic propositions of religion. And no one who has looked into the subject can doubt that it has already done a great deal towards establishing the reality of these phenomena.

All of which leads me to feel that the occult revival is not so much revival of human gullibility as of human optimism.

As to the present book, it may be regarded as a straightforward introduction to some of the more puzzling phenomena. It makes no attempt to romanticize the "men of mystery." If anything, it goes out of its way to avoid an obviously "popular" approach. The article on Aleister Crowley is by a man who knew him and disliked him. The article on Dashwood contains a great deal of new—and previously unpublished—research. Christmas Humphreys' piece on Madame Blavatsky differs from most writings about her in that he is totally convinced of her genuineness (which is more than I personally can say). The chapter on Uri Geller is written by a couple who have had a chance to study the operation of his strange powers at first hand.

The article on Tesla by Dr. Kit Pedler deserves a word to itself. Probably more than any other article in this book, it is obviously a labor of love. Tesla was not a magician or psychic, but a scientist of genius, and the mystery lies in the nature of his genius. Most great scientists—like Newton and Einstein—have been obsessive plodders, patiently hunting down their quarry over years of hard work. Tesla's genius was a kind of explosion of intuitive brilliance, and it raises precisely the same kind of problem we encounter in the case of "calculating prodigies."

Such prodigies are usually children of no special talent, apart from their freakish ability. Ten-year-old Vito Magiamele, son of a Silician shepherd, was asked to calculate the tenth root of 282,475,249 (i.e. a number that, when multiplied by itself ten times, would give the above figure). After a few moments of thought he replied: "Seven." I have just tried doing the problem the other way around, just to make sure that seven to the power of ten really equals the above number; it took me nearly five minutes even with a sheet of paper.

Now the weird thing is that such prodigies usually lose their powers in their teens and become "normal." Or rather, from the mathematical point of view, sub-normal. Which raises baffling implications. Not just where the power came from in the first place, but where it *went to.* Obviously, we don't *need* to calculate such huge figures to stay alive, which would seem to explain why we don't all have this ability. But why should the perfectly ordinary son of an Italian peasant be born with it? Above all, *what happened* when it vanished? Did some ancestral mechanism in his brain say: "You don't need this—get back to normal"?

Tesla was a prodigy who did *not* lose his powers as he grew older. And he raises again the basic question about "men of mystery." Do we all possess such powers? Is there some part of our evolutionary mechanism that suppresses them because we don't need them? Uri Geller and Matthew Manning can read minds and bend spoons by stroking them; Father Joseph of Copertino had the curious habit of flying through the air; Daniel Dunglass Home could wash his face in hot coals and make heavy tables levitate; Madame Blavatsky could make a room resound with rapping noises or the sound of bells by merely raising her finger. Are such men and women freaks? Or do they offer us a glimpse of what we might all become—indeed, of what we already *are*?

This present book may not answer that question; but it will offer you a chance to form your own opinion.

Rasputin

When the news of Rasputin's murder swept through Petrograd in early January 1917, there was universal rejoicing; people sang and cheered in the streets. He was the most hated man in Russia. Why? What had he done to deserve such loathing? If we wish to be historically accurate, the answer must be: nothing. But the majority of the Russian people believed that he was the Tsar's evil genius—and probably the Tsarina's lover. His photographs lent color to the story—the pale face, the piercing eyes, the matted beard. During his lifetime, many people believed him to be a black magician. After his death, he became known as "the mad monk" and "the Holy Devil." Nowadays there are few people who know the true story of Rasputin, and fewer still who want to know it. The legends of the evil debauchee are more interesting.

Yet the strange, complex reality behind the legend is far

more fascinating than the stories of the alcoholic sex maniac that still pass for history. And in order to understand it, we must go back to the year 1894, the year of the coronation of Nicholas II, the last Tsar of Russia.

For more than three centuries—since the time of Queen Elizabeth—Russia had been tormented by a succession of tyrants and despots, beginning with the legendary sadist, Ivan the Terrible, who once spent five weeks supervising the torture of sixty thousand people. In the nineteenth century, the Russian people began to hit back with bombs and bullets. Police chiefs and government ministers were assassinated; in 1881, the Tsar Alexander II was blown up with a bomb made of nitroglycerine in a glass globe. In 1888, there was a determined attempt to kill his successor when the imperial train was blown off the rails (although some historians still believe this was due to rotten sleepers). The future Tsar Nicholas was among those who escaped.

And unfortunately, Nicholas was the last man to hold together the disintegrating Russian nation. He had immense charm and kindness; but he simply wasn't tough enough. He had the Russian equivalent of the public-schoolboy mentality. When faced with crisis, he firmly made up his mind— then changed it.

This charming, weak character made the worst possible choice for a wife, Queen Victoria's granddaughter, Princess Alix of Hesse-Darmstadt, a beautiful, shy, dreamy girl without a single one of the qualities that would have made a good queen. Instead of dominating her court, as her great predecessor Catherine had done, she fled from it, and formed her own little clique. There is no surer way of getting yourself hated. The courtiers sneeringly called her "the German," and hinted that her sympathies lay with Bismarck and Kaiser Wilhelm rather than with Russia. It was untrue, but the mud stuck.

The first duty of a Tsarina was to produce an heir to the throne. And here Alix—now Alexandra—encountered her usual awful luck. She produced four daughters, one after the other, and the courtiers winked and made unkind jokes. She then had a hysterical pregnancy when her stomach swelled, and she wore a maternity gown; it proved to be little more than wind. The attitude of dislike began to spread from the courtiers to the ordinary people of Russia.

And it was at this point, according to one account, that Grigory Rasputin enters history. In 1903, the Tsar decided to canonize a holy man called Seraphin, who was generally regarded as a saint in his own city of Sarov, near Nijni Novgorod. The Tsar hoped that the saint would repay the compliment by interceding for the birth of a male heir to the throne. At the canonization ceremony, a ragged, bearded pilgrim was seen to be praying with exceptional devoutness. In fact, he seemed to go into a state of trance or rapture. When he awakened—surrounded by a curious crowd—he prophesied that a male heir to the throne would be born within a year. This man was Rasputin, and news of the prophecy came to the ears of the Tsar.

The prophecy came true; in August 1904, the Tsarina gave birth to a boy called Alexey. Bells rang and cannons roared. But in the palace, rejoicing was short-lived. A scratch on the child's navel began to bleed, and it was still bleeding twenty-four hours later. Doctors confirmed their worst fears; the baby suffered from hemophilia, inherited from his mother's side of the family. His blood lacked the coagulant that causes clotting, so that if he cut himself, he was likely to bleed to death. If he stumbled, the slightest impact caused a bruise, and a bad bruise could lead to internal hemorrhage and high fever.

Later in the year 1903, the *staretz* (or holy man) came to St. Petersburg in his wanderings. Perhaps he was hoping to be introduced to the royal family. If so, he was not disappointed. He had met the saintly John of Cronstadt, the Tsar's confessor, and the Archimandrite Theophan, the Tsarina's spiritual adviser; both were impressed with him. Rasputin's reputation as a holy man came to the ears of the Grand Duchess Militsa, the Tsar's sister-in-law. She and her sister—they were known as the Montenegrins because they were the daughters of the king of Montenegro—were much absorbed in spiritualism and mysticism; Rasputin was invited to their homes. When he left St. Petersburg towards the end of 1903,

Rasputin was already something of a minor celebrity and a friend of royalty.

When he returned eighteen months later, the Grand Duchess Militsa was no longer welcome at court—presumably she had had some kind of disagreement with the Tsarina, for the Tsar himself still visited her home. And it was there, on November 1, 1905, that he met Rasputin, and wrote in his diary: "We have got to know a man of God—Grigory—from the Tobolsk province."

Unfortunately, there are no further entries in the Tsar's journal to enable us to follow the progress of this relationship. All that we know is that within a matter of months—perhaps even weeks—Rasputin had become a regular visitor at the royal palaces, and a close confidant of the Tsar and Tsarina. The reason for his influence was simple: he was able to exercise his healing powers on the young Tsarevitch Alexey.

The story of the first occasion when this happened has become something of a legend, and each writer gives a slightly different account. But, taking them all together, the general outline seems to be as follows. In spite of the vigilance of his bodyguard—an enormous Russian sailor—the boy fell down when playing and bruised himself; within hours he was in a fever. Nothing the doctors could do seemed to have any effect. Finally, in desperation, the Tsar recalled the "man of God" he had met at Militsa's; the Grand Duchess had described him as a healer. A messenger was dispatched. In the early hours of the morning, he located the *staretz* in a gypsy encampment on the outskirts of the city. Fiddlers were playing Hungarian czardas and revelers danced by the light of a bonfire. Among these was Rasputin, half drunk and full of high spirits. As the Tsar's messenger rode into the firelight the music ceased, and the dancing stopped. The man inquired for Rasputin, and stated his business. Rasputin advanced into the center of the circle, fell on his knees, and prayed silently. After a while he looked up and said: "Return to the royal palace, and tell the Tsar that the boy will recover. I will come as soon as I can." By the time the messenger returned, the crisis was over; the fever began to abate the moment Rasputin fell on his knees . . .

This is one version of the story. Another simply has him

entering the bedroom of the feverish boy, praying for a few moments, then sitting on the edge of the bed and telling the Tsarevitch stories about Siberia. Since Alexey was only about eighteen months old at the time, this sounds unlikely.

What *can* be said with certainty is that by the middle of 1906, Rasputin had already become famous—or notorious—in St. Petersburg. When the house of the Prime Minister Stolypin was blown up by a terrorist bomb, and some of his family injured, the Tsar offered him Rasputin's services as a healer. Stolypin had heard strange tales of Rasputin, and declined his help. Five years later, in September 1911, Rasputin was to have a kind of revenge. As Stolypin's carriage drove past him, Rasputin suddenly called out: "Death is after him, Death is driving behind him." The same evening, Stolypin was assassinated at the opera.

Who was this semi-literate peasant who eventually became one of the most powerful men in Russia?

Grigory Yefimovitch Rasputin was born sometime in the 1860s in the small village of Pokrovskoe, near Tobolsk. His father was head man of the village. From an early age, Grigory displayed the power of "second sight." This first attracted attention when a group of peasants were discussing the theft of a horse; Grigory lay ill on a bed in the room. Suddenly he sat up and pointed at one of the men saying: "He is the thief." The man denied it and Grigory's father apologized, explaining that his son was in a fever. But two of the peasants were suspicious; they followed the man home, watched him go into his barn, and lead out the stolen horse. They beat him severely and returned the horse to its owner.

Rasputin's daughter Maria speaks of her father's second sight, and tells how, in St. Petersburg, a woman entered the room with her hands folded in a muff. Rasputin shouted "Drop that!," and struck at the muff; a revolver fell out onto the floor, and the woman had hysterics.

In his early teens Grigory became a wagoner, and soon acquired a reputation as a drinker and womanizer. Then came a sudden change of heart. When he was sixteen he was hired to drive a novice monk to the monastery of Verkhoture.

On the journey—which took several days—they spoke of religion. The result was that Rasputin spent four months in the monastery. This life answered a deep need in his nature; he was gripped by an obscure sense of purpose, and a desire to escape into some more significant form of existence than he could find in a peasant village. He was also fascinated by one of the sects he encountered at Verkhoture: the Khlysty, or flagellants. These men were heretics, and were virtually prisoners—their jailers being the more orthodox monks.

The Khlysty were "enthusiasts." They believed that the flesh is evil, and that only the spirit is good. They also believed that Christ keeps returning to earth to rally the faithful. One of their "Christs," Daniel Phillipov, preached that men should seek persecution and martyrdom as a way to salvation. Sexual relations were forbidden. A man could repudiate his wife, and take a "spiritual wife" from among the sect; but although they were permitted to sleep in the same bed, the relationship had to remain pure.

The Khlysty ritual was designed to produce ecstasy—or hysteria. The celebrants danced around a tub of water which, according to the Khlysty themselves, would begin to boil of its own accord. They chanted hymns and flagellated one another, gradually working themselves into a state in which they could be possessed by the holy spirit. They would shout prophecies, speak in unknown tongues, and finally collapse into an exhausted sleep on the ground. Their enemies insisted that these rituals were actually orgies, ending in general promiscuity, and that the Khlysty custom of spiritual wives was only another excuse for adultery. There could be an element of truth in these accusations—since the members of the sect were only human—but there can be no doubt that Khlysty doctrine was rigidly puritanical. There seems to be no possible ground for the accusation most commonly made against them: that they preached a doctrine of salvation through sin—that the harder you sinned, the more you were likely to be able to repent.

We do not know whether Rasputin ever became a member of the Khlysty; on the whole, it seems doubtful. But he was certainly attracted by them. All religion made a deep appeal to his temperament—the more "enthusiastic" the better. From the time of his first stay at Verkhoture, he felt that a new way of life had been opened to him. It is also important to bear in mind that religion was perhaps Rasputin's *only* escape from the featureless life of a Russian peasant. If he had been brought up in a city, there would have been a dozen other possibilities; he might have developed a passion for literature or music or art or left-wing politics; he might have decided to make a career in the army or the church or even the secret police. But in Pokrovskoe, none of these possibilities were open to him. Yet he was no ordinary man; he possessed unusual vitality; he was undoubtedly a member of the "dominant minority." This explains the drinking and womanizing. Yet he was also too intelligent not to feel fundamentally bored with debauchery. Religion opened up new worlds.

But the chemistry of inner transformation takes a long time. Back in his home village, Rasputin continued to drink, dance and pursue peasant girls. On two occasions he was in trouble with the police; in 1891 he was sentenced to flogging and a short term in jail for leaving the wagon unattended, and allowing thieves an opportunity to steal a bundle of furs.

By that time he had married a peasant girl, who bore him a son. Rasputin adored the child and seemed prepared to settle down. The child died at six months. Rasputin was shattered; he went back to the monastery of Verkhoture, and when he returned home, spent hours reading the scriptures. One day when he was plowing, he had a vision of the virgin. He decided to go on a pilgrimage to Mount Athos, in Greece—a two thousand mile walk. From there he went on to the Holy Land. And when he returned to his wife two years later, unkempt and bearded, he was no longer the village rake; he had acquired a strange nervous force, and a compelling and hypnotic gaze. He constructed an oratory in his backyard and spent hours in prayer. He held prayer meetings in his house after dark. Many of the women of Pokrovskoe became his converts. The village priest, Father Peter, observed all this with increasing annoyance, and finally reported him to the Bishop of Tobolsk, accusing him of being a member of the Khlysty. The Bishop came to Pokrovskoe to investigate, but could find no evidence of heresy; in fact, a policeman who was sent to examine Rasputin became a convert. But for the sake of peace, Rasputin decided that it was again time to take to the road. So he made his way towards St. Petersburg, pausing en route to pray devoutly at Sarov for the birth of a royal heir, and prophesying that the Tsarina would bear a son within the year ...

When Princess Alix became consort of the Tsar of Russia, St. Petersburg was in the grip of an "occult" craze. By that time, Russia's most famous occultist, Madame Blavatsky, was dead—and in any case, she had left Russia thirty years earlier—but there were dozens of mediums, spirit-healers, fortune tellers and miracle workers who claimed equally remarkable powers. In the seven years before she produced an heir to the throne, the Tsarina had had a whole series of quack doctors and healers who undertook to guarantee the birth of a boy. The phantom pregnancy was caused by the ministrations of a French hypnotist called Dr. Philippe; after this failure he was loaded with presents and sent back to France—a welcome change from the bad old days when unsuccessful magicians and soothsayers were executed. A deformed creature named Mitya Koliabin uttered prophecies in a state of ecstasy and caused the Tsarina to have hysterics. The gibberings of an idiot woman called Darya Ossipova were found incomprehensible. The only man who seemed to be able to retain the trust of the royal couple was a Mongolian named Badmaev, who claimed to have studied in Tibet; he was a shrewd man who recognized Rasputin as a useful ally, and cultivated his friendship.

As soon as Rasputin was rumored to be a favorite of the Tsar and Tsarina, he became a man of power in St. Petersburg. He was soon surrounded by a crowd of "disciples"—mostly society women. People who hoped for royal favors came to see him. And, since the government was full of ministers who intrigued against one another, and who viewed with suspicion anyone who might exert political influence, Rasputin was soon under police supervision. He actually became friendly with several of the *ochrana* (secret police) agents who were sent to spy on him, and would give them a timetable of his movements to save them following him around.

Inevitably, the legends burgeoned around him. His enemies soon discovered that he had a police record, and that he was accused of being a member of the Khlysty. Those who disliked him—like the Prime Minister Stolypin and the President of Parliament (the Duma) Rodzianko—believed that he used his position to make money, to indulge in political intrigue, and to seduce hysterical women. There was a widespread belief in his hypnotic powers, and in those days—when George Du Maurier's *Trilby* was widely read—most people were convinced that a hypnotist could paralyze the will merely by staring masterfully into someone's eyes. Stolypin himself, who described Rasputin as vermin, added that he was convinced that he possessed powerful hypnotic powers. A young playboy named Prince Yussupov later described how, as Rasputin prayed beside him, he felt his whole body become paralyzed as if by some powerful narcotic. Rasputin's biographer Fülöp-Miller quotes the story of a young girl who went to ask Rasputin's advice on spiritual matters; she declared that Rasputin's eyes bored into hers until she felt herself sink into a state of helpless paralysis; Rasputin began murmuring indecent suggestions in her ear and steering her in the direction of the bedroom. With a tremendous mental effort she threw off the lassitude; instantly, Rasputin's face became bland and patronizing, and he raised his hand in blessing above her. Another woman quoted by Fülöp-Miller describes how Rasputin simply tore off her clothes, dragged her into the bedroom, then raped her while she was unconscious.

There were equally startling stories about Rasputin's power to perform miracles. He is credited with innumerable cures—even with causing a cripple to stand up and walk—and with causing a rose to blossom spontaneously by holding it in his hands. There are equally startling stories about his incredible capacity for vodka, and his physical strength. One biographer tells how Rasputin was attacked by three ruffians, and killed two of them by lifting one in each hand and smashing their heads together. The stories of healing have some basis in fact; the others are inventions. Rasputin drank fairly heavily, but he preferred sweet wine and seldom touched vodka. And the number of occasions on which he was roughly handled by his enemies suggests that his strength was no greater than the average.

What is certainly true is that Rasputin became involved in various right-wing movements. This was almost inevitable. For hundreds of years Russia had been a feudal estate ruled by absolute despots; by the time Rasputin came to St. Petersburg in 1903, the lid was about to blow off the caldron. People with mildly revolutionary opinions were likely to find themselves sentenced to Siberia. Protest marches were fired on by the police; in January 1905, Cossacks charged a peaceful demonstration outside the Winter Palace and cut the workers down with swords, then a cannon opened fire on those who fled; 150 people were killed and 200 wounded. When told the news the Tsar asked: "Are you sure you've killed enough people?" When told that another of his regiments had fired on unarmed workers he commented: "Fine fellows."

Like England's Charles I, the Tsar firmly believed that he ruled by Divine Right, and that any attempt at liberalization was a surrender to forces of stupidity and chaos. He was a gentle, good-natured, intelligent man, yet he regarded all leftwingers as Torquemada regarded heretics. By conviction, he was what the left would now call a fascist.

Now since most leftists were also militant atheists, it follows that the Russian Orthodox Church sided with the Tsar. John of Cronstadt, Bishop Hermogen, Bishop Theophan, were all truly devout and good men; where revolutionaries were concerned, they had no hesitation in recommending the bullet and the sword. (Most Russian prelates were also anti-Semites who believed that the Jews were quite as dangerous as the Anarchists, and that an occasional pogrom was the ideal way to keep them in check.)

When Rasputin became the Tsarina's favorite, he agreed whole-heartedly with these extremist views. As the years went by, and he saw more of the corruption of the ruling classes, and the incompetence of the civil service, he began to change his mind. He had always loved the Russian peasantry; as the years went by, he began to feel that the salvation of Russia might lie with them rather than with the rulers and the bureaucrats. The irony is that when Rasputin was murdered, the leftists and populists rejoiced because they felt that an "enemy of the people" had been destroyed.

Rasputin's career as a public figure was a series of ups and downs. From the beginning, his democratic manner scandalized the palace servants. The governess of the princesses reported to the Tsarina that Rasputin used to walk into their bedroom to kiss them goodnight—often without knocking. The Tsarina was incensed that anyone should suspect Rasputin of sinful thoughts—let alone intentions—and sacked her. Rasputin promptly seduced the nurse of the princesses at the baths. (Rasputin was extremely fond of the public bath.) The nurse told her confessor, who advised her to tell the Tsarina. Again the Tsarina declined to face the truth; she dismissed the nurse.

It is impossible to doubt that much of Rasputin's unpopularity was due to his bad manners. Even his friend Simanovitch refers to his "incredible insolence." He treated his female disciples like slaves, and enjoyed humiliating aristocrats who came to him to beg favors. Moreover, he enjoyed boasting about his friendship with the royal family—particularly when drinking. Inevitably, this came back to the ears of the Tsar, who soon recognized that their "man of God" was something of a rascal. If he had any doubts, then he was probably convinced by reports of the secret police, which revealed that Rasputin managed to spend most of his nights with different ladies—in one case, the wife of a captain in the local regiment.

But if Rasputin was a rascal, he was not a scoundrel or an opportunist. Like most dominant males, he enjoyed sex and would take it when it was offered. But he was not interested in money; he might accept a bundle of notes from a businessman who hoped for a government contract; but ten minutes later he would hand it to some poor peasant woman who had come to beg for help. It seems doubtful whether he was even really interested in power. In St. Petersburg, information was a valuable commodity, and Rasputin had access to a great deal. With dubious associates like Simanovitch and Maniulov—both adventurers—he traded information and pulled strings. But it was seldom for his own advantage; he simply seemed to take a naïve delight in playing games and being the center of attention.

And he remained a strange, paradoxical man with a deep streak of mystical religion. His diaries written on pilgrimages—for no eyes but his own (and only discovered after his death)—reveal that there was nothing bogus about his religion. So when the Tsarina insisted that he was a truly holy man, she was by no means mistaken. Her mistake lay in supposing that a religious mystic would be incapable of seducing the princesses' nurse.

Throughout 1908 and 1909, the disciples multiplied—particularly among society women. The Tsarina and the princesses presented Rasputin with embroidered blouses and shirts; other admirers gave him velvet trousers and patent-leather boots. He became something of a dandy. The Tsarina thought he was a saint, and the Tsar once described him as a "very Christ." It was all enough to turn anyone's head.

Yet it hardly took a prophet to realize that the times were dangerous, and likely to end in disaster. Contemporary memoirs seem to be full of a brooding feeling of foreboding. Police chiefs and government officials continued to be assassinated. In spite of the secret police and the Peter and Paul fortress, revolutionists and agitators dared to preach their doctrines openly. Liberalism was a rising tide. Level-headed ministers—like Stolypin and Rodzianko—did their best to walk the razor's edge, trying to check popular agitation while gently steering the Tsar in the direction of more liberal policies. Again and again the Tsar agreed to introduce something more like democracy—and again and again changed his mind at the last moment. When Parliament became exasperated, he dissolved it and tried to govern alone.

Then there were foreign problems. In 1905 there had

been the disastrous Russo-Japanese war, when the Russian army was defeated at Mukden and the Russian navy sunk at Tsuchima. In 1908, Austria annexed two Balkan states, Bosnia and Herzegovina. Russia was prepared to go to war. And there seems to be little doubt that it was Rasputin who averted the war by telling the Tsar that the Balkans were not worth the life of a single Russian soldier. If the Tsar had followed the same advice six years later, the Great War would never have happened.

Meanwhile Rasputin's enemies increased. It was the influence of powerful friends in the Church that had been responsible for Rasputin's original introduction to high society: men like Bishop Theophan and Bishop Hermogen (both of whom belonged to a reactionary organization called The Union of True Russians). Now they saw his growing influence, heard the ugly rumors of his debaucheries, and began to wonder whether it might not be time to withdraw their support. The monk Illiodor, another ardent patriot with dreams of building a "spiritual fortress," went with Rasputin to visit Pokrovskoe, and was shocked to see Rasputin embracing and kissing his female converts. Rasputin was amused by Illiodor's priggishness and advised him to get rid of his virginity as soon as possible. (In fact, it seems fairly certain that Illiodor was homosexual.) Illiodor found himself wondering whether Rasputin was a saint or a devil. For the moment, he kept his doubts to himself.

The Tsar's ministers began to feel that Rasputin's influence was evil. Stolypin, the Prime Minister, talked frankly to the Tsar about Rasputin's misdemeanors, and he was delighted when the Tsar looked thoughtful and asked him to draw up a full report. But when the report was prepared, the Tsar dropped it into a drawer and told Stolypin to go and see Rasputin for himself. According to Stolypin, Rasputin made a determined attempt to hypnotize him; but he resisted the mesmeric gaze, and roughly ordered Rasputin to leave St. Petersburg as soon as possible. Under different circumstances, Rasputin might have resisted and appealed to the Tsar. But as it happened, the idea suited him. He was getting sick of being spied on, and he suspected—rightly—that his life might

be in danger. So in 1911, he went off on another pilgrimage to
the Holy Land. He continued to write to the Tsarina, who
preserved all his letters; her replies show that she still regarded her teacher with almost mystical adoration. When he
returned from Palestine, he went back to Pokrovskoe. The
Tsarina sent her friend and confidante, Anna Vyrubova, to
stay with him—partly to find out whether stories about his se-
ductions were true. Anna was impressed by the "biblical simplicity" of Rasputin's home life, and made a thoroughly
favorable report.

In September 1911, Stolypin was assassinated, and the
Tsar lost his most competent minister. There were various
successors, each worse than the last. And each of them
brought nearer the day of the ultimate collapse of the Russian monarchy.

When Rasputin came back to Petersburg, his enemies
were all waiting to pounce. The monk Illiodor had finally decided that Rasputin was a devil, and told Bishops Hermogen
and Theophan about his debaucheries. He assumed—mistak-
enly—that the two bishops would be more than a match for
Rasputin. Hermogen sent for Rasputin, asked if the tales of
his sex life were true, and when Rasputin admitted it, beat
him with a cross and ordered him to stay away from women.
It was clear that he meant to denounce Rasputin to the Tsar.

But Rasputin got there first. His story was that the monk
Illiodor had tried to rape one of his penitents, and had then
accused her of trying to seduce him and had her beaten. The
woman protested to Rasputin, who promised to speak to
Bishop Hermogen. But Illiodor had already poisoned Hermogen's mind against him ...

The Tsar immediately issued an order banishing Hermogen and Illiodor to different monasteries. Hermogen took his
banishment quietly. Not so Illiodor, who traveled about the
country, denouncing Rasputin as a devil incarnate. He was
caught and imprisoned in a monastery; he escaped and compounded the offense by declaring that the Tsarina was Rasputin's mistress. Finally, he had to flee the country. His book
The Holy Devil—full of the lies of a mind unbalanced by hatred—began the Rasputin legend.

The simple truth was that Rasputin was becoming a kind of scapegoat for all the abuses of the Tsarist regime, a symbol of oppression. Suddenly, he was hated by every liberal in Russia. Newspapers denounced him. Someone published a pamphlet accusing him of being a member of the Khlysty. Even the Tsar began to turn against him, finally convinced by stories of his debauches.

And then fate intervened again. In September 1912, the royal family went to their summer resort near Grodno for a holiday. Anna Vyrubova actually smuggled Rasputin onto the royal train, but the Tsar heard about it and ordered him to be put off and returned to Pokrovskoe. But just as Rasputin's enemies were chortling about this latest disgrace, the tide turned. The Tsarevitch slipped as he was jumping from a boat and hit his knee; a hemorrhage turned into blood poisoning and the doctors despaired of his life. The Tsarina asked Anna to send Rasputin a telegram, asking him to pray for the boy's life. Rasputin telegraphed back: "The illness is not as dangerous as it seems. Don't let the doctors worry him." As soon as the telegram was received, the fever abated and the recovery began.

This story, like so many others, makes it difficult to accept that Rasputin was some sort of charlatan. Anna Vyrubova later had occasion to observe his powers at first hand. In 1915 she was in a railway accident; her legs were crushed and her head trapped under an iron girder. In hospital, doctors declared there was no hope for her life. As soon as Rasputin heard of the accident he rushed to the hospital. He was in disgrace at the time, so when he walked into her room he ignored the Tsar and Tsarina. Anna Vyrubova was unconscious, but when he took her hands, she opened her eyes and said: "Grigory, thank God." He concentrated on her for several minutes, then released her hands, saying: "She will live, but she will always be a cripple." He was pale and exhausted, and as he walked out of the door, collapsed. But Anna's recovery began from that moment.

In 1912, Rasputin told the Tsar: "While I live, your throne is safe. If I die, you will lose your throne and your life." Even in that year, international storm clouds were gathering. In England and France, most far-sighted politicians expected a war with Germany. Austria, like Russia, was a top-heavy monarchy ruled by bureaucrats and an old-fashioned despot. The Balkans seethed with indignation about the takeover of Bosnia and Herzegovina, and young patriots dreamed of avenging the insult. Their opportunity came on June 28, 1914, when Archduke Ferdinand, the heir to the Austrian throne, paid a visit to the Serbian town of Sarajevo. He had a strong premonition that he would be murdered. At eleven o'clock in the morning, Ferdinand and his wife were driving in a carriage when a young Serbian patriot stepped up and fired two shots, killing them both. These two shots launched the Great War.

One man could have prevented that war—Rasputin. He alone of all the Tsar's advisers might have had the influence to prevent the order for full mobilization. Yet, by an incredible coincidence, Rasputin himself was the victim of an assassination attempt at precisely the same moment that Ferdinand was shot. As he walked out of his house to catch the postman, a peasant woman accosted him as if to ask for alms; as he reached into his pocket, she took out a knife and stabbed him in the stomach. She was seized by neighbors and dragged to Rasputin's house screaming: "I have killed the Antichrist."

There are fifty degrees of longitude between Pokrovskoe and Sarajevo, so that 11 A.M. in Sarajevo would be 2:15 P.M. in Pokrovksoe. It was at precisely 2:15 when Rasputin was stabbed. He was rushed to hospital, losing blood; his intestines had been exposed by the blow. His immense vitality saved him. But when he lay helpless, events moved to their inevitable conclusion. When he heard news of the Tsar's order for mobilization he sent him a telegram begging him to change his mind. It was too late. Austria had declared war on Serbia, and when the Tsar mobilized, Germany declared war on Russia. The Great War had begun. The last act of the Russian tragedy was beginning.

When war was declared the Tsar suddenly became the most popular man in Russia. Even the intellectuals and leftists applauded. And this was not because they were patriotic or belligerent; it was because they were bored. Russia was the most backward country in Europe, and it was full of small, dirty, isolated towns which were like stagnant ponds. All the major Russian writers of this period convey the same awful sense of futility, the feeling that nothing would ever change. In that mood, people would have welcomed an earthquake.

Russia went to war in its usual bumbling, inefficient manner. They had plenty of men, but few rifles, and they were fighting the most highly industrialized nation in Europe. The minister of war boasted that he relied on the bayonet. Rasputin, with astonishing shrewdness, had once begged the Tsar to improve the railways, because they were the lifeline of Russia, but the Tsar had ignored him. And it was eventually the failure of the railways—and therefore of the food supply—that finally brought the Revolution. Meanwhile, thousands of men armed with old-fashioned rifles were sent to the front in dilapidated cattle trucks. There were a few notable victories, but the war soon began to go badly.

It was unfortunate for the Tsarina that she was a German. Everyone assumed she was a supporter of the Kaiser; the Tsarevitch was jokingly reported as saying: "When the Russians lose, daddy looks gloomy, and when the Germans lose, mamma cries." It was the Tsarina's fate to spend her life being libeled and misunderstood. She needed her friend more than ever. Rasputin was at the royal palace almost every day. Events like his "cure" of Anna Vyrubova revived the Tsar's faith in him. But the reconciliations were never long lived. Some police spy would remark that Rasputin had got drunk in a public restaurant in company with a prostitute, and had spoken familiarly about the royal family, and for the next week or so, the Tsarina would have to meet her friend secretly in Anna Vyrubova's little house. The tension lessened when the Tsar decided to go to the front and take charge of the armies himself. It was widely believed in Russia that the Tsar took Rasputin's advice on military matters, but this seems unlikely. What *is* certain is that when the Prime Minister—the incompetent Goremykin—was dismissed, he was replaced by one of Rasputin's sycophants, Stürmer.

At the beginning of the war, a young Russian nobleman, Prince Felix Yussupov, had escaped from Germany. When he returned to Russia he was horrified by the state of the country. Rumor declared that Rasputin was responsible for the Tsar's absurd decision to become commander-in-chief of the army, and that Rasputin and the Tsarina, his mistress, were plotting to seize power. It was universally believed that Rasputin was a German spy, and that he periodically made the journey to Berlin to report direct to the Kaiser. Understandably, members of the government began to brood on the idea of murdering Rasputin. Hvostov, the Minister of the Interior—who owed his appointment to Rasputin—sent one of his minions to buy poisons, and some of it was slipped into the milk in Rasputin's house. The cat tasted the milk and died instantly; Rasputin wrongly assumed that the murder attempt was engineered by another of his "friends"—a homosexual intriguer named Andronikov—and broke with him. But the incident put him on his guard. Hvostov even planned to bring Illiodor back from Norway to kill Rasputin, but the scheme came to nothing.

The war dragged on. Food was short; soldiers at the front talked openly of revolution. When Hvostov's murder plans were uncovered, he was dismissed, and another Rasputin sycophant appointed in his place.

In December 1916, a member of Parliament named Purishkevich was driven by desperation and anger to deliver a violent speech, denouncing Rasputin and his various appointees. Prince Yussupov was in the audience, and Purishkevich's frantic sincerity made a deep impression. There and then, Yussupov decided to murder Rasputin.

And Rasputin himself suddenly had a premonition that the end was near. After Purishkevich's speech, he became moody. One day as he walked along the Neva, he had another vision—the river seemed to be red with the blood of Grand Dukes. One day he wrote a strange letter, headed "The Spirit of Grigory Rasputin," in which he prophesied his own death, and said that if he was murdered by the Russian people—the peasants—then the throne would be safe for hundreds of years to come. But if he was killed by the nobles, di-

saster would follow; brother would kill brother, and none of
the Tsar's family would remain alive for more than two years.
The legacy of hatred would last for the next twenty-five
years. Rasputin sent the letter to the Tsarina, who decided
not to show it to her husband. It came to light after her
death.

On December 29, 1916, Prince Yussupov invited Rasputin to his home for a midnight supper. Yussupov's wife Ir-
ina was a famous beauty and Rasputin was anxious to meet
her. In fact Yussupov had plotted with Purishkevich—and
three other conspirators—to murder Rasputin. When Rasputin mentioned the invitation to Anna Vyrubova, she
begged him not to go, convinced there was danger. Nevertheless,
when Yussupov arrived in his car at midnight, Rasputin accompanied him back to his palace.

They went down to the basement; when Rasputin asked
after his wife, Yussupov explained that she had visitors and
would be down shortly, and offered Rasputin wine or tea; he
refused both. According to Yussupov, he then persuaded
Rasputin to eat a number of cakes that had been heavily
laced with cyanide. These should have killed him within seconds. But to Yussupov's amazement, Rasputin went on eating
and talking as if nothing had happened. Yussupov began to
wonder if this man was truly demonic.

He made an excuse to go upstairs, where the other conspirators were waiting, and told them that the poison had
failed to take effect. One of them handed Yussupov his revolver. When he went downstairs again, Rasputin said he was
feeling ill; his throat was burning. Then he proposed that
they should leave and visit the gypsies. Yussupov suggested
that he should say a prayer in front of the crucifix; as Rasputin turned, Yussupov shot him in the back. He gave a roar
and collapsed on the carpet, and the other conspirators
rushed into the room. One of them, a doctor, felt Rasputin's
pulse and pronounced him dead. Yussupov and Purishkevich
went upstairs, congratulating themselves. Yet Yussupov felt
uneasy; he had a feeling that Rasputin might rise from the
dead. He went downstairs, bent over the body, and shook it.
To his horror, Rasputin's eyes opened; he stood up, and tore

an epaulet from Yussupov's shoulder. Then, as Yussupov ran upstairs, he began to crawl after him on all fours. He came to a locked door, burst it open, and rushed into the courtyard. Purishkevich fired at him and hit him with two shots; Rasputin collapsed. Purishkevich kicked him in the head, and Yussupov battered him with a steel bar. The body was then bundled into a car, taken to a hole in the ice on the river, and pushed through. Perhaps the most astonishing part of the story is that when the body was later recovered, a post mortem revealed that Rasputin had died of drowning.

The next day, the story of Rasputin's death was all over St. Petersburg (now called Petrograd). The Tsarina ordered Yussupov to be confined to his house. Two days later, an urchin discovered Rasputin's boot by a hole in the ice on the Neva; the police investigated, and soon found the body. Rasputin's hands had been tied when he was thrown into the river, but he had managed to raise one of them to make the sign of the cross. A post mortem revealed no sign of poison in the body—it is possible that Yussupov was lying about this, in an attempt to dramatize his own inglorious part in the murder. (He escaped from Russia after the war and dined out for the rest of his life on the story of how he had killed Rasputin.) Rasputin's body was buried in the royal park, and later on, dug up and burned.

The conspirators believed they had altered the destiny of Russia by murdering the Tsar's evil genius. In fact, nothing changed. In March 1917, food shortages caused riots in Petrograd. Police fired on crowds. The army mutinied. A provisional government was formed, and the Tsar was advised to abdicate. In August 1917, Kerensky—who was in charge of the provisional government—sent the royal family to Tobolsk, and the Tsar actually refused to cooperate in a plan to get him out of Russia, believing that he would eventually be restored to the throne. In November, the Bolsheviks staged their coup, and Russia became a communist regime. On July 16, 1918, the Tsar and his family were all murdered in a cellar in Ekaterinburg. Rasputin's strange prophecy had come true.

Gurdjieff

On the morning of October 3, 1948, a Harley Street physician named Kenneth Walker made his way to an apartment in the rue de Colonel Renard in Paris; he was on his way to meet his master and teacher, George Gurdjieff. For exactly a quarter of a century, Walker had been deeply influenced by Gurdjieff's ideas—ever since an evening in 1923 when his friend Maurice Nicoll took him to a lecture given by P. D. Ouspensky. Ouspensky was Gurdjieff's leading disciple, an indefatigable propagandist for his ideas; yet in the twenty-five years Walker had spent attending his lectures, he had never glimpsed Gurdjieff. Now Ouspensky was dead, and Walker decided it was time to meet the fountainhead, the founder of the Institute for the Harmonious Development of Man, the teacher whom his disciples regarded as a kind of god, and whose enemies denounced him as a charlatan.

The apartment was jammed with incongruous odds and ends, and had the appearance of a junk shop. A crowd of disciples listened for over an hour as someone read aloud from the manuscript of that vast and incomprehensible masterpiece, *Beelzebub's Tales to His Grandson*. Then Gurdjieff came into the room, a small man with a bald head and gray handlebar mustache, and invited everybody to lunch. Walker and his wife sat opposite Gurdjieff at the low table—Gurdjieff dined Eastern style—and so had an opportunity to observe him closely. Walker comments: "What an astonishing man he was, entirely different from anybody I had previously met. Now that the *kalmak* (headgear) had been removed the full splendor of his clean shaven head was fully revealed. It rose to an immense height above the level of the ears, reaching its zenith at a point midway between the front region and the occiput. The next most remarkable feature about this head of his was that although he claimed to be over eighty years of age, his face was completely devoid of wrinkles. His olive-colored face was smooth and serene, and at the same time charged with virile power, a face that recalled to me the Lohan figure which had made such a deep impression on me at the Chinese exhibition before the war." And later, when Walker and his wife Mary returned to their hotel, he asked her what she had thought of Gurdjieff. "He's the most astonishing man I ever met," she said. "The chief impression he gave me was an impression of immense vigor and of concentrated strength. I had a feeling that he was not really a man but a magician."

Yet even Walker's straightforward description of Gurdjieff raises problems. Gurdjieff claimed to be over eighty; yet another disciple who knew him intimately—J. G. Bennett—was fairly certain that he was born in 1872, which means that even when he died in the following year, 1949, he was still well under eighty. Claiming to be far older than you actually are is one of the well known tricks of bogus magicians. Yet the answer may be more straightforward. Gurdjieff was born in Kars, on the Russo-Turkish border. This small town has been destroyed again and again as it passed from the Russians to the Turks and back again. In the East, there is a less urgent sense of time than in the West; many people have no idea when they were born, and in Gurdjieff's case, the records were almost certainly destroyed when the Russians again invaded the town in 1877 and massacred the Turkish inhabitants. (Fortunately, Gurdjieff was a Russian-Greek.) Gurdjieff told Bennett he thought he was born in 1866; Gurdjieff's sister told Bennett she thought it was 1877; Bennett's independent inquiries finally led him to settle on 1872. There was probably no conscious deceit on Gurdjieff's part; just vagueness about time.

Bennett met Gurdjieff in 1923 in Turkey, and his own first impression is worth quoting: "When we were introduced I met the strangest eyes I have ever met. The two eyes were so different that I wondered if the light had played some trick on me. But Mrs. Beaumont afterwards made the same remark, and added that the difference was in the expression, and not in any kind of cast or defect in either eye." We may compare this with the remark of an anonymous pupil, who met Gurdjieff in Moscow about 1913: "His eyes particularly attracted my attention, not so much in themselves as by the way he looked at me when he greeted me, not as if he saw me for the first time, but as though he had known me long and well." Others have said that Gurdjieff gave the impression that he could look through people, or read their thoughts.

Was Gurdjieff a "magician"? In the accepted sense of the word, probably not. But that may be because the accepted sense of the word is misleading; we think of someone like Merlin, or Tolkien's Gandalf, waving a magic wand. Yet there can be no doubt that Gurdjieff spent many years traveling in the East, and studying the occult and mystical traditions, and that as a consequence he had acquired certain curious powers, including the ability to communicate by telepathy, and to exercise a form of hypnosis. A story told by his disciple Fritz Peters will serve as an illustration. A Russian family came to his Institute at Fontainebleau. Gurdjieff told his followers that their daughter was susceptible to certain musical chords, and that if a certain chord was played, she would go into a trance. The unsuspecting girl came into the room with her parents; Gurdjieff's pianist, von Hartmann, played the piano. As he played a certain chord, the girl fainted, and it took a long time to revive her. Gurdjieff persuaded the girl to repeat the demonstration several times later, and Peters says that her bewilderment and hysteria when she woke up was always too obviously genuine for any suspicion of fraud.

Gurdjieff has given us some details of his early life in a book called *Meetings with Remarkable Men*. As a child, he became interested in what we would now call "paranormal"—a young man who could accurately predict the future when he went into a hypnotic trance, a Yezidi boy trapped in a circle that had been drawn in dust around him. In his teens, Gurdjieff visited monasteries, studying tales of miraculous cures, always trying to discover the secrets of the occult. He became a stoker on the railway, and was asked to accompany an engineer to survey the route of a new track; Gurdjieff made a great deal of money by approaching mayors of the towns the railway was scheduled to go through, explaining that their town was not on the route, but that he could fix it.

In his first book, *Herald of Coming Good,* Gurdjieff tells how, as a teenager, he became increasingly obsessed by a desire to understand the life-process of all living creatures. Gradually, he says, this itch came to possess his whole being. He and a friend named Pogossian set out to seek for "secret knowledge" in monasteries of the Mediterranean and Central Asia.

Yet one of his most important discoveries came from his friend Pogossian. Pogossian was always swinging his arms, marking time with his feet, snapping his fingers; he explained that he wanted to accustom his whole being to *work*, to drive out laziness. This could be regarded as the foundation of all Gurdjieff's ideas. The central trouble with human beings is that we are passive, mechanical creatures, little better than robots; we march through life in a kind of trance, and consequently make use of only a fraction of our potentialities. You could say that what fascinated Gurdjieff was man's curious *limitedness*, his narrowness. Yet of all creatures, man ought to be the least limited. You can understand why a dog or a cow should be limited; there is nothing much for it to do apart from eat, drink, sleep, excrete and reproduce. But man has built cathedrals and opera houses, created poems and novels and symphonies. His potentialities seem so tremendous. And his actuality so narrow and dull. It is as if he is suffering from some kind of sleeping-sickness. *This* is the problem that fascinated Gurdjieff. Like some spiritual Houdini, he wanted to unpick the locks and unwind the chains.

The first forty or so years of Gurdjieff's life seem to belong to legend. Rom Landau records that a lady who saw him declared that she had seen him years before at the court of the High Lama of Tibet. All that is certain is that he traveled widely and sought knowledge. Then, shortly before the First World War, he appeared in Moscow, and organized a ballet called *The Struggle of the Magicians*, in which his pupils performed complex dances that derive from the dances of the dervishes. An anonymous pupil who wrote a manuscript called *Glimpses of Truth* described being taken to meet Gurdjieff—with considerable difficulty (Gurdjieff believed that we are inclined to devalue anything we get too easily); it was he who spoke of Gurdjieff's eyes and their quality of penetration. This man was an occultist,* and Gurdjieff began his conversation with a discourse on the structure of the universe, its different kinds of energies, and so on. He then moved on to his real concern: the fact that the human "factory" is so inefficient. Man possesses extraordinary powers; yet he fails to utilize them. He wastes his potential. When the disciple asked him about occultism, Gurdjieff answered that most of it is valueless, except as mental exercise. Man must get to grips with reality, and this involves a precise understanding of our own mechanisms.

Peter Ouspensky has also described his own first meeting with Gurdjieff, at roughly the same time. Ouspensky was another seeker who had already written a book called *Tertium*

---

*In fact, according to Ouspensky, this article was written by two of Gurdjieff's pupils, at his own suggestion.

Organum, and was about to write *A New Model of the Universe*, when he met Gurdjieff. He was impressed by the lack of mystical mumbo-jumbo in Gurdjieff's approach; Gurdjieff spoke precisely and quietly, like a scientist. What he had to say was hardly comforting. Man is fundamentally a machine. He thinks he lives and thinks and makes decisions; in fact, he has not more control over his destiny than a river has. If a river possessed consciousness it might imagine that it had chosen its own route, that as it rushed down hills or meandered across plains, it was hurrying or dawdling according to its inclinations. Man, said Gurdjieff, is in precisely the same situation. He thinks he possesses a controlling ego, an "I." In fact, different I's take over from minute to minute, each one with its own motives and desires. This is why life is so chaotic. It is like a book written by two dozen people, each writing a single sentence in succession.

"Can one stop being a machine?" asked Ouspensky, and Gurdjieff replied: "Ah, if you'd asked that more often we might have got somewhere."

For although Gurdjieff seems to be so totally pessimistic about human beings, he also believes—he would say "knows"—that there *is* a small spark of freedom in man that can be developed. It is immensely uphill work, but it can be done. The first step is to study ourselves very closely, until we have come to recognize just how much we "drift." We wake up in the morning and proceed to go through certain rituals. We may have a sudden flash of desire to do something new, something creative. In fact, we tend to run like trains on railway lines, thinking and doing basically what we think and do every other day. So when most people reach the age of seventy-five, they are no wiser than a train that has run on the same line for seventy-five years.

And how can man escape this automatism? This was the whole aim of Gurdjieff's work. One of our basic troubles is laziness. Religious teaching has always recognized this, and tried to combat it with ascetic practices. The yogi pursues the way of knowledge, the monk pursues the way of prayer and religious emotion, the fakir pursues the way of physical discipline. None of these is enough. Man must *combine* these three into a fourth way, which Gurdjieff sometimes calls "the way of the cunning man."

The basic enemy is habit, the "robot." It is this that robs us of our freedom. So Gurdjieff's method aimed at freeing man from the robot, or rather, making him less dependent on it. This was the aim of the complicated dervish dances. I have seen these dances—at J. G. Bennett's "school" in Sherborne, England, and they are visually quite stunning. The dancers, all dressed in white robes, make incredibly complicated movements. If you try rubbing your stomach with one hand while you pat your head with the other, you will quickly see how difficult it is to make the two hands do different things. But Gurdjieff's dancers could do different things with each arm and each leg, and something different with the head. The sheer difficulty of acquiring this technique "wakes people up," gives them a new degree of freedom. But, as one of Bennett's pupils admitted to me, when you have mastered it, you get no more freedom from it; it becomes automatic.

Then Gurdjieff believed in keeping his students in a perpetual state of intense alertness. He might go into the dormitory at four in the morning, and clap his hands; within seconds, every student was expected to be out of bed and in some complicated and difficult position. He set great store by alertness, a perpetual watchfulness and readiness.

But all these things—and the tremendously strenuous physical work he expected his pupils to perform—were only aids. The really important part was to strengthen the mind, to strengthen the consciousness, man's "essential" self. Man is full of dozens of I's—probably thousands; every real effort, every time he calls upon his deepest resources, a few of these I's fuse together, so he begins to acquire something like unity.

The aim is freedom. Everybody knows what this is. It is the flash of sudden absurd joy. Wordsworth talked about "intimations of immortality." You feel more alive, more awake; the whole world seems an immensely fascinating place; meaning seems to stretch out in all directions, like great lighted avenues in a huge city. When you are in such a state of aliveness, and you think back on your usual state, it seems, quite simply, that we are usually *blind*. The meaning is always there; we just don't see it. We keep on striving for various things because achieving them makes us feel more alive—money, possessions, sex, fame, power. Yet all these things only bring a momentary *intensification of consciousness*. It never strikes us that we would do far better to direct our efforts single-mindedly at intensification of consciousness. But it struck Gurdjieff, and he devoted his life to teaching it.

As the First World War progressed, conditions became more difficult in Russia. When the communists came to power in 1917, Gurdjieff realized that he could no longer work in Russia. It was not the materialism of communist ideology that bothered him—he regarded himself as a kind of materialist (he even insisted that knowledge is material)—but its simplistic crudeness. Gurdjieff knew that when all the economic problems of life have been solved—whether by communism or by capitalist free enterprise—man will still be as un-free as ever. So he left Russia for Finland, and during the next few years traveled a great deal—Bennett met him in Turkey in 1923—and finally settled, as far as he ever settled, at Fontainebleau, south of Paris, in an old Priory (the Prieuré), which became his Institute for the Harmonious Development of Man. He traveled to America several times, and presented his "ballets" in theaters—he was an accomplished showman. Although he had no wish for fame, his name became increasingly known. At one point, D. H. Lawrence thought of becoming a resident at the Prieuré. Men like Orage—editor of *The New Age*—and Maurice Nicoll abandoned their careers to follow him. Katherine Mansfield was one of his pupils; inevitably, her death from tuberculosis was blamed on Gurdjieff.

In fact, as the years went by, an increasingly powerful anti-Gurdjieff movement developed. A book called *M. Gurdjieff*, edited by Louis Pauwels (Paris, 1954), starts from the supposition that Gurdjieff is a charlatan and a dangerous monomaniac, and Pauwels describes an encounter with two of his female pupils who were emaciated, exhausted and on the verge of suicide. Yet for anyone who understands the essence of what Gurdjieff was trying to do, the whole book appears to be a travesty, a crude and distorted picture by someone who has not taken the trouble to find out.

In 1934, after a serious car accident that almost killed him, Gurdjieff gave up the Prieuré, and moved to the apartment in the rue de Colonel Renard. There were still fairly frequent trips to America, until the war came. In spite of the insistence of his disciples that he move to Free France, Gurdjieff preferred to remain in Paris; he stayed there until his death in 1949.

Gurdjieff and Ouspensky—his most important follower—had gone their separate ways after leaving Russia. Temperamentally, they were miles apart. Ouspensky was cool, precise, almost pedantic; he has been described repeatedly as a kind of scientist. Gurdjieff was an altogether more complex character. His system was complex and sophisticated, yet he himself remained oddly simple. He believed in God and often used the name of God. Ouspensky, if asked if he believed in God, would probably have replied that he neither believed nor disbelieved; it is completely irrelevant to the matters that interested him. Gurdjieff struck many people as an actor; he seemed to regard people from a distance, as if he was observing them. He would roar with laughter or lose his temper as he felt inclined, simply to influence those around him. Yet he also struck people as a warm, kindly man. He once told a disciple that anyone who loves his parents is fundamentally good; Gurdjieff himself showed an oriental respect and devotion to his parents.

On the other hand, he showed considerable skill as a demogogue and a cult leader. He always made it difficult for people to get to see him—or to see his representatives in various countries. (The Gurdjieff movement, incidentally, had great success in America.) He insisted on secrecy. His pupils were not allowed to talk about "the work" to outsiders. After meetings, they were told to disperse quickly and quietly, as if they were conspirators. He made his pupils pay as much as they could afford for lessons—not, apparently, because he had any desire for money—he lived simply and frugally—but because he believed that people only value what has cost them an effort or sacrifice. In fact, we are slaves of the robot, which

takes over and quickly devalues anything we get too easily.
Everything in Gurdjieff's teaching was directed to driving his
pupils to make more effort to stretch the robot.

This may explain why he could be so infuriating. Fritz
Peters describes how they would set off on lengthy jaunts,
with Gurdjieff driving the car. Gurdjieff was an impossibly
bad driver—perhaps he wanted to shock his pupils into wake-
fulness with a sense of danger. He would dawdle during the
day—when not driving too fast along narrow roads—so that
they always seemed to arrive at hotels when they were closed,
and embarrassed pupils would have to batter on the door to
awaken the landlord. Gurdjieff would lean out of the car,
shouting instructions in Russian about how many bedrooms
were required, and how many meals. It sounds as if he deliberately set out to stretch the patience of his disciples to its
limit.

In his second book, *Gurdjieff Remembered*, Fritz Peters
has an uproarious description of the tribulations of taking a
train journey with Gurdjieff. In the summer of 1934, Peters
decided to go to Chicago, and felt proud when Gurdjieff said
he would like to accompany him. Peters went to collect Gurdjieff with plenty of time to spare, but Gurdjieff was not
ready, and they arrived at the station with only ten minutes to
spare—to be met by a hoard of Gurdjieff's followers with important messages. Gurdjieff ordered Peters to talk to some official and get the train delayed; staggered and rather
resentful, Peters nevertheless succeeded. Finally he pushed
Gurdjieff onto the moving train—then had to take part in a
kind of W. C. Fields comedy. Gurdjieff complained loudly
about being interrupted in his farewells, and sat down to
smoke a cigarette. The conductor said there was no smoking,
and requested that they move—about 12 cars further down to
their sleeping accommodation—begging them to do it quietly.
It took about three quarters of an hour to get Gurdjieff to his
berth, loudly complaining, and they woke up everyone on the
train. Then Gurdjieff decided he wanted to eat (it was now
about one in the morning). The commotion was so great that
the porter and guard had to threaten to throw them off at the
next stop. Gurdjieff settled in his bunk—then loudly de-

manded a drink of water and a cigarette. And so it went on until four in the morning, when he finally consented to sleep. The next day it was worse. In the dining car, Gurdjieff raised every possible objection to the food, and demanded yogurt; after driving everyone to a frenzy, he quietly ate a large American breakfast. During the day he constantly offended the passengers by smoking (presumably it was a non-smoker), drank heavily, and kept producing vile-smelling cheeses. When passengers became angry he would soothe them with profuse apologies—then find some new way of upsetting everybody. In Chicago, Peters announced he was leaving—for good. Gurdjieff—in front of an audience of Chicago disciples—raised such an outcry that Peters had to promise to go with him. Gurdjieff pathetically described how cruel Peters had been to him on the journey, and the disciples were disgusted. Finally Peters stalked out of the apartment, and declined all appeals to take Gurdjieff back to New York.

What are we to make of all this? The simplest approach would be to accept it all at its face value, and assume that Gurdjieff was a querulous old charlatan. But a glance at any of the serious books about him dispels that impression. He was, undoubtedly, one of the greatest men of his time, probably less of a charlatan than any other contemporary messiah. No, Gurdjieff was acting again. To understand what he was doing, you only have to glance at two of his books, *Beelzebub's Tales* and *Meetings with Remarkable Men*. *Beelzebub's Tales* is written in such a weird, convoluted style—with a dozen unnecessary dependent clauses in every sentence—that it seems either inept or pretentious. *Meetings with Remarkable Men*—which is admittedly straight autobiography—is lucid and direct. Gurdjieff deliberately turned his writing into a kind of obstacle course, to keep away the dilettantes and force the faithful to grit their teeth.

His basic idea can be explained in terms of what William James calls "vital reserves." We all have a great reservoir of energy which we can call upon when an emergency arises; its most familiar form is the phenomenon of second wind, when exhaustion suddenly changes to new vitality. Gurdjieff was trying to push his followers to call upon second wind. Most of

us hate chaos, but most of us love order for the wrong reasons—like a prim, middle-aged maiden lady who goes through
life with a we-are-not-amused expression on her face. To escape their limitations, people have to push themselves further
than usual, to make efforts they are not normally willing to
make. It was the equivalent of throwing them in at the deep
end. The psychiatrist Viktor Frankl tells of an obsessive patient
who had a morbid horror of dirt, and would wash his hands a
hundred, two hundred times a day. Frankl cured him by making him empty all the bed pans in the ward and clean out the
toilets. Gurdjieff's technique was not dissimilar.

Gurdjieff seemed to have possessed, to a large extent,
this power of calling upon his vital reserves. Possibly his curious behavior was an outburst of sheer mischievous vitality.
Certainly it was intended as some kind of test for disciples
like Peters. In *Boyhood with Gurdjieff*, Peters mentions how
Gurdjieff gave him the task of cutting the lawns at the
Prieuré, and forced him to work progressively harder and
harder until he could perform the apparently impossible task
of mowing acres of lawn in a single day.

On the other hand, his method had an understandable
lack of appeal to many people, like D. H. Lawrence. For the
practical part of life at the Prieuré was just hard work. Gurdjieff wanted to get his students used to pushing themselves
beyond their normal limits. So they worked—at gardens, interior decorating, household chores—from morning till night,
and meanwhile made strenuous efforts to "observe themselves," and to learn new and ever more complicated dance
movements. One of Gurdjieff's basic concepts was "self-remembering." He pointed out that if you close your eyes, you
become aware only of you, as if your attention was an arrow
pointing inward. If you look at your watch, your attention is
an arrow pointing outward. But now try to look at your
watch—or anything else outside you, and try to retain awareness that you are looking at it—in other words, try to make
the arrow point in and out at the same time. A little practice
quickly reveals that it can only be done for a few seconds at a
time. Yet it is also clear that those moments of inner-freedom,
Wordsworth's "intimations of immortality," are moments

when you are self-remembering. You have the feeling: "What, *me*, here?," and you are as intensely aware of yourself as of your surroundings. Gurdjieff's pupils had to make constant efforts at self-remembering as they worked.

Occasionally, the effect could be revelatory. In his autobiography *Witness*, Bennett describes such an experience. He had been suffering from dysentery, and felt exhausted. Gurdjieff made them practice some particularly difficult new movements when he was in this state, and Bennett found that it was costing him a supreme effort of will. It became agony to continue. At this point he felt that Gurdjieff's whole attention was directed on him, ordering him not to stop if it killed him. And then, "suddenly, I was filled with the influx of an immense power. My body seemed to have turned into light. I could not feel its presence in the usual ways. . . . My own state was blissful beyond anything I had ever known." He had "broken through." He went to dig in the garden, and deliberately worked on at a pace that would normally have exhausted him within minutes; he was able to maintain it like a machine for half an hour or so. His pains had all vanished. He went for a walk in the woods, and found that he had a new and extraordinary control over his emotions. "I said to myself, 'I will be astonished.' Instantly, I was overwhelmed with amazement, not only at my own state, but at everything that I looked at or thought of . . . Then the thought of "fear" came to me. At once I was shaking with terror . . . I thought of 'joy,' and I felt that my heart would burst from rapture."

The description gives us a new insight into what Gurdjieff was aiming at. When I am dull and tired, my attention seems to be dragging itself over the surface of reality like a wounded beetle. In such a state I may do something that normally delights me—listen to a favorite piece of music, watch a favorite TV program—but somehow I get little or nothing out of it. In order to enjoy music—or anything else—I need to be somehow "above" it, seeing from a kind of bird's-eye view. And in this state I am somehow aware of its relations with other things, as if seeing them from above. To thoroughly enjoy my experience, I need to "take off" like a hovercraft. And in this state, my *imagination* seems to wake up; it is easy to remember the exact quality of almost forgotten experiences. I become aware that imagination is not another name for day-dreaming, but is an actual *faculty* for connecting us with other realities. (In order to underline this distinction, I have elsewhere coined the term "Faculty X.")

In these occasional states of inner-freedom, of Faculty X, we see clearly that one of our main problems is habit and laziness, our desire to find the simplest and most convenient way of doing things, our desire to avoid unexpected obstacles. In fact, if enough expected obstacles appear, we finally arouse ourselves out of this "spoiled" state of sullen rejection, and begin to enjoy solving the problems. We have "broken through." And—if we are very good at self-observation—we may also realize that our chief enemy is a state of haste, a de-sire to economize on effort. You become impatient. You can even notice it in your breathing; instead of long, deep breaths you take short, hurried breaths. And your inner-breathing, your connection with your own energy supply, also become short-winded.

This is what Gurdjieff's "magic" was all about: energy. And it seems fairly clear that Gurdjieff himself knew some basic trick of calling upon vital reserves; not only that, but of transmitting them, when necessary, to other people. Again, Peters tells a significant story. During the war, he was in the U.S. army. In 1945 he was in Paris, on the verge of a nervous breakdown. He went to see Gurdjieff, who instantly saw that he was sick. In Gurdjieff's kitchen, Peters sat slumped at the table, exhausted. Then suddenly: "I began to feel a strange uprising of energy within myself—I stared at him, automati-cally straightened up, and it was as if a violent, electric blue light emanated from him and entered into me. As this hap-pened, I could feel the tiredness drain out of me, but at the same moment his body slumped and his face turned grey as if he was being drained of life." Gurdjieff went out to meet guests, apparently exhausted. "It also became obvious within the next few minutes that he knew how to renew his own energies quickly, for I was equally amazed when he returned to the kitchen to see the change in him; he looked like a young man again, alert, smiling, sly and full of good spirits.

He said that this was a fortunate meeting, and that while I had forced him to make an almost impossible effort, it had been—as I had witnessed—a very good thing for both of us."

This last remark is highly significant. Obviously, Gurdjieff himself *was* willing to make the kind of superhuman effort he was always demanding of his pupils. But his comment to Peters implies that he had temporarily forgotten it, and had been reminded by the demands made on him by Peter's exhaustion. It seems clear that Gurdjieff himself was no superman. He had a certain vital knowledge, yet it had not penetrated to every corner of his being.

All these stories about Gurdjieff make it plain that he was a strange, highly complex, sometimes extremely irritating character. Revered, almost worshiped by disciples, he had no desire to be treated as a god-like being, and exaggerated his quirks and oddities. Like the Buddha, he insisted on being a normal—slightly more than normal—human being. He smoked and drank heavily, and tried to make everyone else do the same. The friend who introduced Kenneth Walker to Gurdjieff in Paris explained that Gurdjieff forced everyone to eat and drink heavily because he had to make quick assessments of many people, and we drop our defenses when full of food and drink. Whatever the reason, these endless lunches and dinners were practically gluttonous orgies, and everyone had to drink some twenty-three toasts in vodka—requiring the consumption of about eight glasses of vodka. Walker quickly observed that Gurdjieff's health was not all that it should be, and warned him that unless he had immediate attention, the consequences might be serious.

Unlike Ouspensky, Gurdjieff was also apparently a highly sexed man. (This was only one of many differences in their temperaments that makes it clear why they had to separate—especially if Gurdjieff subjected Ouspensky to any ordeals like the train journey to Chicago.) When his wife died—at the Pricuré—Gurdjieff promptly took a mistress, and slept with other willing female disciples. It is even conceivable that Gurdjieff used sex as a way of testing female disciples as he used inconvenience to test the males. Peters tells of a young female dancer who taught the dances to newcomers but whose prime reason for being in the "work" was a desire for authority. One day when she contradicted Gurdjieff, he told her that he would have to give her a personal answer to her question later. He then told Peters to ask the young lady to come to his room at three in the morning, where he would show her some wonderful things. The girl declined scornfully, saying she recognized a proposition when she saw one, and left the group. Gurdjieff laughed heartily; this was precisely what he had intended her to do. But, he added, he would probably have gone through with it if she actually turned up. It was just as well she didn't, because he would not really have had time to deal with the reverberations that would have followed a sexual relationship. Gurdjieff understood that there are hidden laws of nature, and that we cannot simply do what we like without consequences. There are always consequences—sometimes pleasant, sometimes otherwise; but they cannot be escaped.

Kenneth Walker's warning came too late. Gurdjieff delayed the recommended operation—to release dropsical fluids from the abdomen—until he arrived in Paris. There he was rushed into hospital, seemed to recover after an operation, then had a relapse and died, presumably of heart failure. Ouspensky was already dead. In the following year, 1950, the long silence imposed on Gurdjieff's followers was broken when Ouspensky's book *In Search of the Miraculous* appeared. (It was originally entitled *Fragments of an Unknown Teaching*.) Gurdjieff had, of course, insisted that book learning is useless. When he first met Bennett, Bennett had evolved a theory about the fifth dimension, which he felt explained the mystery of the universe. Gurdjieff replied: "Your guess is right. There are higher dimensions or higher worlds where the higher faculties of man have free play. But what is the use of studying these worlds theoretically? Suppose that you could prove mathematically that the fifth dimension really does exist, what use would that be to you so long as you remain here?" Gurdjieff was interested in how to make the voyage to the fifth dimension.

Helena Petrovna Blavatsky

When writing a life of one long dead it is not difficult to remain objective; but when writing of a living person whose life is still, or was recently, in the public eye, one's appraisal may be more subjective, and probably in conflict with the opinions of others possessing the same material.

In this case I find myself on the median line. I never knew Madame Blavatsky, who died in 1891, but in 1920 I joined the Theosophical movement which she founded, and soon knew well a number of persons who had worked with her in various ways and in some cases published their reminiscences after her death.

My own views on this powerful and controversial figure are based partly on the memories of these men and women, partly on long study of her voluminous writing, and more profoundly on the experience gained from her teaching as viewed in the wider field of comparative religion and philosophy. More and more, as she prophesied, these doctrines and principles are being ratified, and in no case to my knowledge has one of them been successfully disproved.

The story of her life is, in essence, that of a woman, a unique book, the teachers who trained her to present its teachings to the West, and the early history of the movement which she founded for that purpose.

She was born in South Russia on August 12, 1831, and died on May 8, 1891, in London at the age of sixty. Her father was Colonel Peter von Hahn. Her mother, Helena de Fadeef, was a famous woman novelist, daughter of Princess Elena Dolgorukov, but she died when her daughter was eleven and Helena was brought up in her grandmother's house. She was an exceptional child; a remarkable linguist, learning classical languages from her grandmother, a notable artist, as we know from many of her paintings, and a first-class pianist, being taught by one of the great masters of the day. She was at the same time a tomboy, a rider of half-broken horses, preferring life in the open fields with her father's men to toys and dolls in her own room with her governess. All noted her extraordinary psychic powers, and her sense of oneness with nature about her. From an early age she had a remarkable sense of dedication. She was obviously concerned with something that she had to do, and it was not very long before she realized what it was.

When barely eighteen she married. It is said that this was not out of love for the middle-aged Russian civil servant, Nikifor V. Blavatsky, but because her governess was always telling her that if she continued to behave as she did she would never marry anybody, not even this friend of the family. This was a challenge to the young Helena. Within three days she made him propose, and only when she was married did she regret what she had done. In any event, the marriage was a complete failure; it was never consummated, and she soon after ran away. Her father supported her in her travels in the years that followed, sending her money when she needed it. From that time onward she lived alone and was moving towards her destiny.

She traveled all over Europe, and in 1851 was in London at the Great Exhibition. There she met, first for a moment or two and then later at length in Hyde Park, her personal Master, the Master Morya. She had known him in her inner life for years, but now met him face to face. They had a long talk, and he told her something of what she had to do. He told her she would have to be trained for the work, and what that training would mean; what utter sacrifice of self it would involve, and the inevitable vilification that comes to everyone who teaches Truth. She realized what was coming and accepted it, and from that moment was only concerned with the training given her.

What had she to do? First, to attempt to stem the tide of materialism already sweeping over the West, breaking up on the one hand the dogmatic theology of the Christianity then current, and the dogmatism of current science; and secondly to re-teach something of the esoteric teaching which had been preserved for untold ages by those who are in every sense masters of that wisdom. She had to teach man altruism, holding up an ideal nobler than the materialistic ideas of the day.

It is not difficult to accept that at the heart of all religions is "the accumulated wisdom of the ages, tested and verified by generations of seers." All who impartially study the basic teachings of such find a common set of principles, whether expressed explicitly or in allegory and symbol. In the third century Ammonius Saccas of Alexandria called this Theosophia, the Wisdom of the Gods, and the name was adopted in New York at the first meeting of the Theosophical Society on November 17, 1875.

Nor is it difficult to accept the existence of highly advanced men who are masters of this common wisdom, under whatever name known, and that together, in the light of their spiritual development, they form a brotherhood beyond the differences of race or color. Tibet has for long been the home of its own schools of Buddhism, and some of the teachings now revealed as being taught from time immemorial in that country may well be older than the "Buddhism" which is the Western name for the doctrines re-proclaimed by Gautama the Buddha.

It was two of this brotherhood, known in Theosophical literature as the Masters M (for Morya) and K. H. (for Koot Hoomi), who undertook the difficult task of training Madame Blavatsky for the great enterprise they had envisaged, and for which she was to be the spearhead for the West.

In the middle of the nineteenth century, these two Masters, then living in Tibet, decided to make an attempt to promulgate at least an outline of this immemorial Wisdom, the Tree of which all religions are branches, to the Western world. They needed an agent, with not only a first-class mind and awakened intuition, but highly developed psychic powers. Such a person would have to be a loyal and willing servant of the Masters' purpose, and ready to bear the inevitable disbelief, vicious libel and vile vituperation which usually follows such revelation. They chose "H.P.B.," as she came to be widely known, as possessing all these qualities.

Her basic training was in Tibet, apparently in two periods of about three years. The training was twofold: first, to teach her brilliant intellect the basic principles of the Wisdom, so that she in turn might teach the West; secondly, to develop in her the exceptional psychic and spiritual powers which would be needed to carry out the task the Masters had given her. They needed, and had great difficulty in finding, a person with such spiritual and psychic development that they could communicate with her, in detail and accurately, at any time and place, using her as the outward instrument of their own teaching. Yet she must never at any time be a mere negative medium; always what she did for her Master must be done in full and willing consciousness. In brief, once chosen, she had to be trained to move from the negative psychism of the spiritualistic medium into the developed powers by which she could consciously represent the Master, whose voice and pen she would use.

She traveled all over the East, as far as Japan, as well as in the West, and made several attempts to get into Tibet before she finally succeeded. Over the ensuing years she was traveling constantly, meeting a wide variety of people, learning languages, developing her inner powers and her incredible knowledge of the subjects which she later taught.

The details of these travels will never be known. Not only was she unwilling to discuss them, for fear, she said, of ridicule and disbelief, but she went further, and in an undated letter to A. P. Sinnett, apparently in answer to specific questions, she wrote "from seventeen to forty" (which would be 1848 to 1871), "I took care during my travels to sweep away all traces of myself wherever I went." But it is a long letter and she does mention many places and much adventure, sometimes dressed as a man, as in the battle of Mentana in 1867 when she was wounded, and in a shipwreck near the port of "Speggia" (Spezia?) when the vessel was blown up. Often penniless, she received money from time to time from a member of her family, but it was not until July 1873 that in Paris she received orders from her Master to go to New York. She was not told why, but she went.

At that time there had arrived on the field of Western thought a force which was destined itself to affect, to an appreciable extent, the materialism both of theology and science. This was Spiritualism, then rampant in the United States, with its claims that after death those who had died could still be in touch with those still living. To challenge both theology and science, H.P.B. had an immensely difficult dual task to perform; on the one hand to prove that the phenomena were genuine, by showing that she could herself do anything that a medium could do, and in full consciousness; and at the same time to show that the claims of the Spiritualists to be in the least "spiritual" were unfounded, and that the psychic plane on which they functioned was only one degree above the physical plane on which we normally live. She had to prove, in other words, the existence of a spiritual plane with its spiritual powers, and to re-teach something of the total make-up of man, including the place of the psychic plane in his sevenfold being.

But things went wrong. The public did not want a spiritual teaching; they wanted phenomena, and the more of it the better, but in Spiritualism there was so much fraud that inquirers were disgusted with the fraud and failed to see the genuine phenomena. H.P.B. tried to prove that a positive mediumship was possible, and to show the knowledge that lay behind it, but few could follow what she had to say, that mediumship, as she wrote in *Isis Unveiled*, is the opposite of Adeptship. The medium is the passive instrument of outside influences; the Adept actively controls himself and all inferior potencies.

The understanding of the psychic plane as a level or "wavelength" of consciousness—as different from the physical as the physical is from the mind—is small even today, but in the nineteenth century it was nonexistent. It was therefore either labeled fraud or relegated to the realm of sorcery and witchcraft and other unhealthy practices of the human mind.

Even today, when there is still some unwillingness to accept extrasensory perception, the very remarkable powers exhibited by H.P.B. are difficult for those trained in materialistic science to understand, and the casually produced phenomena of a Uri Geller are still for the public either fraud, insanity or to be ignored. The warning given to H.P.B. by her Masters of the violent reaction the display of such powers would arouse, was well advised.

When she arrived in the U.S.A. in 1873, at the age of forty-two, she was in full possession of her powers and almost incredible knowledge. She met, as was clearly planned, two remarkable men: Colonel H. S. Olcott, an American who had fought in the Civil War and was a lawyer interested in the new phenomena, and W. Q. Judge, an Irish lawyer who was equally interested. Those three, having been brought together, realized soon what their immediate work was to be, to found some kind of society to study the phenomena of Spiritualism, to see what it meant, how it could be used and what were its limitations. From the group so planned there was born in New York on November 17, 1875, the Theosophical Society. Colonel Olcott was elected the founding President, and H. P. Blavatsky became then, and was never more than, the Corresponding Secretary. Her task was to be a channel for her Master's wisdom and the teaching she had been trained to give the West. The organization was left in the hands of others.

Note that the original objects of the Theosophical Society were not as now. At that time the main purpose was the study of spiritualistic phenomena, while the present most important object, "to form a nucleus of the universal brotherhood of humanity," only appeared at the virtual refounding of the Society in India in 1879. But this was what the Masters really wanted, and in this it failed. It succeeded, nevertheless, in its second object, the study of comparative religion, and the present Western interest in the study of religions, in an attempt to find the spiritual truths at the heart of all of them, comes largely from the pioneer work of the Theosophical Society.

A further object, "to investigate the unexplained laws in nature and the powers latent in man," meant at that time learning from H.P.B., and because she was the one person who could write down what these seekers wished to know, she began to write *Isis Unveiled.* These two immense volumes, written in New York and published two years later, have been criticized, not least by the author herself, as containing a number of errors and inconsistencies. True, the writer's English was still imperfect, and she had no experience in writing, but if the student, bearing this in mind, takes the trouble to read it carefully, he will find that in this pioneer work is to be found a vast quantity of remarkable information.

In 1878 she realized that her work in America was over, and on her Masters' orders sailed for India with Colonel Olcott. Why to India? A possible explanation for her Masters' orders to this effect is that while the spiritual development of the United States in 1875 must have ranked low indeed, that of India then was and still is perhaps the highest on earth, in spite of the degradation of the centuries. Sure enough, a large number of the leading religious minds of the day at once accepted the ancient Wisdom she was calling Theosophy as a purified and expanded version of their own esoteric philosophy. In India she threw off all attempts to gain acceptance for the teaching by a display of psychic phenomena, and gave out for the remainder of her life "the wisdom of the gods," which, unencumbered with dogma, ritual and forms, shone with the clear light of the intuitive plane, on which it primarily dwells.

Before she left she became an American citizen, a move which was to prove of considerable value. For on her arrival in Bombay in 1879 she was immediately attacked as a Russian spy, partly because the word Russian then connoted spy; and why else, it was asked, should a woman of her brilliance come to India and teach such curious ideas? Her American passport must have helped her considerably.

In India the movement was an immediate success. One of the first Europeans there to welcome the Founders was A. P. Sinnett, then editor of the *Pioneer*, of Allahabad, perhaps the most influential English-language paper of the day in India. He craved to be put in touch with the Masters who had trained H.P.B. and she agreed. The result of the contact was a unique set of letters from Sinnett to the Masters, of which we have no copy, and their replies, which Sinnett carefully filed in a brass-bound box, now in London in the possession of the Mahatma Letters Trust. These letters, now in the British Library, were sent between 1880 and 1884, and as edited by A. T. Barker may be read in *The Mahatma Letters to A. P. Sinnett*, published in London in 1923.

The *Letters*, and Madame Blavatsky's greatest work, *The Secret Doctrine*, are the principal sources of our knowledge of Theosophy. In a sense they stand or fall together as a new presentation in outline of the wisdom which Ammonius Saccas was the first to call by that name. No one doubts that she wrote *The Secret Doctrine*, for there are many accounts of its laborious writing, in Germany, Ostende and London. But a book was written to suggest that the *Letters* are forgeries, that she wrote them too. The suggestion is absurd, for A. P. Sinnett wrote two books from his reading of the flimsy and often scarcely legible originals, *The Occult World* and *Esoteric Buddhism*, both of which had appeared five years before *The Secret Doctrine* was published in 1888; and Madame Blavatsky was herself writing regularly to Sinnett between 1880 and 1888 as shown in *The Letters of H. P. Blavatsky to A. P. Sinnett*, also edited by A. T. Barker and published in 1925.

Here, then, is the setup for the literary basis of Theosophy, leaving aside the direct teaching to other Europeans, and the support of Indian pundits. The *Letters* from the Masters to Sinnett and hers to Sinnett cover the same period and refer to each other. The handwritings may be compared. His own books written from the *Letters* to him were published long before *The Secret Doctrine* was begun. How, and, more important, why should she write at immense length in duplicate, leaving the forged *Letters* of her Masters to see the light of day when first published thirty years after her death? The suggestion is foolish.

Meanwhile Colonel Olcott was developing an independent line of his own, using his remarkable powers of spiritual healing wherever he traveled on behalf of the Society, and also working, most successfully, in Ceylon in the reorganization of Buddhism.

In the light of the rapidly growing interest in Buddhism in the West, this connection of the two Founders with Buddhism should not be overlooked. They both declared themselves Buddhists before leaving the United States, and in Ceylon in 1880 both 'took Pansil' in a monastery in Galle, amid scenes of intense enthusiasm, thus again formally declaring themselves Buddhists. It is of interest to compare this with remarks on the Buddha made to Sinnett by the Masters in their *Letters* to him, where the Buddha, for example, is described as "the patron of the adepts, the reformer and codifier of the occult system." For them the Buddha was "the greatest and the holiest man that ever lived." As I wrote in a review of *When Daylight Comes*, the latest life of Madame Blavatsky, by Howard Murphet, "the totality of the universe, the presence in every form of the Light of the Buddha-Mind, the supreme force of compassion, karma and rebirth, and man as the 'pilgrim of eternity' on his way home, these were principles interesting London twenty years before Buddhism as such was known to any but the occasional scholar."

In 1882, the two Founders, who had been living in Bombay, bought an estate at Adyar, near Madras, which is the world center of the Theosophical Society today. There they worked for the rest of their time in India. In 1884, Olcott was going to London on behalf of the Buddhists of Ceylon, and H.P.B., exhausted and ill with overwork—they worked at Adyar for sixteen or seventeen hours a day—came with him, leaving, as she thought, the Theosophical Movement in India on a sure foundation. In Europe, she was almost mobbed. Her range of knowledge, her conversation, the brilliance of her mind and her extraordinary powers took London by storm. Ill though she was, she produced a visible effect on the thinking minds of the day.

Meanwhile, the hand of Karma was about to fall. With the backing of Christian missionaries in Madras, an attempt, which nearly succeeded, was made to smash the movement. A certain Coulomb and his wife, servants at Adyar whom H.P.B. had left behind, proceeded to forge letters in her name and sell them to Christian missionaries in Madras. The Society for Psychical Research in London was immediately informed, and sent out a young Australian named Richard Hodgson to investigate. He, who it seems never saw the letters, alleged them to be forged; he, who never saw any phenomena, said they were false; seeing nothing, he produced a report which to this day is the foundation of every ignorant and vicious attack on H. P. Blavatsky. Fortunately, although the report nearly killed the Theosophical Movement, it has now been belatedly destroyed by a volume written by Adlai Waterman, pseudonym of a well-known worker for Theosophy in America, called *Obituary: The Hodgson Report on Madame Blavatsky: 1885-1960*, published by the Theosophical Publishing House. That is the answer which will satisfy any intelligent person that the remarks, still being made, about "that old fraud," are utterly unfounded.

The attack nearly killed its victim, already exhausted with overwork, and in London she was very ill. She went back to Adyar to challenge the attack, to prove the letters to be forgeries, and to say what she had to say about the Coulombs whom she had long and generously befriended. She found that before the spurious letters were shown to the missionaries that the Coulombs had been dismissed, by the committee she had left in charge, for proven blackmail, forgery and fraud, but they were still believed by those who wished to believe them. She was, however, persuaded not to bring a libel action on the ground that, however the action went, it would hurt the movement, and she feared it might drag the

Masters' names into the mud. She resigned her appointment and left India, never to return.

Note that the attack was on the genuineness of her psychic phenomena which, as a means of spreading Theosophy, had been largely abandoned in New York; it was not against the teaching later to be set down in *The Secret Doctrine*. Her writings stand for all to read. Not one word of it has been disproved; more and more has been proved by the standards set by science for its own limited field, to be true. She was right indeed when she prophesied in 1888 that "in the twentieth century scholars will begin to recognize that the Secret Doctrine has neither been invented nor exaggerated but simply outlined."

She lived at first in Würzburg, in Germany, with her great friend, Countess Wachtmeister, and later in Ostende. In 1887 she went to London, where she finished her greatest work, *The Secret Doctrine*. Begun in Würzburg in 1885, and finished in London with the help of Bertram Keightly and his nephew, Archibald, this was an amazing undertaking for any woman at any time. It was written in longhand, 1,300 pages of it with almost as much rewriting, with thousands of quotations which she wrote in first and then asked to be verified. Sometimes the quotation would be found in a book in the vaults of the Vatican, or be later proved to have come from a manuscript of which no copy could for a long time be found, and no one has explained how she could produce such a vast amount of information with a reference library which scarcely covered the mantelpiece.

The Secret Doctrine was published in 1888, and was immediately sold out. It is a strange fact that, when first published, *The Secret Doctrine* of H. P. Blavatsky was, is still today, and looks like remaining for years to come, unique. No other published work in any language contains a comparable range, depth and sense of authority on the subjects therein treated, the origin of the universe and man. Written and rewritten over 1,300 pages of laborious writing, over several years and in three countries, it finally appeared in two volumes and was an immediate success. Much of the material is a renewed attack on the dogmatic science and theology of the day, which followed up her *Isis Unveiled*, published in New York in 1877, and it has been possible to remove much of this now dead material to produce *An Abridgement of the Secret Doctrine* (1966) in a mere 250 pages. As the work stands, it was never claimed to be more than an "outline" of its vast subject, a description of the tree of which all religions are the branches, large and small. It is in no sense a pastiche or collation of principles to be found in extant religions, and may fairly be regarded as the inherited wisdom of mankind in which, as she said, "the various religious schemes are made to merge back into their original element, out of which every mystery and dogma has grown, developed and become materialized." Yet this "outline," in the totality of its range and the clarity and vigor of its expression, goes far beyond the published teachings of any one religion, or indeed the whole of them together. It does seem to be, in the strict sense of the term, unique.

Also in 1888 H.P.B. founded an Inner Group of Theosophical students, later known as the E.S. In the following year she published, in the form of question and answer, some of the basic principles of Theosophy as *The Key to Theosophy*, and in the same year *The Voice of the Silence* appeared, being "Extracts from the Book of the Golden Precepts" which she had learned by heart while under instruction in Tibet. This is surely one of the finest scriptures extant, worthy to rank with the *Bhagavad Gita*. As the *Theosophist*, published in Adyar, was no longer under her control, she published in London a new magazine called *Lucifer*, the pages of which, as those of the *Theosophist*, contained much of her most powerful writing. When to these works and her voluminous articles are added the *Mahatma Letters* from her own Master and the Master K. H. to A. P. Sinnett, and her own letters to him, we have a body of teaching which, even taken as a series of working hypotheses, is enough for any of us for this life, and it may be for lives to come.

The Blavatsky Lodge of the Society was founded when she came to London in 1887, and in 1889 she attended some of its meetings. There she answered questions on the first few stanzas of *The Secret Doctrine*, and these were later published as *Transactions of the Blavatsky Lodge*, which may be read with profit in conjunction with the major volumes. They have recently been reprinted in Volume X of her *Collected Writings*, edited by Boris de Zirkoff.

On May 8, 1891, she died at home, the funeral oration at her cremation being read by G.R.S. Mead who later, with Annie Besant, edited the third edition of *The Secret Doctrine*. But H.P.B. was the truth she taught; she had no successor. None with her occult powers has appeared to replace her as the direct agent of her Masters' teaching. It is for the present members to carry on the work with the help of her writings, her memory and their own ability to learn and teach the wisdom which she lived and died to proclaim.

Who, then, was H. P. Blavatsky? Who was "H.P.B."? The answer may be different, for the latter was to some people more than an intimate name for the former. She was her Master's pupil, utterly devoted to him, body and soul, from the moment she met him in the flesh in 1851 to the moment she died. She was literally his instrument, in a way that we cannot affirm of any other teacher known to us. If she was sometimes just a sick and irritable woman, she was, at other times, as many of those present recorded, sometimes very much more. For at times her Master used her himself, in her full consciousness, to teach and write as directed. We know this from the Master K.H. who wrote to a German doctor with reference to *The Secret Doctrine* that, whoever might help in its preparation, it was nonetheless the writing of three people, her Master (meaning the Master M), "H.P.B.," and "Yours sincerely K.H."—in other words, the two Masters behind the Theosophical movement and their instrument, H.P.B.

What a woman! Living in a tired old body, misunderstood, vilified and abused, and yet with a brilliant, cultured and deeply learned mind; the very soul of generosity; a woman of direct speech and action, refusing to talk the pious platitudes and nonsense that we chatter under the guise of socially good manners, but offering the truth for anyone who wanted it. If they were hurt by the truth that was their own affair, they hurt themselves. Ruthlessly honest, she hurt the feelings of many, but those who wanted truth remained, and those who left she did not wish to retain. Breaking conventional rules deliberately, smoking her hand-rolled cigarettes all day, she could at times be thoroughly bad-tempered. Yet, when the victim of her language was almost broken by her treatment, suddenly, because he was doing his best to understand, or to help her, she would say with a lovely smile, "Do you see what I mean?"

This was the way she taught her pupils, and she said so. Those strong blue eyes could see into the character of every man and woman who came to her, and even see by whom she would later be betrayed. This was a remarkable quality of mind, that she would help from her meager funds (and she was always poor), all those in need, even though she knew at the time that they were planning to smash the cause she had given her life to serve.

She was never neutral, or the same to all. She made a great number of friends who would die for her, and enemies who would kill her if they could. She tried to control her developed psychic powers but at times, as related by friends, she failed to do so. This psychic-spiritual combination seems to have been unique. Yet, in spite of her own great spiritual development or because of it, she was, as several wrote in tribute after her death, "unknown to egotism" in any form. Her energy was endless. Sick and dying, by her own doctor given up as "this woman cannot live," she spent twelve hours at her desk, writing and rewriting her books and articles and correspondence. Indeed she cared just nothing for herself; only for the Masters and their cause, and so, desperately ill, she labored until she died.

What did she teach? In *Isis Unveiled* she broke down dogmatic theology and science, and so paved the way for a constructive teaching. In *The Secret Doctrine* she taught the Ancient Wisdom and something of its guardians, the Masters of the Wisdom. She taught cosmogenesis, the coming into being of man; the dual evolution of spirit coming down and matter building up, until the two met in man. She taught the tree and its branches; the original esoteric doctrine and some of its branches extant in the various religions of the world.

She taught one life in every form, and the sevenfold nature of man. She gave out the truth in detail about life after death. She taught the doctrines of karma and rebirth, older than Hinduism or Buddhism, and by teaching them here in the West made it easier for the Buddhist movement when it arrived. She set out in detail the potential future of mankind; it is for mankind to seize that opportunity.

This teaching is difficult, and no book written by any human being, now or at any time, can make it easy. As she herself said in the Introduction to *The Key to Theosophy*: "To the mentally lazy or obtuse, Theosophy must remain a riddle, for in the world mental as in the world spiritual each man must progress by his own efforts," thus echoing the words of her Master's Master, Gautama the Buddha who, as he lay dying, exhorted his disciples: "Work out your own salvation with diligence." *The Key to Theosophy* is the nearest we have to a manual in the Theosophical movement. *The Voice of the Silence* is to some the noblest scripture extant.

What of the influence of H.P.B. and her Masters? As a speaker she was magnetic; she never lectured, but she would talk, and those who heard her could think of nothing else. In 1920, when I came into the movement, I knew, as I have said, a number of people who had known her well, and on this they were agreed, that after meeting her nothing was quite the same again. As a writer, she caused a sensation with everything she wrote. She aroused new interest in comparative religion. She taught in karma and rebirth a twofold doctrine which many, with fading faith in the Christian God, found an excellent substitute, more reasonable and more acceptable to the average Western mind. These basic principles, which run through all her writing, have percolated deeply into Western thought, though not, it may be, under the name Theosophy. This does not matter. The label is unimportant if the truth as such be known. What matters is the Teaching, and as Truth it may be found in a thousand forms.

Thinkers today are accepting as never before the teachings of an ancient Wisdom, and are prepared to recognize it wherever found, whether in the scriptures of extant religions, in mythology and folklore, in the writings of thinkers of all times and climes, or in the modern "discoveries" of science and psychology. But Theosophy, let it never be forgotten, is not a pasted-up collection of such fragments, but a re-exposition, complete though in outline, of the Ancient Wisdom of which all religions are but the sad remains.

And what of the movement she came to found? It ought to have been "a nucleus of universal brotherhood." "That is all I ask," she said again and again, "a nucleus." Where is it? Even in her lifetime there were splits, with arguments and rival personalities. After her death, there were splits again and again. Where is today a nucleus of universal brotherhood, caring nothing for distinction of race and sex and caste, of class and color, caring nothing for personalities, without rivalry as to who shall lead, or teach, but only striving to serve mankind? That is the nucleus which the Masters are still, apparently, willing to help wherever they find it. There has been a decline from the spiritual to the psychic plane and the personal; too little understanding that psychic phenomena have nothing to do with spiritual principles and spiritual powers. Where today in the movement do we find Madame Blavatsky? There has always been a "Back-to-Blavatsky" movement, trying to preserve and teach and apply the teachings that she gave. It has long been a minority, but larger than some seem to think. The various Theosophical organizations do not alone comprise the Theosophical movement, which also includes thousands of earnest students who do not wish to join an organization of any kind. They are concerned with the teachings, and the application of the teachings, of H. P. Blavatsky.

The Theosophical movement today is far from expended, and is showing life in a surprising variety of forms. Even as the tide of materialism creeps across the Western world, so there is a counter-movement of the spirit. Science, Marxism and the American worship of the almighty dollar are three forces which among them are destroying the spiritual awareness of the West. What is to be put against them? The answer is to be found not only in the continuing, but fading, efforts of organized religion, but in small groups, mostly without a name, which meet together in halls or in someone's house to hear and discuss some aspect of the wisdom offered by someone who has himself experienced it. They are looking, these good people, Masters unconsciously, for the bricks of personal experience with which to build the temple of some "new" religion, some new presentation of what is in fact the Secret Doctrine which H.P.B. was sent to the West to reproclaim. This future religion will not be Buddhism or Hinduism or Christianity; not even Theosophy. It will create its own form, but it will be the same wisdom, for this wisdom, the common heritage of all mankind, is one.

Nikola Tesla

On a winter evening in 1882, two young men were walking in the city gardens of Budapest. The sun was about to set and the sky was so spectacular that one of the walkers began to quote aloud from Goethe's *Faust*:

> The glow retreats, done is the day of toil;
> It yonder hastes new fields of life exploring.
> Ah that no wing can lift me from the soil;
> Upon its track to follow, follow soaring...

The man who spoke was Nikola Tesla and the other, called Szigeti, scarcely reacted since he was already well accustomed to his friend's eccentricities. But what happened next made him draw back in alarm.

Tesla suddenly stopped speaking and then froze, his

head thrust forward and his eyes staring directly in the fiery glare of the sun. As Szigeti moved forward to touch him, Tesla began to speak again, but his voice had changed; the words came out harshly and flat as if from an automaton. "Watch me, watch me reverse it!"

Szigeti remembering the words of Goethe and fearful of his friend's sanity, assumed that Tesla was talking about reversing the movement of the sun—to pull it up into the sky again. For a second time he tried to remonstrate with his friend to get him to rest on a nearby bench, but Tesla brushed him aside and continued to pour out a confused jumble of words, steadily growing more and more excited in the process. "Don't you see! Don't you see! How smoothly it is running. Now I will throw this switch and it reverses. See, it goes just as smoothly in the opposite direction. Now I stop it, I start it. There is no sparking, nothing to spark."

Szigeti was by now thoroughly alarmed: "I see nothing at all—no sparks. Are you ill?" Tesla swung round, staring through his friend, ignored the question and then immediately rushed on with a full and detailed description of what has now turned out to be one of the most important inventions in the history of electrical science. By the time he had finished he was mentally exhausted and apparently in a semi-ecstatic state.

At the time of Tesla's visionary experience, it was dogma that electricity could only be used in direct form, that is to say with fixed and unchanging positive and negative charges on two conductors. Alternating electricity is different in that the positive and negative charges on the two conductors reverse rapidly sometimes hundreds of times every second. At the time, several scientists had unsuccessfully attempted to construct alternating current motors, but because of the rapid changes in polarity, the energy in the current was dissipated in ineffective vibrations of the central rotating part of the motor called the armature. Tesla's great and simple idea was to feed the alternating current to the motor in more than one wave, each one out of step in time so that each crest and trough pulled the armature round to a new position. In this way the motor spun smoothly and silently just as he had fore-seen in his vision.

A mere technical description of an advance in electrical science sounds prosaic enough, and it is easy to find equally academic accounts of this discovery in the scientific journals of the time. But the fact remains that the subsequent development of what are now known as "polyphase" currents revolutionized the entire basis of electrical engineering and led directly to the long-distance transmission of electrical power.

Again this seems merely to label Tesla as a gifted and original scientific thinker. So where is the special quality, why do I believe that Tesla was a completely different and mysterious human individual?

Contemporary science is now beginning to divide into two separate and largely incompatible systems of thought. On the one hand we have what I call institutional science with its highly developed and essentially mechanical sense of reality and, on the other, a nascent and more fragile belief system which proposes that nature does not break down at all into fully describable systems which when fitted together make a complete and understandable whole. This second category of belief also holds that institutional science is inadequate, narrow and self-limiting and produces biased descriptions of reality which can only fit the method itself and all its limitations. Instead it questions the myth of objectivity and proposes that there are alternative frameworks of reality and that these essentially depend on the attitude and perceptions of the individual. Although it is an oversimplification, it suggests that the individual is an integral and creative part of the fabric of nature and that his own being and existence would, if fully developed, make this reality just as "real" as the external, physical and allegedly objective version used by the institutional scientist. This new science, which I hold to be so important to the development of man, is easy to talk out of existence and I know this from personal experience.

I worked for many years in various institutional laboratories and it is only recently that I came to doubt and then reject the basic assumptions of orthodox institutional science as both limiting, misleading and inadequate. Had I been asked to describe Tesla at that time I would doubtless have produced the appropriate epithets to create an image of him which would have made him acceptably unimportant. I would have called him: "maverick," "showman" and "populist" and then having made sure that his wholly unique properties posed no real threat to the probities and dogma of my own speciality, I would have closed the laboratory door behind me with a definite sigh of relief.

Nikola Tesla has provoked more controversy than almost any other scientist living or dead. He was responsible for a prodigious series of original inventions ranging from small electrical machines up to Wagnerian devices thrusting great metal towers hundreds of feet into the air to draw power from the sky and to send bolts of electrical energy ringing round the substance of the planet.

He oscillated between penury and riches, he was a socialite and yet solitary, he enjoyed the company of women but shunned any close personal relationship with them. He was fully aware of the financial consequences of his inventions and yet gave away patent rights which could have made him as rich as Rockefeller. He invented and described guided missiles, aircraft without wings and interplanetary communicators. He probably discovered cosmic rays, X-rays and the fundamentals of radio transmission well before the scientists who are normally credited with their discovery.

He was described as magician and showman, a Dr. Faustus in league with diabolical forces and as a poet toying with artificial lightning.

But to begin at the beginning.

In the summer of 1856, a second son was born to Reverend Milutin Tesla and his wife Djouka. They lived in Smiljan which was then a part of an Austro-Hungarian province called Lika, which later became part of Yugoslavia. Milutin was village pastor and Djouka, his wife, was illiterate but nevertheless intellectually brilliant. She was also a highly practical inventor of many household devices, including her own design of loom, and she possessed an abnormally retentive memory which seems to have acted as an effective substitute for literacy and enabled her to acquire an

extraordinary and widely based education. She could recite
thousands of verses of national poetic sagas and whole books
of the Bible from memory. She was also widely known for her
artistic needlework and weaving and her son insisted that
when she was over sixty, she could still tie three knots in an
eyelash using only her fingers.

His father, Milutin, was entirely a different character. A
sensitive individualist, quick to offense and slow to forgive, he
started life in the army and finding its crude and brutalized
lifestyle intolerable, resigned his commission and entered the
church. A poet and philosopher, he was also highly aware of
the social and political problems of his age and so was just as
likely to preach a sermon on labor relations and economics as
he was on some aspect of Christianity.

Nikola was one of five children and had one other
brother, Dane, who was also exceptionally gifted, but who
died in an accident at the age of twelve and it is often as-
serted that the death of the elder child forced Nikola to imitate his brilliance. This must have been a factor, but I believe
it is quite trivial when considered in the whole development
of this unique and mysterious human being.

During his childhood and schooldays Nikola seems to
have shown all the qualities of a born experimentalist, sometimes with near lethal results. For example, he became fascinated by the flight of birds and taking his ideas on to the
performances of a logical experiment, launched himself from
the roof of a barn suspended from an umbrella. The result
was a severe shaking and six weeks in bed.

At about the same time he was discovering the delights
of public acclaim. In his home town of Gospic a new fire service had been created and the populace turned out for a demonstration of the fire-hoses and water pump. There was a
ceremony; speeches and music. The end of the hose was im-
mersed in the river, the men began to work the handles of the
pump and people waited expectantly for the spray of water.
Nothing happened. The men sweated and pulled harder at
the pump; still no water. Tesla, at seven years of age, was
watching and suddenly blurted out, "Keep pumping" and
rushed down to the water's edge and found a kink from the

intake hose which he unbent. Water shot from the hoses and
the seven-year-old boy was chaired round the town; the hero
of the hour.

So now we have an exceptionally able and gifted boy
who was already inventing and building his own devices. He
already had a water-wheel, a primitive vacuum pump and a
machine powered by insects to his credit. But now we begin
to see the first evidence of a really strange quality.

Everyone has the ability to visualize to some degree. If
we close our eyes we can see things in what we call our mind's
eye. We can all create, to a varying degree, an internal visual
model of an object or a place. In the case of Tesla, this mental
property was different, not only in degree, but also I believe
in kind and relates to what I have said about the sciences. But
to get some idea of the sudden and strange vision he experienced in the park in Budapest, we can get some help from accounts of his schooldays.

In the mathematics classroom, his teacher rapidly began
to suspect that he had invented a new and unusually clever
system of cheating, because it mattered not at all whether he
wrote his sums down on a piece of paper, went to the blackboard to write them or just sat quite still looking at his fingers. He could produce the correct solution to a problem
almost instantaneously, however complex and in however
many stages.

Much later he described the process as he saw it. He was
able to see the calculation as a reality in front of him and the
development of the solution would actually happen in succes-
sive stages as writing on the board, much more rapidly than
he could possibly write it down. The image of the writing was
just as real as the board. Again it is quite possible to say, as
his teachers certainly did at the time, that he was just exceptionally good at mental arithmetic, but this ability recurs
again and again in different forms during his life and requires
an entirely different interpretation. For example, if he imagined some machine or other invention, he many times said
that it would literally appear in front of him and that he
could freely move his own viewpoint in and around all of its
structure. He could also see and record all the movements of

the machine together with its dimensions and tolerances. Much later in life when he was at the height of his fame, he told a colleague that he had just invented and built several electrical machines and that they were already working and on test. The machines in our sense of the term did not exist, they were all in his mind's eye or, as I prefer to state it: in his own framework of reality. While the machines were spinning in his own real world, he again said that when the tests were complete he would be able to measure and report on any breakdowns or wear which had occurred. This extraordinary quality not only proved to be true when the machines were eventually built, but also frequently exasperated his assistants because he never bothered to make drawings of his inventions, but carried all the shapes, tolerances and stress figures within his own frame of reference. He could, at any time, produce any physical measurement without recourse to any document or drawing.

So powerful was this particular property that Tesla himself wrote that it was sometimes impossible for him to distinguish between what we would call reality—the hard edges of tables and chairs—and what his mind showed to him—an entirely different world of continuous invention, where machines could be created at will.

Again it is perfectly possible to conclude that Tesla just had a strong and unusual ability to visualize whatever his imagination created and indeed institutional science has developed words and labels to describe such phenomena. Many learned articles on "eidetic" images, or "hypnagogic" and "hypnapompic" experiences describe aspects of this quality, but looked at in detail, these descriptions carry no problem-solving power at all. They are mere tautologies lamely trying to create a believable taxonomy of the inexplicable.

One of Heisenberg's great contributions to knowledge and one which had now spread well beyond his own sphere of theoretical physics was to show that it is not possible to examine a situation or system without altering the system by the act of examination. By the same token, we can try and analyze and codify Tesla's abilities by imposing highly structured descriptions but by so doing we only create a picture which suits our own cultural values and mechanical view of nature and we are just as far away from an understanding of his own framework of reality as we were when we started.

Earlier on I suggested that there is a growing dichotomy in scientific thought: the institutional approach which is motivated towards hard-edged objectivity and the second, which supposes that the human observer is himself an essential and creative part of the reality he observes. The great scientist and philosopher Eddington must have understood the second approach when he wrote that "the universe looks less and less like a machine and more and more like a great thought."

This brings me to my first conclusion. I believe that Tesla was a man who was in touch with a particular and quite mysterious part of reality which is not normally accessible. To write such a statement is for me a profoundly important experience and one which still sends shock waves rushing through my institutionally conditioned mind, but nevertheless, I believe it to be true. Tesla seems to have had a reality framework around him which was entirely different in kind from ours.

I have by no means yet justified such an extreme and dogmatic statement, so I want now to examine some other aspects of his character.

One single property of his stands out as a consistent thread extending through the whole of his life and that was an unwavering sense of purpose. For example, when his elder brother died, his parents naturally tended to overprotect their younger son. At the time he was developing a strong interest in engineering but because this entailed a long and arduous college training, his father wanted him to enter the church instead. At about the same time Nikola was doing especially well at his studies, particularly in the sciences. Then he contracted what may well have been cholera. The attack was serious and he gradually sank lower and lower until, it appears, he was almost at the point of death. Ahead lay two alternative courses of action, a compulsory period in the army and then the church. Finally his father relented and said to the dying boy that he could study engineering. From that point on, as Tesla later recounted, he felt able to draw on the strength of his family and made a rapid and complete recovery. It was as if his mind and body were in complete consonance and behaved as a single entity expressing his own drive and single-mindedness. Once again, it is easy to find orthodox medical explanations. Doctors might talk of the psychosomatic element, or the effect of mind on body in his recovery, but again this is completely nonexplanatory and serves only as a redescription. Moreover, it introduces a conceptual bias suggesting that it is mind that is affecting body. This may well occur just as the body obviously affects the mind, but it is entirely unnecessary to talk about either polarity. In the case of Tesla the only route to understanding is to assume that his mind and body were one individual unit and that during the illness his whole will and purpose was to influence events so that he could become an engineer.

Throughout his life Tesla set himself impossible standards of work. He always became totally committed to any new project and would deliberately whittle down his sleeping period until he was in his bedroom for a mere five hours, only two of which were actually spent in sleeping.

There were so many strange episodes in Tesla's life it would be impossible to refer to them all, but one in particular strongly reinforces my belief that he had access to an aspect of nature or frame of reference which is denied to most of us. At the time, he was working for the Central Telegraph office in Budapest and had, in an amazingly short space of time, created a profusion of improvements to the telephone system. But he was also beginning to become obsessed with the alternating-current motor which was then thought to be a technical impossibility for reasons I have already described. He finally worked himself to the point of total collapse and fell ill, but his symptoms were so extraordinary that doctors at the time were totally unable to categorize, let alone treat, his complaint. Contemporary medicine would also have nothing useful to say about his condition at the time.

As he lay in bed he was subject to an intolerable increase in the power of his senses. He complained of the ticking of a watch three rooms away, the vibrations of the city traffic became so harsh and painful that rubber pads were placed under his body to dampen transmission from the street outside. Someone speaking made a noise like a series of explosions and a slight touch had all the power of a blow. Sunlight shining through the window burned his eyes and in the dark, he described the ability to see an object as far away as twelve feet by means of a "curious" sensation he experienced in his forehead.

Once again it is perfectly possible to redescribe this experience in ordinary terms and say that it is quite common for people to feel a sudden heightening of sensitivity. It is a matter of common experience that during a fever, the sheets feel hurtful to the touch, the body as a whole reacts painfully to almost any movement. Also Tesla had a highly developed sense of the dramatic and, as we shall see later on, was quite capable of embellishing a quite ordinary event with all the techniques and flamboyance of the theater.

But in the context of his prodigious and strong abilities, I believe that this particular experience was an integral and vital part of what followed, because it was almost immediately after his recovery and his senses had returned to normal, that he was walking in the park with Szigeti and saw his great vision of polyphase currents.

Look back at the lines from Faust that he quoted at the time:

> Ah that no wing can lift me from the soil;
> Upon its track to follow, follow soaring...

Throughout his life he was consistently driven to struggle free from his ordinary human state—to soar on a wing away from the soil perhaps. He possessed a quite superhuman urge to see into the unknown fabric of the universe which was quite different from the more prosaic and codified inquiry of the ordinary scientist. One description of him written towards the end of his life seems particularly apt, "a Dr. Faustus who cared nothing for Marguerites, a philosopher filled with a vast discontent, a poet who toyed with artificial lightning...." But so differently from the stricken Faustus, there is nothing to suggest that he was trying to cheat death and everything to indicate that he wanted to control the forces of nature he had discovered for the benefit of men.

It is difficult to know where to choose the next facet of this massively talented and mysterious person. The easy course would be to conclude that he was a completely single-minded and highly talented individual who pursued an extremely carefully planned course through life without deviation. A man who saw his plethora of abilities as an important source of alleviation for mankind's suffering. All this is a matter of record. He said many times that he could supply all the energy needs of the world by means of his global power transmission systems. He could stop war by the creation of what would now be called a doomsday machine and he would harness the actual structure of the globe for universal communication between peoples.

But slowly and with increasing certainty, I have become convinced that orthodox psychological and scientific descriptions are not only insufficient to understand Nikola Tesla but actually block understanding.

Earlier on I referred to what I believe to be the emergence of a new and more fragile science. One in which the universe is not merely observed and categorized from a so-called objective viewpoint with all its arrogance and *hubris*, but one where all the perceptions and persona of the individual become an integral part of reality.

Perhaps the greatest mistake we have made in our own Western culture has been to assume that our science is real and valid because our technology appears to work efficiently and repeatedly. Because Apollo lands successfully on the moon, we assume that our view of nature is also correct. We forget that the Apollo spacecraft is merely a super-efficient tool showing our very powerful and successful control over the raw materials of the universe. As we probe, dissect, analyze and build with the elements available to us, we are steadily reinforced in the belief that we are progressing in our more general understanding of the universe and its workings because we are good toolmakers.

I now believe this view to be fundamentally mistaken and moreover one which will at worst destroy us as a species from the destructive results of our toolmaking within a very short space of time, or at best destroy our position of dominance on this planet probably forever. I also think that Tesla knew this, but knew it in a way which was unique to his own existence. From his earliest days as a child right up to the time of his death, he seems to have had a consistent vision of how we could take what energy we needed from the earth without damaging its fabric.

Energy is now our most urgent preoccupation and we all know that we have exploited and drained our very small planet to a point where little more will ever be available. How was it that in an industrial age of apparent plenty Tesla came to realize that energy was the basic building block essential to our survival and that it was strictly finite?

Again there are clues in his childhood, but once more they can be seen from two entirely different viewpoints.

On one occasion, for example, he was climbing a snow-clad mountain with some schoolfriends and they were bombarding each other with snowballs, most of which just embedded themselves in the snow or rolled a few feet downwards. But one in particular began to roll and roll growing bigger and bigger by accretion and gathering speed and momentum as it bounced its way down the mountain. Finally it swelled into a booming avalanche thundering down the mountainside sweeping trees and rocks aside and finally landing in the valley with such force that it sent a shock wave reverberating back through the whole mountain.

Imagine a group of thoroughly frightened schoolboys aghast at the result of their game: not Tesla. To him the event symbolized the concept of amplification. That by injecting a very small force into a poised system containing a larger force, the large force could be released. One flick of a forearm could move the side of a mountain. His muscles were the switch to the energy amplifier.

On another occasion he was watching a thunderstorm and saw great arcs of fire flash downwards immediately followed by a torrent of rain. He drew the natural but mistaken conclusion that the lightning caused the rain and much later in his life designed large electrical towers to precipitate rain artificially. An obviously mistaken idea but one which was deeply linked with his obsession with electrical power and global energy.

Also while he was experimenting with super-powerful crossbows, a vacuum pump and other inventions, he seems to have discovered how to produce a state of euphoria for himself without access to drugs or alcohol. A physiologist would call the phenomenon hyper-ventilation and would show that by deep, regular and repeated overbreathing, excess carbon dioxide in the bloodstream is voided and more than the usual amount of oxygen is taken into the body and distributed to all the corners of the brain inducing a heady sense of well being. This technique is well known in some religious rituals as a means of achieving a state of ecstasy, but for a solitary twelve-year-old boy it is a completely remarkable achievement.

Time and time again the young Tesla seems to have been brought face to face with demonstrations of the mechanisms of the universe, and the relation of his own body and mind to it. And it is perfectly easy to conclude that the experiences were purely random and fortuitous. On the other hand, as his principal biographer O'Neill records:

> Nature seems to be constantly engaged in staging spectacular demonstrations for young Tesla revealing to him samples of the secret of her mighty forces.

I believe that the structure of the universe is not just a gray neutral framework of atoms, radiation and galaxies but is a sentient, living whole which is subject to a continuously evolving design process of which we have no overall concept, but which some individuals can glimpse in brief flashes. This view can easily be dismissed as a thin restatement of Pantheism, but I believe that at times Tesla experienced this connection and communication with the language of the universe. I do not at all mean that he was subject to great visions of a personal God who spoke to him, but that he was able occasionally to understand or to have revealed to him aspects of a living integrated whole. I cannot understand how

the knowledge could have been codified, what language was
used, but it seems likely to have been a visual metaphor. That
just as he could see nonexistent machines spinning in his own
frame of reality, so could he visualize some of the anatomy of
the living universe.

He was also quite capable of writing complete cant.

At times his self-importance grew to quite extraordinary
heights and in one immensely confused article published in
America in 1900 he concludes that the human race can be totally explained in terms of mass, momentum and velocity and
that the best way to improve the human lot or mass is to
make sure that no germs ever get into the drinking water!
Having concluded a diatribe on the evils of whisky, wine and
tea he goes on to thunder: "for every person who perishes
from the effects of a stimulant, at least a thousand die from
the consequences of drinking impure water. This precious
fluid, which daily infuses new life into us, is likewise the chief
vehicle through which disease and death enter our bodies.
The germs of destruction it conveys are enemies all the more
terrible as they perform their fatal work unperceived. They
seal our doom while we live and enjoy."

It is probably true that water in those times was much
more likely to contain pathogens than it is now, but even so
his views about it and about personal hygiene were so extreme as to be seen as no more than a personal quirk.

But in the same article, there is a brilliant and original
description of how alien life might appear on another planet
which walks straight through conventional biological descriptions of life. Also there is one of the first accounts of a subject
now called alternative technology, and this in 1900! Dealing
with the problem of food shortage, he describes ways of fixing
atmospheric nitrogen for fertilizer by means of high voltage
discharge and goes on to make a plea for power to be generated from the wind and the sun. He also seems to have perceived the waste of the planet's resources involved in the
growth of cattle for food and recommends a vegetarian diet
as a consequence, a regime to which he adhered in later life.
In our present deodorized, bleached, sterilized and super-
white world, I believe that exposure to more bacteria would

be beneficial to us in re-establishing basic immune structures in our bodies which we have probably lost from a biologically parched environment. But Tesla's view of the evils of impure water, although pompous and didactic, is still of interest because he had an almost religious respect for the body and his dogma about the drinking water may simply have been another metaphor whereby he sought to understand and then protect its delicate systems: "Everyone should consider his body as a priceless gift from one who he loves above all, a marvelous work of art of indescribable beauty and mastery beyond human conception, and so delicate and frail that a word, a breath, a look, nay, a thought may injure it."

A thought may injure it! Now we can begin to understand the strange hypersensitive condition of his senses he experienced just before he had the vision of the polyphase current system in the park in Budapest. There is no need to involve psychic or soma, because here was an individual who was fully aware that his physical substance was a delicate system of infinite balance susceptible to the slightest external influence.

He seems to have gone into some sort of resonance with the forces of nature, much as a tuned circuit in a receiver goes into resonance with incoming waves. His whole body seems to have become an antenna system vibrating and oscillating in tune with a raging flood of stimuli pouring in from the outside world. If Tesla could feel light, the spoken word and traffic vibration to be intolerably powerful, what other more meaningful information entered his consciousness at the same time?

What did he see without the aid of his eyes?

At the age of twenty-nine Tesla arrived in the United States penniless and without personal effects having, incredibly, left all his luggage behind in Europe by mistake. Within just a few days he had met and joined Edison who was already working on his own direct-current generating system. He was relegated to a small routine job having immediately clashed with Edison about the relative merits of alternating- and direct-current systems. But gradually his abilities surfaced and he produced a bewildering cascade of designs for

new electrical machines. For one, Edison promised him
$50,000 and when he perfected it, Edison laughed in his face
and told him that the promise of money was just a joke.

Tesla resigned immediately and almost at once fell into
the hands of business promoters who succeeded in ruining
him financially in a very short time.

Then followed one of his lowest points in life. He was
broke and had to take a job as a laborer digging ditches at
two dollars a day. Finally, through a highly educated works
foreman also down on his luck, he got a job with Western
Union and was given a laboratory to develop his own alternating-current machines.

Once again his prodigious creativity took over and he produced design after design culminating in a lecture to the American Institute of Electrical Engineers showing that alternating
current could be transmitted over long distances, whereas Edison's direct-current system was limited to small urban areas. In
the audience was another pioneer of electrical science, George
Westinghouse, who without any hesitation offered him a job
and one million dollars cash for his growing pile of patents.
Tesla agreed at once provided that he received one dollar per
horse-power generated by his own designs. Again he set to work
with a total dedication that left a string of exhausted and incredulous assistants behind him and a shining new series of electrical machines in his laboratory.

Now it was Westinghouse's turn to fall into financial dif-
ficulties and he also came under control of promoters who put
pressure on him to renege on his one dollar per horse-power
deal with Tesla. When asked diffidently by Westinghouse to
reconsider, Tesla actually took the written agreement and
tore it up saying that his sole interest was in the development
of his idea in the service of man. This genuinely magnan-
imous gesture certainly cost him at least twelve million dollars.

Throughout his life nothing seriously deflected Tesla
from his course. Living within his own view of reality he simply forged on brushing aside relative trifles such as penury,
riches or fame or opposition.

Now freed from the irritating constraints of commerce,

he returned to his old laboratory in New York and at once began experimenting with higher and higher frequencies and voltages of electricity, leading upwards towards the frequency of radio waves and light.

Again came a flood of inventions including the now universal "Tesla-coil" and a reciprocating dynamo powered by a unique free-piston engine. His reputation steadily grew throughout America, and then Europe, and he became the center of attention of an increasingly astonished scientific world. He also became the pivot point of affluent New York society and guest of honor at many a glittering social function. In return he would stage elaborate gourmet dinners at the Waldorf-Astoria Hotel and was often to be seen prowling the kitchens beforehand sampling and tasting and advising— doubtless to the chagrin of the chefs.

After the meal he would take his guests down to his laboratory for demonstrations and now we can see the real magician at work. Consider what he looked like. Here, for example, is a contemporary description:

> No one can look upon him without feeling his force. He is more than six feet tall and very slender. Yet he possesses great physical power. His hands are large, his thumbs abnormally long and this is a sign of great intelligence. His hair is black and straight, a deep shining black. He brushes it from over his ears, so that it makes a ridge with serrated edges. His cheekbones are high and prominent, the mark of the Slav; his skin is like marble that age has given the first searing of yellow. His eyes are blue, deeply set and they burn like balls of fire. Those weird flashes of light he makes with his instruments seem also to shoot from them. His head is wedge shaped. His chin is almost a point ... When he talks you listen. You do not know what he is saying but it enthralls you. You feel the importance without understanding the meaning.

Imagine the scene. A darkened laboratory full of great copper coils, spinning machines and rows of switches and batteries. A huddled group of expensively dressed socialites waiting in considerable awe in spite of the fortification of good food and wine. Enter a man looking more like Mephistopheles than any actor would have dared present. He begins to throw switches, dynamos start spinning. There is a low hum rising to a tense whine. The hard staccato blast of electrical discharges begins. Sparks begin to stab the air between terminals. The noise grows, the sparks develop into great branching trees of electrical flame crashing and exploding between points on the ceiling and on the floor. The air grows heavy with the disinfectant reek of ozone. There is smoke. The cannonade of power swells. His childhood dream of artificial lightning is realized! Excelling Prometheus he pulls down another deafening battery of discharges and then with a final flourish, allows hundreds of thousands of volts of high frequency electricity to flash harmlessly through his body to light bulbs and tubes held in his hand. Just as suddenly as it began, the noise and flashing brilliance subsides and there is silence.

It is not the fictional setting for the entrance of Baron Frankenstein, but a talented dramatist giving a performance of his own inventions which would have driven a professional actor to despair. So much power was released into the neighborhood from his demonstrations that on one occasion someone drew a one-inch spark from a tap streets away! One might be reasonably suspicious of such melodrama, if it were not for his astounding originality and sheer weight of invention. For example, it took a 495-page book to describe all his inventions and researches.

At the crest of a wave of acclamation and success in the United States, Tesla made a triumphant tour of the major European capitals, managing to survive an almost continuous process of lionization, and also a series of malicious accusations suggesting that he had plagiarized the ideas of an Italian engineer. Just before he left once more for America, his mother fell ill and he reached her bedside only a few hours before her death, after a remarkable and documented premonition of her illness.

On return to America again he abruptly abandoned all public life. The socializing, the parties and the demonstrations gave way to a period of fiercely intense work in his laboratory.

One would have thought that by that time he would have sensed some peak in his achievements and rested on his laurels, but it was not the case. Not in the least content with his massive and powerful electrical machines now beginning to cover the world, he began to conceive the entire substance of the planet as a manageable system and began to draw up Promethean plans for the global transmission of intelligence and power.

Still using his basic concepts of high frequency waves, that is to say, radio waves, and lower frequency power waves he would have done away with the necessity for the national electrical grid with its ugly regiment of pylons stalking across the green land.

He continued to be fascinated by the phenomenon of resonance. Just as the bowing of a violin string at a certain note will shatter a nearby glass if the material of the glass is of a form and mass that will vibrate in harmony with the note, so will one frequency of transmitted waves from a radio station cause the tuned circuits of a radio receiver to resonate or vibrate in tune. No one, however, had foreseen the possibility of transmitting useful amounts of power by the same means. Once again, an experiment he performed seems to have provided the basic visual image. Another tableau provided by nature perhaps?

He was at the time discharging a very large coil and the air of the laboratory was once again laced with an exploding profusion of electrical fire. Then he noticed that sparks began to spray into the air from another uncharged coil far away in the corner of the room. It had resonated to the frequency of the large coil and discharged power. Power had been transmitted across space.

It would be easy to go on describing his increasingly Wagnerian creations, a 180-foot wooden tower surmounted by a sixty-foot cupola of interlaced steel wires for global radio transmission actually built in 1904, another jutting steel mast firing enormous electrical bolts down at the ground with such explosive violence that the great bank of copper coils supplying its power finally melted. This list is endless, but now what of the strange, remote figure behind the inventions? What of the small boy from Lika who saw visions of a planet with limitless and pollution-free energy and who gradually came to realize that his gifts could make the visions happen?

In later life Tesla often said that he had no fear of death since he was certain to live for at least 120 years and far from being empty bombast it is clear that this is what he actually believed. Although he actually died at eighty-three, he saw himself as a continuous and virtually immortal creator of new aspects of nature.

Many writers have described him as a superman and in many ways the word is fitting, but not in a dominating or aggressive manner, but perhaps more in line with the much-maligned concepts of Nietzsche. A man who, by concentrated inquiry, continuous internal development and rejection of cultural values, is able to transcend his ordinary humanity and walk a little nearer to the gods.

In this context, it is strange to read that biographers have written that Tesla regarded man as an automaton. His own words were "meat machine," but it is quite clear that he did not mean this as derogatory, neither was he using it to describe man as a mere protoplasmic robot. He had created what seems to be an elegant and simple image to explain the difference between living and nonliving material. He described the meat machine or living body as inextricably related to the inanimate, since it is consistently taking in and putting out matter in the form of inanimate atoms and molecules and yet the "machine" itself lives. The body therefore, as he described it, was only a machine in the sense that it is an input-output system with the musculo-skeletal, nervous, digestive and cardiac systems as parts of an integrated whole. For example, in a description of one of his psychic experiences wherein he recounted the feeling of acute physical pain when a friend was hurt by others, he goes on to say: "We are automata entirely controlled by the medium" and his use of the word medium is only to describe the physical continuum of nature and the continuity of the body with the medium. He goes on: "being tossed about like corks on the surface of the water, but mistaking the resultant of the impulses from the outside for free will." This last phrase is important for he is not suggesting that we exist in some rigidly preordained network of certainty, but that the behavior of the physical body is linked to the substance of nature. He also thought that if we keep our whole mind-body complex in what he called perfect order, we can bring ourselves into a balanced communication with the substance and processes of nature:

> A very sensitive and observant person, with his highly developed mechanism all intact, and acting with precision in obedience to the changing conditions of the environment, is endowed with a transcending mechanical sense.

In later years he went on to develop the concept of resonance to explain this effect. He described his own sense of sometimes total continuity and identity with the natural order as a resonant or tuned state.

It also seems as though Tesla had several experiences which many have called psychic. He firmly rejected the description, but in the same breath said that he was certain that mind could communicate directly with mind, and that it was possible to see forward in time. His rejection of "psychic" as an explanation, although an apparent paradox, stemmed from the current use of the word which then involved vague and romantic notions of spirits and souls. He preferred to see the phenomenon as one which would ultimately be explainable by an extension and enrichment of the scientific method.

At one of his parties, for example, he was suddenly overcome by the obsessionally recurring thought that a group of his friends should stay with him that night. He apparently restrained some of them almost by force. They finally stayed and found later that they would have all traveled on the same train which later that night crashed with many casualties.

On another occasion, towards the end of his life, he was living in a hotel room in New York where he had installed elaborate cages for pigeons which he delighted in feeding as they flew in through the open window. Feeding the birds had been an obsession for many years and he would go to ex-

traordinary lengths to ensure that the birds were regularly fed
if he was to be away for any reason. One bird in particular, a
white dove, became for him a real and very beautiful symbol
of love and devotion. Listen to his own words:

> Yes I loved that pigeon, I loved her as a man loves
> a woman and she loved me. When she was ill I knew
> and understood; she came to my room and I stayed be-
> side her for days. I nursed her back to health.

And again:

> No matter where I was . . . I had only to wish and
> call her and she would come flying to me.

Finally:

> One night she wanted me, she wanted to tell me
> something important; so I got up and went to her. As I
> looked at her I knew she wanted to tell me she was
> dying. And then, as I got her message, there came a
> light from her eyes—powerful beams of light. It was a
> *real* light, a powerful, dazzling, blinding light, a light
> more intense than I had ever produced by the most
> powerful lamps in my laboratory. When that pigeon
> died, something went out of my life. Up to that time I
> knew with a certainty that I would complete my work,
> no matter how ambitious my program, but when that
> something went out of my life I knew my life's work was
> finished.

The psychologist will produce gray, academic and totally
nonexplanatory descriptions of the dove as a female symbol
of a celibate recluse and the vision researcher will point out
that there are no light-emitting organs in the eyes of a pigeon,
just receivers, but I believe Tesla experienced the phenomenon he described as real and that he was neither deluded nor
senile. Neither do I think that the experience can be described just as a part of Tesla's "inner reality." It was an integral part of his frame of reference and had any of us been

there within that particular framework at the time, we would have experienced a similar event.

The choice of interpretation is uniquely our own. Occam's razor shows with devastating clarity that there is no external objective world which we can all agree about as consistent and whole. Each person's view of the universe filters in through his own senses and goes out again as language to which has been added his own mental and cultural biases.

Tesla was a unique and marvelously endowed person, but also I have said that he was a totally unusual individual.

I see individuality as a temporary separation from the fabric of nature. The best picture of this that I can imagine for myself is to see a plane or sheet of infinite extent. The sheet is flexible and individual humans and animals emerge rather as if someone had pushed a finger against the reverse side of the sheet and made a bulge. The bulge becomes a sphere with a thin neck still attached to the plane. Then the neck parts and the individual is free, but just for a lifetime.

At the time of death, the sphere goes back down to the plane, reattaches, flattens and flows out into the whole until there is finally no trace of it. But the temporary individuality has not been lost but has merged with the living entity of nature. We are given a brief leasehold on a separate enclosure. I believe that during the lifetime of some rare humans the neck between the plane of the universe and the sphere of the individual remains actively open during their lifetime and that communication can occur along it both ways between the entity of the universe and the cognition of the individual. I think Nikola Tesla's vision sprang from this connection and that he could translate the patterns of nature he saw into our own mechanistic frame of reference. I mentioned earlier that the new science will enable us to use our own individual properties to see different aspects of nature which are more complete than the fragmented and mechanical descriptions offered by the old science and that this must involve the whole of our own experience. So for me it is very rewarding to be able to conclude this chapter by recording that my experience and standpoint has been materially changed in this direction by the act of writing it.

Aleister Crowley Rest In?

Devil? . . . but when I met Aleister Crowley in the room I had found for him to die in, he was no devil.

I had first met Crowley when I was three; my infant hand in his; my trust in him absolute. Now, in my late twenties, and his old age, I feared him: but who could dislike an old gentleman to whom one had done a good turn, as on Senior Citizens' Day? The magician looked charming in green plus-fours, mandarin beard, silver buckles on his shoes, and tinkling Tibetan bangles that had the added advantage of keeping his stockings up. Who could not feel a condescending concern for an old gentleman who excused himself in the middle of supper to pump heroin into his veins, enough to kill three men; enough to keep Crowley's old limbs moving and his conversation flowing?

My father had, some weeks before, asked if I could find a

quiet room in Hastings for Crowley who was thinking of retiring. It was the last year of the Second World War. I wandered around, asking landladies if they would house a magician. I asked in the dressing-room of the local repertory theater, where I was acting, and one of the players, who had opened an intellectual guest-house, leaped at the chance of adding to the attractions of weekend discussions. The rent was paid for Crowley by a sect in California which revered him as their master, or, at any rate, felt he had the copyright of their religion: they sent him enough to keep him in caviar, whisky, latakia, and the hottest curries.

I was bewildered by Crowley—whom I had not talked to for twenty-six years—surprised by this magician who had made evil his god. He was intelligent, with an intelligence that dried the air. I had expected a pretentious warlock, a dangerous clown, and I found an intelligent man. To make conversation, I asked him how his magic was getting on: he offered to sell me a set of books for a hundred pounds. There was an element of slapstick in all we did, that did not seem compatible with "The Great Beast." I took him up to the hall of this guest-house, and as we entered, every person in it got up in horror and left. At least it looked like that: afterwards I was told that, at the precise moment we opened the door, a discussion session had ended: but Crowley seemed hurt. Looking at him directly, as I left, instead of giving him the shy, bird-like glances of my previous confusion, I could see what a formidable person he still was. His eyes were bright, with particular intensity: he was relaxed in a reptilian way; his voice varied from dry rustle to caressing charm. His whole personality was focused, he was completely in control: of more than I could see, no doubt. My awe was increased by my mistaken idea that he was in his nineties; he was in his seventies.

What was Crowley?

We need a new assessment; one that goes beyond the sycophantic, or disparaging, or scandalized or condemnatory. I have no intention of making such an assessment. I hold up pieces of the man.

Crowley's disciples, victims and most of his associates

give the same impression of him as a profane bull of a man wrapped in a cloud of magic and sex: he is the Great Beast. The phrase "the wickedest man in the world" had been coined by the periodical *John Bull,* when reporting the death of a young Oxford man, Raoul Loveday, in Crowley's Sicilian Abbey: the Abbey that Crowley had called "Thelema" in imitation of Rabelais' creation where "Do what thou wilt shall be the whole of the Law." "Enticed to Abbey" ... "Driven to Suicide by Devil-worshippers" ... "Dreadful Ordeal of Young Wife" ... (she wrote a book about herself, later, called *Tiger Woman*) ... "Drugs, Magic, and Vile Practices." Vile practices there were, enough to make "each particular hair stand on end like quills upon the fretful porpentine"; but Crowley indignantly protested—and sued. The notoriety of the libel action, the infamy, made him a household name. He is a household name now, though "household" seems a sober description for a name that is identified—especially among the young—with black magic and the stirring up of the universe with the Great Wand.

Published photographs of Crowley give much the same impression; like the work of a brilliant publicist: which Crowley was. It would be wrong, though, to dismiss the photos as superficial studio poses; they give the truth, unmistakably, that this body had long been the incarnation of evil: that cannot be faked.

I have three of the photographs by me now. One, in the front of *The Collected Works of Aleister Crowley: Volume I*—published in 1905 when he was thirty!—bound in what looks like the white skin of a goat or a child, shows him as a handsome young man, with dark eyes, hypnotic but not glaring; a face softened by the full fleshed lips; a noble forehead under hair that is dark and thick, correctly cut as that of the most unaesthetic undergraduate; his clothes of a thick cloth as handsome as his face; he wears a poetic, over-large cravat. The second photo is of "the Beast" in his prime; powerful with thick, cultivated brutality around that sensitive mouth; a sensitive hand raised conjecturally to his chin, as though he had been surprised by his own greatness in the glass; the eyes as luminous as when young, but his left eyebrow lowered as though to ward off the remnants of his inherent delicacy; the head a shaved dome; he might be wearing the same cravat as before, slightly trimmed to suit his formidable authority; the clothes are still well cut. The third photo is of an old man whose serenity is in the beadier eyes, bright in their slits, hypnotic, calm, powerful; the mouth thicker, clown-like, made so by the lips' clasp on the horn pipe of latakia tobacco that drags the face down to a crease in the cheek; the cravat looks the same, only larger like the bows of artists in fiction. There is another photo of Crowley: Crowley in 1910, when he was thirty-five, the husband and father, a pleasantly meaty young man, a loving man, one might think, nicely shrewd in a city job, and ready, no doubt, to join the local part-time regiment, even at the cost of being less with the little daughter he holds, like a shepherd, across his shoulders, and less with the serene wife who shelters under his arm.

Crowley was born in Leamington, England, of a rich Quaker father and an oriental-looking mother. The father became a fanatical member of the Plymouth Brethren: the mother lived in constant fear of the Lord's coming. It was the mother who first called her son, "the Beast." When his father died, Crowley was brought up by Christian sadists. It is said that he turned to the Devil for strength. He also found strength in mountains; graduated in magic; matured into a poet: his wit was original, his humor sometimes puerile, his jokes were practical, his way of spending fortunes so impracticable that they took on a logic of their own by which the lost millions returned to the squandering hand. If he was not a millionaire in his old age by the sea at Hastings in Sussex, he lived as though he was. In food and drink he always showed judgment, marred by his eccentricities in the matter of blood and strong spices. He was an excellent chessplayer. At Hastings, he wandered into the well-known chess club, the first afternoon of his retirement, and beat the local champion.

A new assessment of Crowley should include all this—each in its right place, and in the right pattern—his poetry, his puerility, his charlatan tricks, his religion, his worldly appetites, his unworldly scattering of millions, his calculations in magic, and that refinement of brutality that came from seeking, with a strong mind, the truth in the dreadful freedom of man. Aleister Crowley has earned himself a place among the remembered names of the world. He deserves more than the interest we might give to a two-headed sheep at the fair.

To start a new assessment of Crowley, I supply two contradictory views of him.

In 1917-18 New York, my mother Frances, who had been in the Imagist group of poets, in Philadelphia, with Ezra Pound and "H.D.," met Crowley through his friendship with her husband, Louis Wilkinson—Louis who often wrote under the name of "Marlow," an Englishman well known as a lecturer in America. Frances loathed, abhorred and understood Crowley. She tried her utmost to end her husband's friendship with him. She had many stories about Crowley.

There was the one about their first dinner-party together with Crowley; when they found the address to be a skyscraper of offices all shut; the elevator out of action: walking up, past a violently shattered door on the fifth floor, they found Crowley on the sixth robed like a priest of Osiris with a saucepan in his hand, and in a temple rather than an apartment; and Louis, who had such an appreciation of wine that he never got drunk, began to talk extravagantly, and foolishly, quite unlike himself; while Crowley looked silenty at Frances over the dinner he had superbly cooked; and her husband laughed uproariously at nothing at all. Nothing terrible, in fact, happened. Louis was himself next day, and remembered only an excellent dinner. Yet, Frances never, after, underrated Crowley's powers; though she did not think them magical.

New York in 1918 was sinister enough, with too many crimes hidden under official sanction; but Crowley added his own melodrama. He seems to have acted the part of the "master criminal" of fiction. Crime, on its own, as a dull way of earning a living, or as a policy and way of life, was contemptible and shoddy to Crowley who was much more concerned with the universe. Even so, he must have been one of the few people to have had the attributes of the "master mind." He had medical knowledge, was a brilliant mathematician, a profound student of philosophy and metaphysics, understood ancient and modern languages, showed indifferences to extremes of hot and cold, and—to add the necessary decorative touch for the "great villain"—he carried a walking stick, a malacca cane, or a stick carved by an African sorcerer, with a demon's head and magical characters; he was also as much a master of disguises as any international crook. He needed the disguises. The authorities were after him even in 1918. Later, he was, of course, barred from some countries. For Crowley to have been a criminal, however great, and to have been nothing else, would have been small-time, and incompatible with the world he lived in, that is reflected in Crowley's own poem *Aha!*, published in the *Equinox* with an Invocation of the Spirit of Wisdom:

> Strange drugs are thine,
> Habit, and draughts of wizard wine!
> These do not hurt. Thine hermits dwell
> Not in the cold secretive cell,
> But under purple canopies
> With mighty-breasted mistresses
> Magnificent as lionesses—
> Tender and terrible caresses!
> Fire lives, and light, in eager eyes;
> And massed huge hair about them lies.

It was not a side of Crowley that Frances saw, or would particularly have respected; one suspects that she saw a very clever and horribly dangerous small boy. One of her stories about Crowley is of the time she and Louis dined with Crowley in a restaurant, and he chose to sit with his back to a window with long blinds: when two men entered, and moved among the tables, Crowley tipped his chair back, pulled the blind down in front of him, and the detectives passed a few feet away.

It is apparent, in all her stories, which all skirt the edge of nightmare, that no harm comes to her or her family. That might have been due to Frances, as much as to luck and Crowley's attitude to Louis. One of the most frightening of her stories is of how, when at home, she entered what she

thought was an empty room, and found a bald man at the
table. The man put on his hair, and turned into Crowley.
Picking up a case—in which Frances saw changes of hair as
other men have changes of shirt (the man she had seen, a moment before, had a completely shorn head)—Crowley de-
parted. He must have been as startled as Frances. Having
been left by Louis in what he thought was the empty house,
he had not expected to be disturbed. One forgets the nervous
tremors of monsters. It had happened so quickly, that
Frances doubted what she had seen; but she tentatively told
her husband; and Crowley as tentatively suggested she was
mad. A little later, in fact, when he had played on her fears,
Crowley helped to get two doctors to certify her; but Frances,
more intricate and intelligent a person than Crowley had realized suspected the plan, knew in good time that she was
being taken, not to a private home, but to a private asylum,
and avoided the trap. She had a strong spirit, but a weak
body: and with her greatest fear that Crowley would harm
her children, she became ill. Crowley did not relent. It was
this man whom Frances, returning home, still very weak, saw
at the top of the stairs, holding the hand of her three-year-old
son. Crowley waited for her and seeing her speechless, led
mother and child to the next room, to the fire, murmuring:

"I met a silly woman yesterday. . . . She had not approved of my friendship with her husband. . . . She returned
home to find . . . her two lovely babes—on the mat . . . in front
of the fire . . . in extraordinary positions—she *said* . . . without
their heads. This woman could *imagine* . . . her babies rolling
on the carpet—*rolling*! . . . cut off in their infancy. . . . Poor,
mad woman—she imagined *I* had done it. . . ."

Frances might indeed have gone mad. Instead she forced
an interview with one of the doctors used in the attempt to
certify her, and confronted Crowley and her husband with
the threat of his evidence. One hopes that she scared Crowley
as much out of his wits as he said she was out of hers. It is
doubtful that she did; but her husband became nervous; and,
at any rate, it was a threat that Crowley understood. He, also,
knew that Frances was waiting her chance to tear off his hair.
His visits became less frequent. They ended: but he told

Frances that he would follow her wherever she went and whatever she did. In a sense, he did.

I remember the terror we felt at the stories about Crowley told by my mother in old isolated houses in England, where we later lived. I was eight when I determined to hunt Crowley down and kill him for the fear he caused my mother, and the evil he brought into the world. The writer Henry Williamson once told me that he, too, was a grown man, had felt the same way, that he had traveled to Paris with a revolver to shoot Crowley, but had found him away from home. It was difficult to find Crowley, who so often was out of his home, when wanted, and sometimes, by transcendental meditation, out of his own body.

It may be thought that Frances, because of the treatment she received from Crowley, would believe any fantastic story about him. Crowley may, indeed, have thought up the story of the headless babes, to frighten Frances. It is a mistake, though, to think that Crowley did not, frequently, put imaginings into practice. That was always his design.

There was also a story, in 1918, told by several people, and even to the police. For this story there was no corroboration except for the drowned bodies of a young couple who had known Crowley. It was said that they had become interested in Crowley and his religion, before rejecting it; though they continued to see him. To be initiated into the most outer circle of secret circles, it is sometimes necessary for a young person to prove devotion to the cause by committing acts outside usually accepted behavior: when that act breaks the law, the young person can be blackmailed into more desperate acts; so led—by the nose—to complete obedience. It may be that this young couple had resisted such initiation. They did, however—unwisely, as it turned out—accept an invitation to a party at a house that Crowley had rented for the purpose on an island in New York harbor. At this party they were stripped, tied up, and the other guests threw darts into them till they died.

Is this story true?

In some writings of Crowley's, found after his death, there is a description of a living black tied to a tree, and of the cutting of a hole in the black's stomach, and of the insertion of Crowley's penis into the opening. Whether this particular description is of Crowley's imaginations or of his practice is not relevant; the mind that conceived such ritual, would have practiced such rituals. There is no doubt that Crowley practiced similar rituals, many such rituals, religiously.

Frances, without condoning Crowley, could see beyond the monstrosities, the sensational trappings, the traps and the clap-trap, to the root. "Crowley was always told that God had given man the freedom to choose between good and evil. So—says Crowley—man has the right to choose evil. So, Crowley chose, He made evil his God—to prove the freedom of man." That freedom that the God whom Crowley abominated had, in the first place, given to man. What literal believers in God Satanists have to be!

Well—in Frances, there you have one point of view.

In Louis Wilkinson, you have another—in his own words from his chapter on Crowley.* To Louis—son of a clergyman—Crowley was a warrior against the moral and sexual hypocrisies of the times, in that same rebellion to which Louis had devoted his life; Louis a bright Lucifer, encased in the triple steel of an English preparatory school, and an English public school, and the oldest university in England. Crowley's freedom in breaking all locks of sexual restraint convinced Louis that the satisfaction of his own great appetites—bisexual appetites till he was well over twenty—was not only a pleasure but a duty. Crowley and Louis did not talk much about sex and magic. Louis was more interested in the whole of Crowley's character, which he admired greatly and critically.

"The pity is that his nose was too small," he writes, "otherwise he would, I believe, have been indisputably a great man, both as a writer and as a religious leader. Vanity was his handicap. He was too sure of his genius to criticize or revise his work adequately. He thought that everything he

*Seven Friends, by Louis Marlow.

wrote must be good. Impatient to see his books printed, and wishing to have them set up and bound in his own lavish way, he rarely tried to find a publisher, so their circulation was strictly limited."

Crowley's books—*The Diary of a Drug Fiend, Moon Child* and at least eighty other works—have had a wider circulation since that was written. Louis Wilkinson suggests that an anthology should be made of Crowley's poetry, some of which is surprisingly light and happy:

> O for a lily-white goat,
> Crisp as a thicket of thorns
> With a collar of gold for its throat,
> And a scarlet bow for its horns . . .

—and there are lines that will surprise some for a different reason:

> Kill off mankind,
> And give the earth a chance;
> Nature may find
> In her inheritance
> Some seedlings of a race
> Less infinitely base . . .

Some of his lampoons, such as one on Alfred Douglas, *To a Slim Gilt Soul,* are masterly. Louis liked Crowley's parodies, too, especially "O English girl, half baby and half bitch . . . "

Crowley's book on the Tarot, illustrated by Lady Harris, is superb. His devotee paid for the publication of his books on magic; Crowley took the money as his due.

"Many of the charges brought against Crowley's wickedness," writes Louis, "are baseless, but of a few there is proof."

As to Crowley's attitude to money, Louis writes, "The inheritor in his youth of a considerable fortune, he spent it all on those richly coloured imaginative manias that can beggar a man more quickly than any mere luxuries. Crowley threw every one of his singular, passionate intensities into spending all that he had. He treated his fortune as a toy. If you fit out mountaineering expeditions and are continually printing sumptuous private editions of your poems ... and buying places in Scotland, and living everywhere like a prince and entertaining like a Maharajah, even a large fortune will not last very long. But what panache, what elan and brio while it does last!"

When Louis Wilkinson first met Crowley, in 1907, that fortune had been spent; but Crowley continued to live as a prince. There was a period, though, in the 1930s, when, I remember, Louis asked me not to give his address to Crowley if I should meet him. As I had not talked to Crowley since I was three, and was developing a YMCA theater, it was unlikely that I would meet witches and warlocks; but Louis was insistent on the point. This may have been because Crowley was living in slum lodgings off Paddington Green in London. Crowley, for the first time and the last, was poor, and looked it; he may have tried to get money from Louis, who was, in most ways, a careful man. In a fairly short time, though, Crowley had turned his back on Paddington Green and turned once more towards Piccadilly and Jermyn Street.

"To some people," writes Louis, "he was certainly dangerous, even fatal. But I doubt very much if he ever 'disintegrated' anyone's 'personality' unless that personality was well on the way to disintegration. . . . Whatever Crowley's morals or lack of them, I should remember with the same deep gratification that he told me, towards the end of his life, that I was his greatest friend."

This is a second opinion, indeed.

Louis describes Crowley's wit in the answer to Theodore Dreiser: "It was in New York during the First World War. Dreiser, after protesting earnestly and at length against the dependence of American letters upon English tradition, asked him 'What have *you* to offer us?' Crowley replied with a single word, 'Patronage.' I still remember Dreiser's rage. It was wonderful. At that time Crowley was experimenting with the drug anhelonium and used to give 'anhelonium parties.' I persuaded Dreiser to come to one. He did so with some misgiving. 'It will take treble the usual dose to move Dreiser,' said Crowley as he prepared it for him. Dreiser none the less drank his glass of the mixture at one gulp, with determined bravado. Then he felt a little uneasy. He asked Crowley if there was a good doctor in the neighbourhood, 'just in case anything goes wrong.' 'I don't know about a doctor,' said Crowley, 'but,' he added, in a tone of genial reassurance, 'there's a first-class undertaker on the corner of Thirty-third Street and Sixth Avenue.' "

Louis also illustrated Crowley's puerile but often funny practical joking. When Crowley was living at Boleskin in the Highlands of Scotland, and was known as Lord Boleskin, he persuaded—in that voice and intonation that was remarkably like Winston Churchill's—a somewhat ingenuous Swiss guest that haggis was a species of sacred ram, and persuaded him to stalk it over the moors.

In that case, Crowley was joking; but when he recited beautifully in an unknown tongue, saying that it was "the language of the angels," he believed what he said.

As he grew old, he felt disappointment; presumably because he, the master, had not achieved more for his master: but the disappointment went deeper than that. "That he really did believe himself to be by destiny a great religious regenerator," writes Louis Wilkinson. "That he had full faith in the religion which he built upon his 'Law of Thelema' to bring the World nearer to what he called 'Godhead,' I have no doubt." Yet Crowley at last called his own life worthless: and thanked Louis, the candid friend, for reclaiming it. No murmur of repentance for his evil ways ever passed his lips: he died firm in his faith: his only regret that he had not done more.

Crowley's belief in the words with which he ended his letters, "Do what thou wilt shall be the whole of the Law," seems inexact for so intelligent a man; for there was always equal emphasis on "The slave shall serve." "Is that the slave's will?" I asked my father. "Yes," he answered without hesitation, "the slave wishes to serve—knows that is what he is fitted for." Which is, of course, convenient for the slave-owner. Compare Christ washing the feet of the disciples.

Neither Frances nor Louis believed that Crowley had

magical powers: but it was sometimes difficult to define what powers he had. After Frances had divorced Louis Wilkinson, we were living in a bungalow on a large estate in Essex, and here Crowley reached her without lifting a wand. Frances found a tramp's sign outside the great gates. These were not like any tramps' signs she had seen, but were like symbols used by Crowley. She was so long looking at them, that we—her mother, and my sister and I—came to her. Frances talked in an even tone, but none of us ever felt before or since such intensity of terror as then descended on us—the two mature women and the two adolescent children—in the hot sun. It was as though Crowley's inversion of belief made a black sun pour cold darkness out of the sky. It was a terror that was above, beyond the rational. Yet the only magic about that is the known fact that all people of great good or great evil create an image that continues to make impact upon the imagination, whether they are there or not, whether they know it or not; even after death.

Crowley often gave a magical impression. In the late 1930s after I had seen Crowley, but had not talked to him, at a luncheon, I pointed him out to my wife, Margaret, as he traveled down an escalator, on the London Underground, while we were moving up: when we reached the top, Crowley was there, at the *top*, his unmistakable figure moving in the crowd. Yet, of course, Dylan Thomas, too, was fond of such tricks. My father once left Dylan Thomas slumped over the bar in a Soho pub, took a taxi, got out at the B.B.C. building, and found Dylan Thomas slumped over the reception desk. Many people have their private or public conjurings.

More tangible proof of Crowley's powers were shown in an incident after the Second World War. I had been speaking at a conference in a Gloucestershire mansion, and had then called on a group of artists in an adjoining house. There, over the fireplace, was a large picture of clergymen being hunted over gravestones by devils: the painter obviously on the side of the devils. "I can almost *see* Aleister Crowley standing against that painting," I said, not knowing if my hosts would recognize the name. "You *would* have done if you had been here when Crowley was with us," said the scene-designer, the

leader of the group. When I, in discussing Crowley, doubted
his magical powers, the scene-designer said, "You would not
have thought that if you had been with us when Crowley was
here. After dinner, we came down to a room on the first
floor—" he took me to the room—a small one for such a large
house—with french windows opening on to rough grass, and
trees beyond. "Crowley sat on his haunches, there by the fire.
One of us sat on the floor, the other side. Two others besides
myself were in the room. As Crowley talked, the man on the
other side of the fireplace from Crowley fell sideways, his
head a few inches from the flames, and stayed there. Another
got up, dropped on all fours, sniffed round the chairs, begged,
barked and whined, scratched at the door ... " At that point I
remembered Frances describing how a man who had called
at the same time as Crowley, that long time ago in New York,
had begun to act like a dog, and how Crowley had continued
to talk, watching with mild interest, till the man recovered,
passing the obscene exhibition off as a joke—which Louis had
accepted, but Frances had not. "Like a dog," the man continued—"and the man over there got up, without a word, rushed
through the window, and didn't come back till noon next day,
his clothes torn, and his face bleeding. I couldn't move for a
while, and when I did, Crowley had gone to bed." "Crowley
might have used drugs," I suggested. "And hypnotism,"
added the young man who was not, I realized, as credulous as
I had thought. That, too, must be remembered, that Crowley
was skillful in the use of drugs; and in hypnotism. "But he
used something else, too," added the young man. "What?" I
asked. "Magic," said the young man.

Magic? Could Crowley raise the wind or make himself
invisible? My father was only once tempted to believe in
Crowley's magical powers, but that was after Crowley's
death, when Louis was one of his literary executors. Among
mementos of Crowley were Rosicrucian cuff links which the
other executors did not, I think, care to wear. Louis wore
them. He was wearing them, a few weeks later, as he walked
to a cottage near his in Dorset. Finding that his friends were
out, he—uncharacteristically, but it was raining and he hated
the damp—tried to climb through the window: became entan-

gled in frame and latch, fell and broke his leg in two places, with his arms caught above him. As he opened his eyes, trussed as he was, upside down, he saw staring down at him, the Rosicrucian cuff links. This did make him wonder a little; so much so that, before he left hospital, and in case Crowley's books of magic should be struck by lightning, he had arranged to move them out of his house and into ours—into the cottage where my wife and I lived with our children in the middle of fields. When they arrived, I looked at the beautiful books, but shut them hurriedly; not out of fear but from determination not to give them the years of study they would need. I would have done the same with books on higher mathematics. What my wife and I did not know, then, was that our eleven-year-old twin daughters used to creep up to the attic, after we supposed they had gone to bed, to study the books of magic, and to follow their instructions as methodically as they did their homework. When they were grown up, they told us how, one night, they were thrown into a panic, when they had followed very closely the instructions and geometric patterns, and the spell had begun to take shape. *What* shape they have never been able to tell us. Anyone, however, who thinks Crowley a charlatan of magic, has only to look at these books: they could have been written only from years of study. Crowley was in earnest. He believed in what he said, wrote and did. He is one of the great originals of the world, and how hard he worked for his god! He is also the abominable little boy whom Frances saw.

My own point of view about Crowley is a compound of my father's and mother's—with greater emphasis on my mother's—and of my own impressions of him during those months by the sea. Surprisingly, when I met him in Hastings, it was not, as I had thought it would be, a meeting of naïveté and sophistication, but more like a clash of simplicities. His point of view was so different from any usual interpretation of life that it sometimes seemed ingenuous. My own simplicity would sometimes, quite unconsciously, trick him. As a reward for my finding him a room in which to die, he sent me what my father assured me, too late, were the most expensive cigarettes in the world. When I confessed to Crowley that I had smoked them all without properly appreciating them, he thought I was asking for more, and sent more. When Crowley—from his room above, when my wife and I with our children called on the actor, his landlord—sent a pot of caviar for us to dip into and return, I thought he was offering the whole thing and took it home. There is comedy about every incident I remember of Crowley. That time when Crowley was having dinner with us, in our coastguard cottage, and he asked to be excused from the table, I had to tell him that our lavatory was across the yard. He said that a lavatory was not essential. This alarmed me, and I offered to bring a chamber-pot into what we called our drawing-room. He waved it aside. I was relieved to see that all the relief he wanted was to stick an enormous hypodermic needle into his arm. I was surprised, but it struck as a human scene, and really, rather allegorical: the Great Magician, vulnerable in his Chinese plus-fours, dependent on a drop of earth's liquid for his old veins. As he left our house, as when he arrived, our dog and cats rolled in loving subjection at his feet. Yet I remained fearful of Crowley. I uprooted my family from Hastings, and we joined a Christian Community in Scotland.

Humor continued to follow Crowley even to the grave, or at least to the crematorium; where savage and beautiful women, and a few great men—including Louis Wilkinson who recited Crowley's *Io, Pan!*—and some bewildering reporters turned the great occasion into high poetic farce.

Paradoxes surround the evil man as well as the good. Why was Crowley, who is said to have sacrificed babes and animals, loved by babes and animals? Why did *Crowley* write:

> For mark you! babes are ware of wiser things,
> And hold more arcane matters in their mild
> Cabochon eyes than men are ware of yet.
> Therefore have poets, lest they should forget,
> Likened the little sages unto kings.

There is also the paradox of that photo of 1910, when Crowley was a contented husband and father: so happy that goodness tempted him to renounce evil. Crowley became good. Catastrophes followed with ferocious and unrelenting regularity. Crowley returned to evil. Having set himself the task of proving man's right to evil, having become more identified with evil than he knew, having become the incarnation of evil to a greater degree than he had realized, he could no longer afford to be good—poor devil!

Hell Fire Dashwood

On a June afternoon in the year 1753 in the courtyard of the House of Commons an assemblage of private carriages, polished lacquer sides emblazoned with heraldic crests, waited in an uncommonly warm London sun. Inside, impatient ladies swatted flies, sipped wine, and fanned themselves. Perspiration trickled down in little rivulets from under masks; for these ladies were reluctant to reveal their identities too casually. Each was a woman of beauty, wit and a liberated point of view. Essential qualities for the destination and purpose that lay ahead.

Somewhat apart stood another carriage, doors lacquered to an improbable shade of crimson, bearing the extraordinary device of Santa Charlotta's Nunnery. In this vehicle four "novices" with the hint of too much paint, gilt ribbon, and more than a sufficiency of floral verdure at the decollatage, peered out towards their more refined sisters. For the moment convention dictated they must neither speak nor acknowledge each other's presence. But by nightfall they would indeed be sisters in the truest sense. None had brought luggage. This occasion would be a kind of "retreat" for which special costumes would be provided. The haven ahead was Medmenham Abbey, but the religion practiced there was no conventional Christianity. Rather, the strange pagan rites of the ancient god, Priapus.

As George II's Parliament wound up its governmental duties for another season, a cluster of distinguished Lords and M.P.s hastened to the waiting carriages. Needing no word of instruction, the coachmen moved out at full tilt towards the Kensington Road. Leading the caravan in a bottle-green coach drawn by two matched pairs rode Sir Francis Dashwood, M.P. for Romney and a leading member of the Tory Opposition Party. Eleven years later he was to become Lord Le Despencer and Chancellor of the Exchequer; later still, Joint-Postmaster General.

At forty-two, Dashwood was already known for his eccentricities: a fondness for the profane and amorous, and a violent leaning towards the bottle. Some called him the Mad Dashwood. Most found him a man of enormous wit and a generous nature. He could well afford it. He owned a vast estate in West Wycombe, Buckinghamshire, and had married a rich widow to boot. His fortune was seemingly as endless as his appetites.

With him rode Paul Whitehead, perhaps his best friend; certainly on occasion his worst adviser. Whitehead's shady but useful abilities as a Tory hack had steered him into the orbit of the impressive and equally easily impressed Dashwood. Although two years younger than the folly, robust peer, Whitehead had early been dubbed "Paul the Aged." Certainly his thin face bore the imprint of a humble, grubbing youth and years spent in Fleet Street Prison for debts. Only a financially rewarding marriage, his wits, and the wit of his acerbic pen had elevated him into the society he now enjoyed.

Never a social snob, wit was one pleasure Dashwood's

money could buy. In the mid-eighteenth century, satire and caricature were the true adornments of the intellect; and so this friendship was of long standing. Whitehead had been Dashwood's guest on several of his early "Grand Tours." Together they had viewed the first excavations at Herculaneum in 1738—and ten years later the excavations at Pompeii, with special attention to "The House of Mysteries" whose walls were decorated with brothel art.

They inspected the equally arousing private rooms of the Cardinal in the Vatican, studied the pagan devotions to Floralia, purchased phallic ex-voti of wax in Naples in the names of St. Cosmas and St. Damian—and in Verona and Venice acquired handbooks of magic spells and incantations. These included grimoires (magicians' books for calling up spirits), *The Isagoge* of Arbatel, Agrippa's *Occult Philosophy*, the works of Paracelsus (these last two men known to be Rosicrucians).

Dashwood had arrived in Italy on the crest of a resurgence of interest in the black arts. Within the civilized society of the Age of Reason was a reawakening of cultism and belief in the powers of mystical ritual. To a man of Dashwood's vast imagination with a passionate interest in indulging his passions, the voluptuousness of Greek and Roman, Turkish and Indian art had a profoundly liberating effect on his ingrained English puritanism. A man who "wished to taste the sweets of all things," Dashwood conceived an idea which would become a lifelong avocation and intrude on the social structure of his society for the next fifty years.

Down the Kensington Road, along the infamous Chiswick Highway and on through Maidenhead the coaches traveled. Past the Bear Hotel not pausing for repast, Dashwood's coachman kept a sharp lookout for the notorious highwayman, Page, who, disguised as a gentleman, terrorized the travelers. Soon the caravan branched off the main road towards Hurley and on down the hill to the River Thames, raising clouds of dust as they approached the low slung roofs and ivied walls of the Abbey. The secret Brotherhood, the Order of the Friars of Saint Francis of Wycombe were about to plunge into their first Summer Festival in worship of the gods Panus and Priapus.

Surely there has never been a time when men didn't congregate into some form of secret society whether in the quest of truth or sensation, revelation or diversion, love or organized murder, God or the Devil—or merely for the sense of special privilege gained by excluding others. Fraternities, sects, cults, and clubs have flourished best in a ritual drenched atmosphere. Mithrics, Brahmins, Druids, Tongs offer an elitist sense of togetherness enhanced by mystery. Some have been so secret they never admitted their very existence. Most religions (including Christianity) began as secret societies shut away from prying eyes in catacomb and cave and monastery. Dashwood found his haven of privacy in a similar environment.

Not that there had ever been a shortage of clubs or cults in England. Since Elizabethan days rakes had banded together for the purposes of eating, drinking, conversing, or more riotous frivolities. The Mohawks and the Makaronies were more destructive in their day than their descendants the Teddy Boys and Hells Angels. In 1720 Philip, Lord Wharton, founded the first Hell-Fire Club. They met at a tavern for the usual purposes: "drinking, gambling and blaspheming." Similar clubs mushroomed throughout England; so many and so offensive to society in general that in 1721 a Royal Proclamation banned forever all Hell-Fire Clubs. But they persisted with the same cast of characters under different names. The Edinburgh Sweating Club, the Dublin Blasters, the Demoniacs, all dabbling in Satanism. The Mollies Club, where men of fashion dressed as women of fashion, evoking the inquiry:

> Tell me, Gentle hobdehoy!
> Art thou girl, or art thou boy?

Dashwood had been one of the original members of the Dilittanti founded in 1732 "for the purpose of promoting the arts." To join, one had to have been on the Grand Tour. He was also a founder of the Divan Club (exclusively for those who had traveled in the Ottoman Empire) and was painted in elaborate costume as El Faquir Dashwood Pasha. But even such esoterica proved too tame for Dashwood taste.

Somewhere around 1742 he and Whitehead began meeting with a select few cronies in more private quarters; a tavern in Cornhill, London, at the corner of St. Michael's Alley called The George and Vulture. On the surface it seemed not too unlike the other clubs—an innocent gathering of rakes, hell-bent on a good booze-up and an exchange of wit. But perhaps it was no accident that this ancient pub had been the home of Wharton's original Hell-Fire Club—and that the landlord was suspected of practicing Black Magic. He owned a collection of metaphysical curios, one of which still exists: an Everlasting Rosicrucian Lamp.

This large crystal globe was encircled by a tail-biting serpent carved in pure gold; the twin symbol of eternity and cosmic energy. Twisted snake chains hung from the globe and a silver winged dove perched on the top. Dashwood, who seemed to have overlooked nothing of the exotic, had studied Rosicrucianism, and no doubt borrowed from its teachings in building his personal philosophy. Beneath that mystical lamp in the cellar of The George and Vulture he must have dabbled in the black arts. And here long before the Brotherhood began to meet at Medmenham Abbey, he came by the sobriquet, "Saint Francis of Wycombe."

Paul Whitehead ("Brother Paul of Twickenham") was elected High Steward and Secretary Treasurer when the Order was officially founded. Among its first members was George Bubb Dodington, later Lord Melcombe Regis. This wealthy eccentric was, at sixty-two, already a caricaturist's delight from a life of total indulgence. Here was ripe fodder for the philosophy that preached: "Do what thou wilt."

Dodington had built himself a county seat at Eastbury which he called La Trappe in parody of that monastic order known for its silence. Perhaps he first suggested the monastery idea to Dashwood. Bubb, sometimes known as Silly-Bubb, lacked Dashwood's finer flair for the classic. His home was a monstrosity of purple and orange silks topped off by too much gilt wood. His fortune was as bottomless as his taste, yet he was of a quixotically frugal nature, refusing to hang paintings because he considered them an extravagance.

He would cut up his embroidered silk waistcoats when they grew too small for his expanding belly and have them sewn into a carpet for the state bedroom at La Trappe. Prince Frederick, who was a frequent visitor, no doubt was among those who tripped over the button loops.

The aging Bubb and the dashing Dashwood may have seemed an odd pair, but they were strong political allies. The puffy peer, wheezing and snorting with gout, was not only friend but adviser to the young Frederick, Prince of Wales, and consequently wielded tremendous political power. On one occasion at least he got a laugh out of Charlotte, wife of George III. Bowing deeply before her he was brought up hastily by a loud riiipp! in his satin breeches. No doubt the offending garment found its way into his State Bedroom carpet.

Another of the original monks (Brother John of Hitchingbroke) was John Montagu, Earl of Sandwich, later First Lord of the Admiralty; according to his contemporaries, one of the most debauched and depraved men of his day. Ten years younger than Dashwood, he could spend twenty-four hours at the gaming tables without stopping for a proper meal. He'd call for a slab of meat between slices of bread, bequeathing a new word to posterity: sandwich. He also gave his name to a troup of islands discovered by his protege, the explorer Captain James Cook. For a man who was described as "mischievous as a monkey, lecherous as a goat, universally hated, mean to his mistress and treacherous to his friends," Sandwich seems to have exerted a vast circle of influence.

He had met Dashwood sometime on the Grand Tour and probably witnessed the incident described by Horace Walpole.*

On Good Friday, each person who enters the Sistine Chapel takes a small scourge from an attendant at the door. The chapel is dimly lighted, only three candles, which are ex-

---

*Memoirs of the Reign of King George III, Horace Walpole, ed. Marchant, 1845.

tinguished by the priest, one by one. At the putting out of the first, the penitents take off one part of their dress. At the next, still more, and in the dark which follows the extinguishing of the third candle, "lay on" their own shoulders with groans and lamentations. Sir Francis Dashwood, thinking this mere stage effect, entered with the others dressed in a large watchman's coat, demurely took his scourge from the priest and advanced to the end of the chapel, where in the darkness ensuing he drew from beneath his coat an English horse whip and flogged right and left quite down the chapel—the congregation exclaiming, "Il Diavolo! Il Diavolo!"—thinking the Evil One was upon them with a vengeance. The consequence might have been serious had Dashwood not immediately fled the Papal dominions.

A more mysterious story from Dashwood's early travels concerns the Empress Elizabeth of Russia. In 1733 Dashwood is said to have posed as the war-like Charles XII of Sweden, deadliest enemy of Russia (and already dead!), and at the Court of St. Petersburg, tried to win the hand of the twenty-four-year-old daughter of Peter the Great. Elizabeth is reported to have granted Sir Francis the favor of her bedchamber, but was more reluctant with her hand.

Another who attended Dashwood's gatherings at The George and Vulture was the witty, charming, and handsome Thomas Potter. He was the same age as Sandwich and possibly even more debauched. Son of the Archbishop of Canterbury, Potter became Paymaster General and Treasurer for Ireland. While serving as Secretary to Prince Frederick he passed idle hours as a constant visitor to La Trappe and West Wycombe Park. Potter enjoyed watching executions, seduced the wife of the Bishop of Warburton and copulated in graveyards—all of which seems to have had a dilatory effect on his health. He once said, "I know the nothingness into which the genius of a Potter is apt to shrink under a superior influence"—for wherever the glittering Dashwood led, Potter was sure to follow.

And perhaps not so strangely, one of England's most outspoken free-thinkers in politics followed Potter into the

Order. John Wilkes (Brother John of Aylesbury) remained a
staunch supporter until, in 1762, when Lord Bute became
Prime Minister, political differences fractured close ties of the
Brotherhood.

But in the early 1750s Potter and Wilkes amused themselves and the Brethren by writing an anonymous parody of
Pope's *Essay on Man.* They called their scurrilous bit of porn
Essay on Woman. Years later, long after Potter was dead, it
proved the undoing of Wilkes. The poet, Charles Churchill, a
latecomer to the Order, wrote of Potter:

> He drank with drunkards, lived with sinners
> Herded with Infidels for dinners.

Not great poetry, but the meaning is clear.

Another late joiner was the wit George Selwyn, M.P.,
also ten years Dashwood's junior and a great friend of Potter's. Selwyn had been expelled from Hertford College, Oxford, for toasting "queer deities" in his own blood, and shared
Potter's necrophiliac tastes. He customarily attended executions (as did Sandwich) dressed as an old lady. According to a
contemporary, Henry Fox, when Lord Holland was on his
deathbed (he had toxemia from an exclusive diet of breast of
chicken) he was told that Selwyn had inquired after his
health. Holland replied, "The next time Mr. Selwyn calls,
show him up. If I'm alive, I shall be delighted to see him. If
I'm dead, he'll be glad to see me."

Selwyn's sadistic tastes led him to Paris in 1757 for the
pleasure of witnessing the demise of one Robert François
Damiens. That Frenchman had attempted to assassinate
Louis XV and was sentenced to be torn to pieces in the Place
de Grève—after having been tortured with red-hot pincers
and having hot lead poured into his wounds. (Perhaps the
revival of this quaint custom would deter the enthusiastic as-
sassins of our own time.)

Still another recruit was William Douglass, Third Earl of
March, called "Old Q" or more often, "the Goat of Piccadilly." He had all the right qualities being a "foul-mouthed
lecher" who kept racehorses and a harem.

But perhaps the most enigmatic character to present itself was a person called the Chevalier d'Eon de Beaumont, who arrived in England as a French diplomat and was listed as both a monk and a nun at Medmenham. Until his death at eighty-two in 1810 only D'Eon knew whether "it" was male or female. Having served Louis XV as a female secret agent on a mission to St. Petersburg, he reappeared in 1758 in Paris as a Captain in the Dragoons. D'Eon came to London in 1762, the year Dashwood became Chancellor of the Exchequer (an office for which he was totally unqualified). In England the Chevalier dressed as a woman, gave fencing demonstrations, and was involved in enough intrigues to fill a book.

In 1771 a group of ladies gathered at Medmenham Abbey to determine once and for all D'Eon's sex. All of society was betting heavily on the outcome, but no bets were collected. The ladies' verdict was—"Doubtful"! But in 1777, another jury decided D'Eon was a woman. A fragile and bejeweled old lady, Charlotte Geneviève d'Eon Beaumont spent her latter days quietly with a Mrs. Cole. Only at her death did the coroner pronounce once and for all that Charles Genevieve was a man.

Of such promising material were the Monks of Medmenham composed. Originally twelve Apostles met with Dashwood to complete the mystical thirteen. Ordinary friars and carefully chosen guests might swell a meeting to twenty-five or a festival to forty, but only the Inner Circle were indoctrinated into Eleusinian mysteries. Time has only hinted at these secrets, for the Apostles carefully destroyed their private papers.

The renaissance of interest in all things Italian had led Dashwood to his interest in all things pagan. The men he drew to him were leaders of government, men of intellect, not merely impious sensualists, and they believed in the eighteenth-century double standard between manners and morals. They cared nothing for public opinion. The impassable gulf between the classes enabled them to do as they pleased in the firm belief that as long as they did it in private it was nobody's business.

It may seem odd that in the vaunted Age of Reason with its enlightened philosophies and healthy skepticism, its Voltaires, Lockes, Spinozas, there should be a blooming of secret societies dabbling in Devil worship. But was that Dashwood's mysterious secret? Some authorities, unwilling on the evidence to buy satanism as the answer, have suggested the Order was merely a huge send-up. Hardly. Dashwood's Order lasted for at least thirty-five years; too long for a practical joke to remain funny.

More likely the ribald outer trappings insured secrecy for more serious practices. Were these Apostles seeking liberation of the psyche through the cult of Dionysis? Instead of practicing black magic in the satanic tradition, were Dashwood and his Brotherhood practicing sex magic in the Tantrik tradition? Although history has left us a jig-saw puzzle from which certain pieces will be forever missing, some clues remain to be seen in the construction of the Caves at West Wycombe and in the statues that once stood at Medmenham.

In the Hermetic tradition, cathedrals were laid out in relation to the nature of our existence. Crystaline structures, mathematical equations, calculations of the seasons, the stars, all can be reckoned in the stone architecture and art forms of history, dating even further back than the Great Pyramid, whose secrets are now being unraveled.

Like the Pharaohs of Egypt or the de Medicis before him, Dashwood was able to indulge the one vice twentieth-century man cannot afford. He could bring to life his fantasies and concepts in physical terms of art and architecture. Even the gardens of his home at West Wycombe were said to have been laid out in the shape of a female form.

When Sir Francis leased the twelfth-century Cistercian Monastery of Medmenham, it was derelict and sinister. He had the yews clipped, added an artificial gothic tower, had frescoes painted on walls and ceilings, placed his provocative statues, acquired a pleasure boat so the "monks" could glide down a moonlit stretch of Thames towards more private devotions.

The Abbey church was restored into a common room with a peculiarly pagan altar. Dashwood removed the existing figure of the Virgin and Child and placed it in his new tower. He hung portraits of the twelve apostles and a selection of nuns. Everywhere Latin graffiti spelled out in gold and crimson, *double entendres* to confound and titillate the visitors.

In *Journals of Visits to County Seats*, Walpole says, "The decorations may be supposed to have contained the quintessence of their mysteries, since it was impenetrable to any but the initiated."

On the staircase landing was an alabaster group of the Holy Trinity. On the floor above was the "withdrawing room" cosily appointed for the comfort of the good friars and nuns who would share their revelry reclining on green silk damask sofas amid ornate Roman decorations "conducive to conviviality." Two remarkable statues stood guard. At one end of the room Harpocrates peered down, finger to lips. Originally, this deity had been the Egyptian hawk god, Horus. The Greeks turned him into Apollo. The Romans, who customarily adopted Greek gods and renamed them, dubbed him Harpocrates. Whatever his name, his function remained the same: to wage war against the powers of darkness. To the Egyptians, a finger to the lips symbolized childhood. This meaning was lost on the Greeks and Romans who made him the god of silence. As such, he found a home in Dashwood's monastery where silence was highly desirable.

Facing Harpocrates across the room was the figure of Angerona, the ancient Roman Goddess who relieved men of their pain and sorrow. She was the keeper of the sacred name of Rome and its protector. Angerona was portrayed with a finger to her bound lips so the sacred name of the city might never be revealed to its enemies. Her festival was celebrated on December 21 and no doubt Sir Francis honored it at Medmenham. He had first encountered her statue in the Temple of Volupia, goddess of pleasure. In ancient times the priests made blood sacrifice before this statue. Angerona's invitation to silence is repeated in the fresco on the grand staircase at West Wycombe House. This statue also suggests that the same freedoms were to be enjoyed by both sexes, as indeed they were at Medmenham.

Walpole wrote:

> This Abbey is now become remarkable by being hired by a set of gentlemen who have erected themselves into a sort of fraternity of monks and pass two days in each month there. Each has his own cell into which they may carry women. They have a maid to dress their dinner and no other servants. Over the door is written this sentence from Rabalais: "Fait ce que voudras" ["Do what thou wilt"].

Fait ce que voudras is the inscription on the Abbey of Thélèma in *Gargantua and Pantagruel*. This theme was later exploited by one of the true black magicians of our time, Aleister Crowley—and in theory at least, by the Marquis de Sade.

A translation of the *Kama Sutra*, extremely rare in the eighteenth century, was among the collection of novels, poems, drawings, etc., kept in the common room. There was a set of prints of the kings of England, but the face of Henry VIII was covered, for it was he who put an end to monasteries two centuries earlier.

The cellars were stocked with enough claret, port, lisbon, rum, etc., to saturate any orgy, but when the cellar book lists "two bottles drunk by Brother John of Aylesbury," we must remember that in the eighteenth century the bottles were smaller. Beneath their names and places of abode hung the monks' habits. Walpole describes the design as being "more like a waterman's than a monk's"—with a white hat, jacket and trousers. Hogarth, an occasional visitor, painted the three Vansittart brothers wearing blue tam o'shanters with the Order's motto, "Love and Friendship," around the brim. Other portraits suggest that at times the monks wore Franciscan robes. The Prior had "a red hat like a Cardinal's and a red bonnet turned up with cony skin."

The nuns dressed in white habits. They, too, wore the silver badge inscribed with the motto. But friendly or not, it was understood that any nun could remain masked in general company if she so desired. Lady Mary Wortley-Montagu, Mary Wolcot (Dashwood's half-sister), Frances, Countess Vane, and Lady Betty Germain mingled serenely with the girls from Charlotte Hayes's bordello, certainly wiser from the contact. No doubt a "women's lib" equality existed within the Order.

The cells were "fitted out for the private pleasures of each monk." We can only conjecture at Walpole's meaning here. One item is documented: an *Idolum Tentiginis* (a phallic hobby horse used in ancient fertility cults). John Wilkes refers to "libations poured to the *Bona Dea.*" If so, Dashwood was carrying the pursuit of Bacchus and Venus beyond the level of mere debauchery.

In the Roman rites of Bona Dea (a purely feminine ritual in worship of the goddess of creation) erotic flagellation and lesbian acts were performed by the priestesses to produce a frenzy of creative energy. These acts were customarily preceded by ritual feasting and drinking. Alcohol, dancing and copulation were regarded with deep religious awe. Through the Dionysian orgy (and the same with the Tantrik) one "passed beyond oneself" into a state of ecstasy and became one with God. The Greeks and Romans did not consider these rituals immoral any more than the Tantrikas. The rites placed the participant nearer to "cosmic enlightenment" and perhaps could be compared to the mind-blowing drugs of a later age.

A statue of Priapus dominated the Abbey orchard, brandishing a flame-tipped phallus. It bore the legend: "Peni Tento non Penitenti" (a penis tense rather than penitence). But was this just a puerile pun or was it a defiant blast at the "anti-sex" attitude of the church? On Priapus' pedestal Wilkes noted "a whimsical representation of Trophonius' cave from which all creatures were said to come out melancholy. Among this strange and dismal group you might however remark a cock crowing and a Carmelite laughing, and the words, Gallum Gallinaceum et Sacerdotem Gratis." There is a Latin saying that everyone is melancholy after intercourse except a cock and a priest, who gets it for nothing. Trophonius built the Temple of Apollo at Delphi. At the ar-

chitect's death, his spirit inhabited a cave as a terrifying
oracle. Dashwood's ownership of this carving suggests he may
already have been digging his own caves.

A statue which was to cause a great deal of controversy
as a blasphemy against Christianity was a copy of one in the
Vatican—a point missed by Dashwood's contemporaries. It
had a man's body and neck, and a cock's head crowned by a
phallus. The cock's head is the ancient emblem of the Sun
God. Richard Payne Knight says* "the figure represents the
generative powers of Eros, Osiris, Mithras and Bacchus
whose centre is the sun incarnate in man." The ancient inscription read: "The Saviour of the World," which pre-dated
Christianity and was a sex-energy totem.

At the entrance to a small cavern was a statue of Venus
seen from the rear, stooping to pull a thorn from her foot.
The Latin quote was to the effect that entry by the wrong
route was not approved of here.

Wilkes also mentions a "Temple of Cloacina"—which
can best be described as a marble out-house. It was inscribed:
"This Chapel of Ease was Founded in the Year 1760." He
says of it, "The entrance is the same entrance by which we all
come into the world and the door to what some idle wits have
called the door to life."

Much later, after Wilkes had parted company with
Dashwood and Sandwich, he wrote, "How can any man take
such pains to show public contempt of all decency, order and
virtue?"

In evaluating Wilkes's remarks about Dashwood and the
Brotherhood one must consider the political climate in which
they were made. Until John Stuart, Third Earl of Bute, became Prime Minister in 1762, Whig and Tory met in amiable
fraternity at Medmenham. Dodington, Dashwood and Sandwich were on the politically victorious side.

Wilkes and his cronies, Charles Churchill and Robert
Lloyd, were not. Wilkes began taking jibes at Bute and the

---

*Discourse on the Worship of Priapus, Julian Press, New York, 1957.

government of George III in his newspaper the *North Briton*. One edition, no. 45, launched such a bitter attack that a means had to be found to get rid of Wilkes. He had also embarrassed the normally imperturbable Sandwich with a particularly bizarre practical joke. This story has often been cited as proof that the Order was deeply involved in black magic.

The Vansittart brothers had presented the Order with a baboon as a mascot. Wilkes is said to have dressed it up in devil's costume complete with horns and hidden it in a trunk. At a moment in the ritual when (it is said) Sandwich was evoking His Satanic Majesty, out popped the baboon, sending Sandwich into a veritable panic screaming for mercy.

Sandwich took his revenge. He dredged up Wilkes's *Essay on Woman*, written over ten years earlier, and read every word of it aloud in Parliament. Wilkes was banished to Paris and didn't return to England until 1768. The vengeful Sandwich was nicknamed "Jemmy Twitcher" after the character in *Beggar's Opera* who had told on Macheath.

Wilkes's course was not to run smoothly. He returned to London only to be thrown in jail. In the end he was not only vindicated, but was elected Lord Mayor of London in 1778 by an affectionate populace.

But in 1751, Wilkes was one of the Inner Circle and a great friend of Dashwood's. The death of Frederick, Prince of Wales, in that year had turned attention away from London, and back to county interests. In 1745, Dashwood had married Sarah, Lady Ellys, wealthy daughter of Thomas Gould. It had made no alterations in his life-style. He continued his bachelor interests at The George and Vulture until it burned down in 1748.

That same year news of the major excavations at Pompeii no doubt prompted Dashwood's excavations into the prehistoric caves halfway up the hill facing West Wycombe Park. The hill was crowned by a derelict twelfth-century church, but the site had been a place of worship since Druidic times and many legends were associated with it. An ideal location to renew ancient pagan practices.

In 1750, Dashwood decided to build a new road to the village at his own expense, ornamenting it with an obelisk

giving the distance to town, the university, etc. Village workers were paid one shilling a head to lay the road with the
chalk dug from the caves. But Dashwood didn't trust the
locals with his secrets. As he had when rebuilding Medmenham, he imported labor. Cornish miners dug out a strange
pattern of passages as designed by Dashwood. The caves
were heavily guarded and when the work was finished, the
miners returned to Cornwall. After 1751 it is certain that the
Inner Circle, seemingly reduced to nine, held secret chapter
meetings in the caves.

John Hall Stevenson, who owned Crazy Castle in York-
shire and had modeled his Demoniacs after Dashwood's order, penned *A Query into the Strange Events which took Place
under West Wycombe Hill*:

> Where can I find a cave to muse
> Upon his Lordship's envied glory,
> Which of the nine dare to refuse
> To tell the strange and recent story?
> Mounting I saw the egregious Lord
> O'er all impediments and bars
> I saw him at Jove's council board
> And saw him stuck among the stars.

In eighteenth-century slang, the word "star" referred to a
beautiful courtesan—the etymological ancestor of a movie
queen.

Dashwood restored the crumbling Church of St. Lawrence placing a remarkable golden ball "at the top of the
steeple which is hollowed and made so convenient on the inside, not of devotional but of convivial rites that it is the best
Globe Tavern I have ever seen . . . . " Wilkes goes on to relate
that here Dashwood tried to make political deals with his
companions who, even if they didn't yield to his "wise reasons
and dazzling offers were both delighted with his divine milk
punch." This golden globe awards the occupant with a vista
of the valley below through four portholes, NSEW—repeating
the shape of the central hall in the caves below it.

The interior of the Church of St. Lawrence is unorthodox, its ceiling decoration a copy of a ruined Temple of the Sun at Palmyra whose flower motif is a female symbol. The font is circled by a giant serpent chasing a dove. Four more doves perch at the top, in remembrance of the Rosicrucian lamp.

Dashwood built a hexagonal mausoleum open to the sky, an echo of the six-sided Abbey of Thélèma. There, in 1762, Bubb Dodington was laid to rest. Dashwood's wife followed in 1768, leaving no children.

Sometime in the 1760s Dashwood had rented tiny Round Tar Island in the Thames between Cookham and Marlow. Its exact location has been misplaced with time, but a lease dated 1776 still exists. A drawing showing the island with a hut and boathouse appears on a Medmenham wine book of 1769, indicating it was already being used as a retreat. After 1764 Benjamin Franklin was Dashwood's frequent guest and attended chapter meetings as "Brother Benjamin of Cookham." He may have stayed on Round Tar Island.

This friendship has been the object of much speculation. Together, Dashwood and Franklin composed a new Book of Common Prayer, reducing the verbiage to simplified essentials. An inexplicable act for a man who mocked religion? But perhaps mockery was not Dashwood's intent. Perhaps his real purpose was to eliminate the dogma and miasmic ethos which he considered the pagan element of Christianity and return to elementary paganism rooted in man's ethnology.

Whatever his purpose, and this man of mystery's intents are never obvious, the collaboration with Ben Franklin was both a success and a failure. The Book of Common Prayer was ignored in England, but in the American colonies it was enthusiastically received and used as "Franklin's Prayer Book." It became, and remains to this day, a standard text.

It is the caves themselves that may reveal Dashwood's secrets. The entrance runs some 200 feet, moving steadily down into the center of the hill. At certain points recesses have been chiseled out which once may have held heavy wooden bars. A small circular alcove near the entrance may have been a "robing room." High on the right wall Roman numerals were cut deep into the white chalk: XXII—F. Its meaning? We have only a village rhyme, the legend of a secret passage, and a strange story of a girl dubbed "Saint Agnes" who served the monks as a vestal virgin, and possibly lived in the secret chamber:

> Take twenty steps and rest awhile
> Then take a pick and find the style
> When once I did my love beguile
> 'Twas twenty-two in Dashwood's time
> Perhaps to hide this cell divine
> Where lay my love in peace sublime.

The poet Charles Churchill, a frequent visitor, wrote:

> Under the temple lay a cave
> Made by some guilty coward slave
> Whose actions feared rebuke, a maze
> Of intricate and winding ways
> Not to be found without a clue
> One passage only known to few
> In paths direct led to a cell
> Where fraud in secret loved to dwell
> With all her tools and slaves around her
> Nor feared least honesty should rout her.

The tunnel leads to the labyrinth and perhaps a vital clue, for it is laid out in the precise design of the Tantrik "fertilized world-egg"—bisected twice, and once through the center. This egg form, divided into regions and currents of energy, is a symbolic tribute to the great goddess from whose womb, and by whose wisdom, all things in the universe are manifest in time.*

Tantric symbols date back to Paleolithic Europe and have been found in natural caves, circa 20,000 B.C. These same symbols are used by Tantrikas today in meditation and

---

*Tantra: The Indian Cult of Ecstasy, Philip Rawson, Thames & Hudson.

intercourse to raise the level of enjoyment and release a form of spiritual ecstasy. The symbol itself is important. Tantra is a way of seeing the world used by many religions under many names. It triggers a concept of physical release that combines mental and emotional energies to carry one towards enlightenment. Enlightenment! That eternal goal of philosophical man in every age, and searched along so many paths by saints and sinners—holy men and fools. Was this the path that Dashwood was following? If so, he had good reason to keep it hidden in eighteenth-century England.

The mysteries of the labyrinth included another Roman numeral: XXXIV. Beyond it the tunnel leads to the main chapter room, a circular hall some forty feet in diameter with four alcoves placed at the exact NSEW. There can be no question that whether by accident or design, this room is laid out in the schematic Tantrik diagram illustrating the transcendent system of cosmic space, with its absolute directions, NSEW, a form subtly related through layers of matter and space to the human cosmos and to the layout of the world in time and space. It is almost certain that Dashwood, like so many of his contemporaries, visited Calcutta and Bengal where the Indian cult of Tantra began. They would have had ample opportunity to acquire sixteenth-century and seventeenth-century illustrations of these important symbols. Dashwood's design seems unlikely to have been accidental. In the center of the chamber hung the Rosicrucian lamp.

Past this chamber we meet another Tantrik form. It cannot be coincidence that the corridors branch off left and right and meet again to form a wide, perfect triangle—the symbol of the Sacred Vulva, the Mother Goddess (a forerunner of Grave's White Goddess).

This leads down to what is now called the treasure room because some coins have been found there. More likely the space was used for storage of wine.

Some 300 feet below the top of the hill, on a level with the floor of the valley, flows an underground river. Today it is no more than a glassy pool, but in Dashwood's time it must have been much larger and with a strong current, for Paul Whitehead related the following story about it: Ben Franklin, a great practical joker, offered to bring peace to its stormy waters. While Dashwood and his brothers watched by torchlight, Franklin waved his walking stick above the agitated caldron. It became strangely calm. Franklin's "miracle" was performed by pouring oil from a secret vial in his walking stick onto the waters Dashwood had named the River Styx.

Past this river was the Inner Temple. Two curious symbols were recently found carved into the wall at foot level, half hidden by pebbles. One is a bas-relief key some ½ inches long. The other an ovoid representation of a vulva. If Dashwood and his companions were following a sex-energy cult, it seems to have done little to bring them to an early grave.

Most of the brothers lived to be well into their seventies, some into their eighties and one, Dr. Benjamin Bates, to ninety-eight. If virility was the objective, these men appear not to have failed. Dashwood had two children by his last mistress, Fanny Barry, when he was well into his sixties and lived to be seventy-three. Sandwich reached seventy-four. Old Q, eighty-six, John Wilkes, eighty-three. Even Selwyn reached seventy-two. Of the original members only Potter expired at forty-one, but he may have caught his death sleeping on graves. Still, it is a remarkable record for the eighteenth century.

Paul Whitehead died at sixty-four, but then he came back to haunt Dashwood, so one might consider that he actually stayed around a bit longer. At his death, and at his request, his heart was placed in the mausoleum. In November of 1781 Whitehead's ghost was seen beckoning to his old friend, now Lord Le Despencer. Dashwood's sister, Rachel, Lady Austin, wrote to the poet Cowper, "There are few of his Lordship's numerous household who have not likewise seen him [Whitehead's ghost] sometimes in the Park, sometimes in the Garden, as well as in the house by day and night, indifferently."

Another omen—a stain on the marble tablet in the mausoleum to the memory of the first Sir Francis—a stain in the form of five red fingers which wouldn't wash off. On December 11, 1781, Dashwood died. He left his private papers and some of his grimoires to his illegitimate daughter, Rachel Frances Antonia. But he took the true secret of his Order with him to the grave and became a man of mystery for the ages.

Uri Geller

From time to time in the course of the human voyage across the comfortable seas of acceptable reality, there is a spell of turbulence, sudden and inexplicable. Once again, such a storm has blown up and at its center is a young man, Uri Geller. In personality and appearance Uri exudes no immediate quality of mystery. This is no sandled guru. He more resembles the eccentric Romanian tennis player, Iliea Nastase. Poise, style and easy manner scarcely suggest the mystic through whom strong forces work to create what has become known in scientific circles as the "Geller Effect." One is at once struck by the charm, candor and infectious humor of this boyish Israeli with the penetrating, omniscient gaze that belies his age. Then one recalls the feats that have astounded scientists and audiences around the globe. An anachronism? Uri wonders at his powers with ingenuous honesty. Yet he is troubled. "But why am I so materialistic?" he asks—as he bends a spoon merely by looking at it.

Mystic? Fraud? Miracle worker? Conjurer? Names are more easily bandied than explanations. But for the first time in history science has placed a person with truly inexplicable powers under the microscope of investigation and come up with some confounding conclusions.

Uri has been tested under strict laboratory conditions (difficult with paranormal phenomena) in France, Italy, South Africa, Germany, Japan, and extensively in England and America. At Stanford Research Institute (operated by the American Defense Department, not the university) Uri beat test odds against him of a trillion to one. He has demonstrated his powers on the stages of the world, on radio, television, for literally hundreds of millions of people. He is booked solidly for two years in advance—nearly a different country every month. By now the reality of his accomplishments would seem to be beyond the most skeptical of skeptics' doubts. Even the prestigious magazine *Nature* printed the SRI experiments conducted in 1972. The report concluded that "Uri Geller does have psychic powers, as yet unexplainable."

But Uri insists he is no psychic. "I think psychics use their own forces. This power does not come from me, it is being channelled through me." Perhaps then, the most correct category in which to place Uri (without inventing a new one) is that of mystic, for he possesses an immediate and intuitive knowledge and experience of realities beyond man's senses or rational faculties.

In October 1975, we felt a compulsion to see Uri in person at the London bookstore where he was autographing his new book. Without taking time for breakfast, we found ourselves standing in front of a desk, the first to arrive. Then Uri came in. He didn't know us but we had seen him on TV and read Dr. Puharich's book about him.*

Uri, Andrija Puharich, Doubleday (also note: *The Geller Papers*, edited by Charles Panati, Houghton Mifflin).

Jesse introduced us and Uri shook his hand. Then he looked sharply at both of us—and asked us to wait. He felt it important that we talk. We worked our way out of the now pressing crowd and watched from across the room. Uri delighted his public by mounting to the top of the desk and bending a lady's door key.

"Look at your keys, everybody!" he called. "Sometimes they bend in your pockets." Pat dug into her cluttered handbag—to draw out our front-door key. It was now bent like a foot soldier at the approach of an assault—and our rationality was definitely being assaulted. Had Uri asked us to wait? Wait we would!

"Who are you? And why am I here?" he wanted to know when he returned with us to our London apartment. It was the beginning of a friendship that would bring us together daily for nearly three weeks. We taped hours of conversation and gained an insight into an extraordinary mind. We witnessed inexplicable phenomena. True, they didn't occur under scientific laboratory conditions but most of the time at least five people were present. We were to discover that a great deal of what happened was not willed by Uri, who was as surprised as we were. Uri wasn't even in the apartment when some of the events took place. Certain phenomena had occurred before we met and some after he had gone back to New York. It all seemed to bear out Uri's theory that he is a channel for the power he draws upon.

Other witnesses had described Uri's volatile personality and complained that when he is performing some feat it is difficult to keep an eye on him every second because he jumps up, gets excited, stalks about like a confined leopard. It would seem that when Uri senses a surge of his powers he is quick to put them to use. And sometimes he is unable to perform because the powers fail to cooperate.

On that first visit someone asked Uri to bend a key. He declined, saying he was too tired (with good reason, having signed at least one hundred autographs). But when our daughter, Lisa, arrived, Uri jumped up revitalized. "Where is a spoon I can bend?"

In the kitchen a suitable steel spoon was selected; a

heavy one we'd eaten with for many years. We all watched
Uri hold the spoon by its bowl. With a gentle stroke of one
finger at the base, the metal handle appeared to droop forward, curving over Uri's hand into a perfect U shape. Next,
he bent a heavy door key, holding it in front of the refrig-
erator door because, he explained, he drew power from the
metal surface. (He also draws power from water.)

On October 7, Uri arrived after dinner with his secretary,
Trina Vatter, and his long-time friend, Shipi Shtrang. Uri was
standing in the dining-room holding a bottle of milk in one
hand and a tin of cocoa in the other. Pat reached down to a
low cupboard for a glass. At that instant something skimmed
across her hair with the hum of a bullet. With a magnified
"ping" sound it bounced on the tile counter in front of her.
An American Indian silver button. Until that moment, that
button had been attached to a card in her bedroom dresser
drawer—three rooms away! Uri did not know of the existence
of that button, nor had he been in the bedroom.

We hurried to the bedroom to find the dresser drawer
closed, the card intact, with the center button missing.

"Did it travel in a straight line?" Uri asked excitedly. Pat
had felt the line of trajectory as it brushed across her hair. It
did. *If* it flew through the dresser, through three walls, and
possibly through Uri himself.

Then he noticed two silver brooches on the same dresser.
Brooches in the shape of Mexican hat dancers, holding amethyst
maracas. "How unusual!" Uri exclaimed, taking up the male
figure by the feet. Even more unusual, the tiny silver arm holding an amethyst ball started bending towards us! Uri dropped
the brooch. "I do not want to break it," he apologized.

"Bend the other to match," Pat suggested. Uri picked up
the lady dancer by the skirt. One silver hand came towards
us. The other bent backwards. Uri dropped it. "No, it will
break," he said.

He noticed an old watch which hadn't been wound in at
least two years. Setting it on a silver shoehorn (for added
power?) he passed his hand above it. Immediately it began to
tick.

We carried the Mexican brooches into the sitting-room,

placing them on the coffee table. Uri played us his record album (his visionary poetry set to music*). In one verse he says many people have this power. "Think bend ... bend ... bend. ..." As his words came from the record, the Mexican dancer's silver arm began to bend forward again. The brooch was lying at least seven feet away from Uri or anyone else. Everyone (seven people) saw it move. Afterwards, the metal showed odd striations, and a slight crack at the bend.

That same record album when played on Swiss radio had brought calls from hundreds of people to report bent keys, cutlery, etc.

We live in a building converted from a late nineteenth-century town house into apartments. The downstairs door is decorated by a wrought-iron grille featuring two winged dragons. To enter the building, one must pause before this door and be buzzed in. On Wednesday night, October 8, 1975, Uri came up the elevator about 8 P.M. accompanied by Trina and Shipi. At around 9:00 P.M. Betty Kenworthy of Thames Television arrived. While waiting to be buzzed in, she noticed those dragons on the door.

Later, Betty left with the others. When they went out, they rang on the intercom in great excitement. While Uri had been upstairs in our apartment, the outer wings of both dragons had bent forward. Now, the gilded wings pointed straight out.

Seeing them in the morning, the manager tried to hammer them back, but one began to crack. "What vandals have been at this door?" she wondered. The wings still remain, slightly jutting forward.

And that same evening Uri had arrived depressed because his powers had refused to respond during laboratory testing. (Uri devotes 20 percent of his time to scientific research. That is, letting *them* examine *him.*) Though the powers had stubbornly refused to manifest themselves that day, the door was not the only happening of that evening.

---

*Uri Geller, released by Polydor Records.

Earlier, before Uri arrived, Pat picked up a metal comb which Uri hadn't touched or seen. It fell apart in her hand. When she tried to fit the halves together there was a gap. Along the broken edge, the metal showed the same sort of curious striations—and one missing tooth. The comb had been in the bathroom in a metal tray—directly in the path the button had traveled the night before—*if* the button had actually moved in a straight line through those walls. Uri's explanation of what happened to the comb: The metal in the center had dematerialized, taking with it the tooth. Why? His guess is as good as ours.

But the phenomena we attribute to our association with Uri actually began the week before we met him. At the time, of course, we didn't tie events to Uri. Later we were to learn that there is a constantly reoccurring pattern of such phenomena among Uri's friends.

The week before we met, Richard, our son, had lost an important research book. The apartment, and particularly Richard's room, were carefully searched. No book. The day after Uri arrived, the book mysteriously reappeared, resting prominently beneath a chair in Richard's room; a place where we each had looked and where it could scarcely have remained hidden. Betty Kenworthy reported a similar experience of "loss and find."

One week to the day before we met Uri, all the lights on one circuit at the rear of the apartment went out. This happened seven times, one lever in the fuse box unaccountably flipping down. By coincidence (or was it?) that night there was an electrician (who had wired the entire apartment) there to fix our hi-fi. He examined everything including the fuse box, and could find absolutely nothing wrong. After the seventh time, the lights came on and everything returned to normal.

This lights-going-out phenomena appears to be a sort of calling card and occurs often around Uri's comings and goings and other happenings. This same circuit of lights went out again after Uri had returned to New York on the night of October 29. The night a bomb blew up an Italian restaurant less than two blocks away. It shook our building. Had the lights been a warning?

Three months after Uri left, we went on a visit to California. The night before we arrived, the bedroom lights where we were to stay went out. They remained off for several hours, then came on of their own accord. One by one, all the picture lights in that house went out, then came on again. No electrical explanation was found nor has it happened before or since. The day after we arrived, Uri phoned us from New York and was not surprised when we related the event.

In London, the morning the first letter from Uri arrived, our silver letter opener was found bent—and it hadn't even been used to open that letter.

It is generally suggested by modern psychologists that paranormal or psychokinetic powers originate from the subconscious mind of the subject. The subconscious, or superconscious (Colin Wilson calls it the mind's attic), is also credited with producing a variety of other inexplicable phenomena, from ghosts, to poltergeists, to clairvoyants, to faith healers, to water dowsers. Scientists seem to feel more secure with this theory, though it is difficult to know why. This process can no more easily be explained or pinpointed in the laboratory. But as yet, scientists are not inclined to consider the possibility that such phenomena could exist quite on their own, and manifest themselves outside the physical senses of human beings.

Certainly the theory of subconscious control of paranormal phenomena seems no more rational or logical than Uri's theory—that he is a channel for an intelligent form of energy outside our dimension. Other dimensions? That's treading on Einstein territory.

Sigmund Freud (a very distant relative of Uri's) held the theory that certain types of psychic phenomena—telepathy, for one—might actually be a throwback in man's evolution to some prehistoric means of communication. Through hundreds of millions of years this ability was replaced by the tools of speech and language. Science still knows little about the communication systems or psychic abilities of animals.

In the case of Uri Geller, credibility is more stretched by the explanations offered by his detractors. Laser beams, ra-

dios planted in his teeth (he doesn't have one filling), metal-
dissolving acids under his fingernails (which presumably do
not damage his skin). To some minds, such explanations seem
more palatable than the possibility that man has not yet
learned everything about his world, his universe, his galaxy.
One is reminded of the official demand to close down the
U.S. Patent Office at the dawn of the nineteenth century to
save the government money since surely there could be nothing left to invent.

Francine du Plessix Gray* says "altered states of consciousness is a concept absolutely crucial to para-psychology.
The elusive sources of telepathy and clairvoyance are more
readily transmitted in the twilight states of reverie, trance,
hypnosis, dream and meditation." This concept does not
seem to apply to Uri, who does not tune out his other five
senses nor go into any sort of trance state. Phenomena occur
while he is in a normal state of awareness. He describes the
feeling coming through him as a "high frequency vibration."

His metal-bending and watch-starting, etc., never happen unless other people are present. He believes he draws on
their energies. Some, who spend much time with Uri, report a
sudden weight loss. Pat did. Jesse didn't. It is known that certain psychics lose weight during trance. Certainly, in both
cases, energy is consumed.

It would be impossible to relate the countless documented incidents of Uri's powers, but for every incident listed
here, there are dozens of similar examples. Uri "repaired" a
portable electronic calculator for Dr. Wernher von Braun and
broke the scientist's wedding band simply by staring at it. In
Munich, he stopped a cable car in mid-air. The lever pulled
itself down, as did our fuse box. He also stopped an escalator
in front of a large crowd. He bent a heavy metal type-set bar
belonging to the Austrian *Kurier* newspaper. In Canada he
demonstrated to Judy Timson of the *Toronto Star* that he
could not only read her mind, but cause her to read his.

New York Times, August 1974.

When he bent Judy's key as she held it, she could feel it grow warm. She set it down and it continued to bend.

Alan Vaughan, features editor of *Psychic* magazine, and editor James Bolen photographed a fifteen-frame sequence of Uri bending a steel fork by stroking it. Vaughan clutched his key tightly. Uri bent it by resting his hand lightly on top of Vaughan's. When Vaughan opened his hand the key was still bending. Uri passed his hand over a nail clipper. The heavy metal snapped at the joint.

Dr. Gerald Feinberg, Professor of Physics at Columbia University, saw a needle, placed on a plate near Uri, split in two with a loud crack (magnified sound) "as though it had been cut through with a very fine instrument." An attempt to produce a similar break with sharp wire cutters left edges bent and crushed.

Albert Rosenfeld, former science editor of *Life* magazine, says of a "Gellerized" fork: "The deformation that began when I was holding it continued for some time afterwards." For Rosenfeld, Uri also pulled apart a door key "like a stick of chewing gum. The halves no longer fit together." An example of dematerialization similar to Pat's comb?

For Robert Chapman of the London *Sunday Express* (November 1973) Uri bent a key and a metal comb. And the next year, another *Express* reporter's key was bent while Uri was standing several feet away. On a London TV talk show, a lady reporter's brooch snapped in two on her jacket. A jeweler could not repair it because the pieces no longer fitted together.

A group of reporters were gathered around Uri in the VIP lounge at London Airport. One man's whisky glass suddenly developed a dent. Apparently not only metals are subject to the Geller Effect.

Gellerized metal has been examined by Dr. John Chilton of Cambridge University's Metallurgy Department. Chilton could give no rational explanation, stating: "There are no signs of cutting, burning, or the use of acid." On another occasion a Geller-bent key was examined by a firm specializing in testing metal fatigue. They insisted the key had been subjected to at least sixty-three pounds of pressure.

In Israel, West Germany and in California, Uri successfully drove a car through heavy traffic, stopping at all the red
lights while blindfolded, by using, telepathically, the vision of
a brave passenger. He has given up demonstrating this feat
because he says "it can be duplicated too easily by magician's
tricks."

For photographer Harry Dempter, Uri accurately described the living-room of Dempter's Essex home down to the
carpet color, position of furniture, and a seascape painting.
He told reporter Andrew Fyall that Fyall had recently had "a
bad experience involving your car and a white animal." Six
weeks earlier, Fyall had hit and killed a white cat with his car.

Uri has photographed himself through a sealed lens cap;
another feat too easily duplicated by trickery, and so abandoned from Uri's demonstrations. But always around him
there are the things that happen unintentionally. Flying from
California to New York in 1975, the airplane's motion picture
projector jammed and the film spilled out. An accident? This
particular phenomenon happens too often when Uri is
present. He contends that his powers are never really harm-
ful, but only shock and delight people.

Thousands of viewers across the world watching Uri on
TV have reported experiencing the Geller Effect on cutlery,
watches, etc. Perhaps the most bizarre incident was reported
in the London *Sunday Mirror* (March 17, 1974). A housewife
from Jonkoping, Sweden, consulted lawyers wishing to claim
damages against Geller. While watching him on TV, her copper IUD coil bent out of shape, and she subsequently became
pregnant.

An English TV show, aired *after* Uri had left the country,
still had viewers reporting bent spoons and repaired watches.
In March 1974, the *Daily Mail* ran a poll: "Does Uri Geller
have Psychic Powers?" Of the thousands who returned voting
slips, 95.5 percent said yes.

In a San Francisco press interview Uri was handed a
rosebud. He held it a moment; it opened and bloomed. On
another occasion he was handed a bloom; it withered. Uri
doesn't attempt such experiments any more because it is an
aspect of his power that frightens him. While being tested at

Stanford, a young polio victim was brought to him. A touch of his hand brought movement to the girl's paralyzed leg. "It started to move for the first time in years. But that scared me." Uri felt himself unready to attempt healing.

When he bent metal held in the hands of Andrew Weil of *Psychology Today* (December 1975) Weil described the sensation: "I felt a distinct throb inside my hands, like a small frog kicking."

In the SRI tests (November-December 1972) Russell Targ and Dr. Harold E. Puthoff had Uri perform experiments in the following categories: *Dice Box:* Ten throws. Uri looked at the box without touching it and guessed which die face he believed uppermost. He guessed eight correctly. Passed twice. Odds, one in a million. *Hidden Object Experiment:* Correctly guessed twelve times without error. Passed twice. Odds, one in a trillion. *Laboratory Balance:* Geller caused the balance to respond as though a force had been applied. *Picture Drawing:* In an electrically shielded room Uri received pictures being drawn 3,000 miles away, by "information transmission under conditions of sensory shielding." He drew an almost identical bunch of grapes to one target picture; the exact number of grapes—twenty-four—and the exact number of rows. Uri says he receives an image projected on a mental "TV screen" in front of him, eyes open. In the case of the grapes, he saw "drops of water coming out of the picture. Purple circles."

Dr. John Taylor, Professor of Applied Mathematics at Kings College, London, has been carrying out extensive research into the Geller Effect and has recorded his findings in a book.* Taylor says of the grape test: "The odds for him guessing the details of this picture by chance alone are at least as low as one in a thousand million and that is definitely an underestimation." While Taylor was testing Uri in his lab, several metal objects apported from a table to crash twenty feet away across the room. A sealed perspex tube containing an iron rod flew from the table striking Dr. Taylor on the legs.

Superminds, John Taylor.

The rod, still inside, was now bent. Uri had not been close to the flying objects.

During a magnetometer experiment (also successfully conducted at SRI) Uri passed his hand near the probe of a Bell gaussmeter (an instrument designed to measure magnetic fields). Geller deflected the instrument several times, demonstrating that he possesses a magnetic field at least half as strong as that of earth! He caused a compass needle to rotate; iron filings moved about when his hand passed near. In carefully chosen words, Dr. Taylor states: "This does seem to mean that there was perhaps some magnetic effect caused by his presence."

In the target picture tests, SRI found it wasn't even necessary for a living person to draw the target. Uri was able to reproduce a diagram created by a computer—and seen by no one beforehand. So much for mind reading!

Uri was also able to move small weights and register on a magnetometer from a distance—a feat theoretically impossible. Dr. Taylor adds: "Either a satisfactory explanation must be given for this phenomena within the framework of accepted scientific knowledge, or science will be found seriously wanting."

Bryan Silcock of the *Sunday Times* of London wrote: "If people can bend metal by mind power it will mean a revolution in science and our whole way of thinking about the world more profound than anything since Newton."

Like so many people with paranormal powers, Uri finds it difficult to demonstrate in front of cynics. And there are plenty of those. The dissent against him seems to be led by a magician who makes a career out of trying to debunk Uri. He has challenged Geller to a stage duel. Uri has replied that he will gladly meet the Amazing Randi in a scientist's laboratory where the tests can be controlled. Not amazingly, Randi has refused such an offer. *Time* magazine suggested that any conjurer could duplicate Geller's feats. Geller is the first to agree that much of what he has done can be duplicated by conjuring—but no magician dares to reproduce Geller's lab tests, or even his feat on the 1973 Jack Parr TV show. Uri bent a heavy metal spike held by Parr. Randi won't attempt this on

TV—to quote Alan Vaughan, "unless he brings his own spike."

But there are stranger things reported than bent spikes or stopped cable cars. Witnesses have testified that objects have been moved mysteriously over great distances. From New York to Israel and from London to New York. In his book, Uri relates his own teleportation from New York to Ossining, thirty-five miles away. At a certain moment, witnesses saw him in the street in New York. Uri blacked out. A few minutes later he found himself crashing through the top of the window in Dr. Puharich's Ossining home.

What sort of person is Uri Geller? How much does he really understand about what is happening to him? Through him? He rarely drinks alcohol, smokes only the occasional cigar, likes pretty girls. He is nonsectarian, although a Jew by birth and a strong believer in God. He is nonchauvinistic although an Israeli. He is deeply concerned with the need for love and peace as an essential goal for all men. He says:

> Love is here! This earth is beautiful! You've travelled around the world, did you see what a beautiful planet we live on? We could have been born on a deserted planet—on an ice planet. Or inside caves—only darkness—and still have a civilization. But we have a gem in our hands in Planet Earth. Beautiful little nothing, lost between endless planets and stars and the cosmos. We all have love, but we don't know how to use it. We don't know how to turn this planet into a gem. We have to polish it.

Uri shuns the suggestion of any personal messianic destiny, but is haunted by the fear of apocalyptic crisis as an end result of man's headlong drive towards the production of his own destruction. He has an appetite for all the things the poverty of his youth denied him, yet is appalled by his own materialism. He is a visionary with a sense of mission, and one of his missions is to awaken the dormant psychokinetic levels in others—and make people aware of forces outside themselves.

He was born on December 20, 1946, in Tel Aviv. His

mother chose the name of Uri, meaning "circle of light," because "before I was born she had a vision of a man of fire." When he was three, he was playing in an arabic garden near his house.* "Suddenly there was a very loud high pitched ringing in my ears. All other sounds stopped and it was strange, as if time had suddenly stood still. . . ." A silvery mass of light seemed to block out the sun. It came lower.

> I felt as if I had been knocked over backwards. There was a sharp pain in my forehead and I was knocked out. When I woke up I rushed home and told my mother. She was angry and worried. Deep down, I knew something important had happened.

Uri's telepathic powers seem to have developed from that moment. He knew exactly how much his mother had won or lost at cards. When he was seven, he discovered he could will the hands of his watch to move. His parents separated, and childhood became lonely. He moved to Cyprus with his mother and step-father, returning at seventeen to serve as a paratrooper in the Israeli Army. This is how he explained it to a Johannesburg audience in 1973:

> I served in the Israeli Army like everybody else does in Israel. When I left it, I went to work for a textile factory and was earning very good money. One day after working there for a year, I said to myself: "I have these abilities, why don't I use them for something?"
> And the first thing I thought of was maybe going to gamble. Maybe win at the horse races, because if I could read minds I could know that horse would come in first. But it never happened! First of all, Israel doesn't have horse races—but cards. I used to play cards—but it never worked when I tried to win money with it.
> Then I started to demonstrate these powers to

*Uri Geller: My Story, Praeger.

small groups. One day a reporter wrote a little article, and in two weeks, I became a household word in Israel. Even Golda Meir once on the radio—it was New Year's day—they asked her what she predicts for the future in Israel and she said on national radio, "Don't ask me, ask Uri Geller." And that did it! Managers came and signed me up to a contract and I started appearing—like here. Then the controversy started. Scientists wrote that when I bend a key I actually have a laser beam in my belt. Or chemicals. Or the people I call on stage are my friends and it's a collusion.

Then I got a letter from Captain Edgar Mitchell. I was very impressed to get a letter from an astronaut. He said that he believed in these powers but in order to validate them I cannot do it on a stage. Let's face it, any magician can duplicate what I do on a stage very easily. Very simple. If you have a transmitter hidden in your ear, or mirrors stuck on the walls. So to demonstrate on a stage and to validate it is very difficult.

(Edgar Mitchell, Lunar Module Commander of Apollo 14, the sixth man on the moon, was one of Geller's earliest supporters. Mitchell has founded a center for the study of Parapsychology, ESP, etc., the Institute of Noetic Sciences. "Noetic" from the Greek word "nous," meaning mind or consciousness. Dr. Puharich saw Uri in Israel and convinced Mitchell to aid in financing the SRI tests project.)

I was unknown in America or the rest of the world so I went to SRI. One of the biggest think-tanks in America, physicists working for the American Defense Department. While I was doing an experiment—in that same section of the building down in the basement there were computers in shielded rooms that belonged to the Pentagon. ARPA—Advanced Research Projects Agency. I was told that the computers went haywire and one of the tapes, which was a very important tape, was totally erased. Something shook the Defense Department because the next day three people came from

Washington. This was written up in *Time* magazine; it's no secret. If Nixon had me in the White House for eighteen minutes, then he would have been off the hook!

(This drew a laugh from Geller's audience, since it was said at the time of Watergate.)

I believe *Time* was influenced to write a very negative story about me. They put it under the science section. If they didn't believe they should have put it under entertainment. But the article shook America about what was going on at SRI, and instead of finishing me off, it did the contrary. In a month's time, the whole world knew about me. People ask: "Why are you making money out of this? Why are you appearing on the stage?"

My answer to that is very simple. I don't think it's anybody's business how much I'm earning. I don't think anybody wants to be poor. But I'm doing shows because I like doing them, it's not just the money. I like travelling around the world, I like meeting people. And this is the only way I can demonstrate to laymen, to the person in the street, that these powers do exist. Anyone who wants to get into it more deeply, he can turn to the scientific side of what I'm doing.

And the scientific side seems to be having a trauma of its own. Even the scientists who do not doubt Uri's powers and have seen ample proof in the laboratory, give ear to unfounded accusations by magicians that Uri occasionally uses sleight-of-hand. No one has yet proved this.

Edgar Mitchell says:*

For Geller to have cheated (at SRI) under the circumstances that we tested him, he would have needed an army of accomplices hidden in the walls, being ca-

---

The Amazing Uri Geller, edited by Martin Ebon, Signet.

pable of projecting what we were going to do the next day, and using a battery of equipment that is totally unreasonable to assume. So we have pretty much ruled out trickery in most of Geller's work with us.

But Mitchell complains that he feels the controls were not tight enough in the beginning. Why?

For instance, we would attempt a psychokinetic experience under good controls, but *another* psychokinetic event would occur actually somewhere else in the room and only peripherally in our vision. . . . So in the beginning we often found ourselves distracted by an apparent psychokinetic effect, a poltergeist effect, occurring elsewhere, which would divert our attention from the real thing we were looking for.

Real thing? This poses a serious question about scientific approach. What is the real thing they are looking for? Is it the reality of a psychokinetic happening (which chooses its own time and place to happen) or is it that they are looking to create something in their test tube, over which they are master, which will follow rules and laws they know and understand?

Mitchell goes on to say: "With things happening other than where we wanted them to happen, we had to learn to disregard them and go on."

Disregard them and go on to what? While science is worrying about strict protocol, eyes glued to the test tube in front of them, the four walls of their lab could levitate and they must, it seems, disregard it or cry fraud.

Little wonder Geller became impatient at being treated like a guinea pig or child. "It was like getting him interested in a new toy and getting him to play with it," adds Mitchell, with a certain disappointment at Geller's "becoming more and more interested in acquiring power, wealth, money and acclaim." While conceding that laboratory research "needs persons of Uri Geller's capabilities," he complains that "we should now work with those who are spiritually motivated, rather than those who are natural psychics or, in a very special sense, 'freaks.' Many of the lamas, the Tibetan masters, and Hindu masters . . ." would be preferred by Mitchell because they might, he thinks, be more cooperative. Perhaps spiritually motivated people would be more cooperative—but probably they would not be interested in devoting 20 percent of their time to laboratory experiments.

Uri has stated several times in the press that he intends to bring back Edgar Mitchell's camera from the moon. We asked him in February 1976 if he still feels this will happen. His answer: "Yes—when it is the right time and place and the right people are around. Hopefully it would be like a Woodstock atmosphere—it would be incredible with all that energy. Can you imagine?"

But Uri's public image as flashy pop star of the psychic world, celebrity with full VIP treatment and admiring female following, should not overshadow his rare and exceptional quality as visionary. His concept of man's evolutionary future may indeed be prophetic.

"What created us?" Uri asks:

> Some scientists say it's an explosion. Some say it's an expansion. Some scientists believe that the universes are expanding, expanding—and billions of years from now—it's like a balloon—Vooom!!! They will have to collapse.
>
> If you look at how man developed from the monkey, we lost our hair because we learned how to wear clothes. Hair was a nest to proect us from the cold and from the sun. We needed brows because the sun would spoil our eyes. That's how nature made us. The little things, the hairs in the nostrils so when we breathe, we won't breathe dust. The hairs stop the dust inside us. It's nature. It's God. It has created some incredible, barbaric machine!
>
> Now, we have to have eyes to look, a mouth to talk. Now, we still have hands, because we have to touch— move—do—express, all those things. But as the process goes into the future—mechanical, electronic, psychical things are going to take over our physical movements.

Like, I will not reach for an object. I will think about it
and it will come to me. Millions of years will pass. My
hand will not be in that movement, so it will grow
smaller. We'll use it less. We'll start deforming, mon-
strously! Hair will disappear. We won't need any more
protection. There will be inner immunity. There will be
no more sick. We will cure ourselves with our minds.
We'll have temperature controls from inside. We'll wear
no more clothes. We're changing.... Hair will be the
first thing to lose. We will become more clever. Find
new ways to learn better. Knowledge ... Our brain will
expand. Our heads will become taller, bigger; our bodies shrink smaller. The brain will start growing—more,
more, more!

Next phase—we won't talk any more. We'll communicate telepathically. Millions of years will pass; our
mouth will start disappearing. Or, it will be in such a
way that we only use our mouth for an art form. It will
be an art! It will be music. Talking will be a theatre type
thing, otherwise, we don't talk.

Aeroplanes, cars and physical transportation will
disappear totally. The roads will disappear. There will
be no roads on the planet, no paths. There will be nothing. We will teleport ourselves. We will dematerialize
and materialize in other places. The houses will disappear. We could make ourselves smaller, bigger. Then
food is going to start disappearing, because we will feed
ourselves with cosmic food. Cosmic food! Our minds
will create food.

Sure, you will say, where is all the fun? Where is
sex and where is a good pear? Other things will take
their place. We will have all this fun in different forms.
To my eyes a gorilla is monstrous, ugly. Fifty million
years from now, human beings will look monstrous to
me. But they will be more intelligent. They will look at
us as the monkeys, the cave men, as the barbarics, as
the people who had to eat from plates with forks! It's
going to be ridiculous that we had operating tables, hospitals, cars. It's going to be all museum pieces. Not even

museums, fifty million years from now. It's not going to exist! Then—in the far future—billions and billions of years—one day we're going to disappear. Might be an explosion. An explosion of intelligence that started a little molecule, and we're going to disappear and become pure energies. Closer to God. Closer to the Creator.

I think that what is communicating with me has passed this process, maybe several times. Because when we become pure energies, what then? That's the mystery. That's not the end. Because there is no end; maybe only a new cycle. But certain things can stop these from happening: Atomic warfares, natural disasters. Many things could happen to stop this natural evolution. And who decides that?

Nature will decide when "X" will press the red button. If a comet hits the earth and spins it out of circulation. We are controlled by nature, and maybe nature is a sort of arm of God. Or it's a thought of God. Maybe we're not even here, there's nothing here. But it's a split, split second—a thought of God. Evolution! It must be that, because there's no end, only vastness.

We asked Uri what he felt his particular mission was and why he had these powers. He answered:

If I can bend a spoon and you can't, that doesn't mean that my mission is more important than yours or the milkman's, or the shoemaker's. Everybody is born and living for a purpose and a reason. We cannot weigh the missions, because there are no balances to weigh them on. We cannot know which mission is more important. Maybe mine is more advanced, that's all. But not more important because it's very simple. If we have a track, and this is me—this is you—this is the milkman—this, the shoemaker—because I'm more advanced, doesn't mean anything, really. Because we are going to no end anyhow, anywhere. We might never meet up. We have to work on the basis, "why am I more advanced?" This person has the same mission, maybe, that I do—but why am I before him?

Maybe it's because it involves another intelligence. It's as though I'm opening a vast wind tunnel to the sky. The wind hits me. It's like a racing driver. He always sticks to his fellow companion—behind him. Because he can drive faster. Because the one in front cuts the wind for him. When he finds the right place, he'll overtake him! That's what the whole evolution is about. The right thing, the right happening, the right creation. Maybe I'm making a way, but it's still the same mission.

Perhaps time will clarify the forces behind Uri. Whether they are from his own superconscious, or the manifestations of a great undiscovered field of energy and knowledge. Are his bent spoons and keys the floating branches by which a new Columbus is given a hint of a land waiting beyond the horizon? Are they the keys to survival, the hints of potential wonders for the future? Or merely the whims of the clowns of the universe, to whom man on the brink of self-destruction has become a bad joke?

If science is to discover the truth behind Uri Geller, it must not cling to old rules and laws. The scientist has always wished to remain the observer, outside his experiment. He must re-evaluate his concepts in relation to the new phenomena. The future, always an unexplored continent, can only be glimpsed through the visionary minds of men of mystery. Men like Uri Geller.

Franz Anton Mesmer

In 1975, Olga Warrell, the remarkable Baltimore psychic, demonstrated by holding her hands over a dish of water that she could willfully affect the liquid to the point that physicists could measure a difference in its surface tension. Some power, emanating from her hands, was changing the molecular make-up of the water.

Kirlian photography showed rays of energy radiating from her finger tips, an energy capable of curing a variety of human ailments.

Two hundred years before her time this, and more, was done by Franz Anton Mesmer; but there was then no scientific means of proving his thesis. He was therefore treated as a charlatan.

Hypnosis, which he developed, is no longer disputed. It is widely used, as he used it, to anaesthetize a patient.

Acupuncture has shown, as Mesmer claimed, that the human body has a polarity, just like a magnet, with minor nodes for the entry of some energy not yet identified, though described by the Hindu and the Chinese as pulsing through the human body, its harmonious balance, as Mesmer insisted, being a prerequisite to health.

Following Paracelsus, Mesmer supported the Swiss sage's dictum that the spirit is master to a subservient flesh.

More dramatic than pedestrianly historical, Mesmer's story is herewith treated in that vein. The facts and dialogue are generally historical; selected and juxtaposed for continuity.

Great vault of sky. Clouds merging and drifting. Music, clear clean delicious Mozart, played on an unusual, unearthly instrument. The sun's rays slant between clouds to dapple a forested valley, reflected in the spray of a waterfall, in the crystalline dewdrops of a lily-filled pool, in the eyes of wild-life.

A breeze rustles the leaves. The music is flutelike. A man in his thirties, with the wide shirtsleeves of the eighteenth century, moves his hands across a plant whose buds unfold into blossoms.

Reflected in his eyes, clouds form and unform. The woods shiver and whisper as he passes. A fox, caught in a trap, snarls, then licks his hand as it is freed, its leg made whole by a caress.

Through the woods, as if by secret command, a horse canters up to nuzzle its master's shoulder. In their leafy hideouts, forest creatures rise to watch the man canter off to a clearing above the Danube. His horse's hoofbeats pound at Mother Earth, as if to arouse her. By the water's edge a couple making love are brought to a united climax by the drumbeat power of the passing rider.

Ahead is the steeple to St. Stephen's Cathedral, its bells ringing for contrition, its doors belching black-clad suppli-cants into the gutters of Vienna.

Through the twisted sidestreets the Sunday crowds flock to their lurid entertainments, to their vices, unnaturally dressed, unnaturally fed, unnatural in their behavior, dragging snotty children from one grotesque sight to the next, gawking at freaks, at distorted human flesh, at mountebanks, charlatans, prestidigitators, necromancers, beggars, cripples, whores.

In the city hospital, a square building with high ceilings, drafty corridors, and a large surgical amphitheatre, the frock-coated rider is addressed as Dr. Mesmer. The place is pestilential with its gangrenous, cancerous, fetid patients cared for by the medical practitioners of the eighteenth century: bled, bloodsucked, leeched, blistered, clystered, or cut into pieces.

A boy with paralyzed legs is dunked into a tub with an enormous electric eel. The patient Mesmer searches has been taken to the morgue where she lies on the dissecting table, still lovely in death, about to be incised by an autopsist. As the knife parts the skin of her abdomen, Mesmer, with a hand on her forehead, rouses her from her coma, and she is bustled back to the ward.

At the Vienna madhouse, Viennese burghers take their children to stare at the inmates, who, like monkeys in the zoo, pick ticks from each other, scratch and cackle. Others groan in their chains, or scream under the lash. A young man whom Mesmer says can be cured by other means is not to be released. There is no *habeas corpus* for the mad.

From the squalor of Vienna rise the baroque and rococo buildings of the gentry built to parade their vanity. Their Empress's palace, Schoenbrunn, is an attempt to rival Versailles.

At the gates of his mansion at 261 Landstrasse, Mesmer is met by his thirty-year-old stepson Franz von Bosch. The garden is landscaped in the approved manner of the French with geometric aisles, groves, walks, a dovecote, a kiosk, an aviary, a round marble basin with fountain and plenty of posturing statuary. On a slight elevation stands a gazebo with a stunning view of the Danube and beyond it the "Prater," Europe's finest promenade. Among its gorgeous chestnuts, deer graze and gaze at the passing crowds. The cabarets are filled with waltzing bourgeois.

Subtler Mozart, on a weird instrument, comes through the French windows from the ground floor. From an upper window, a girl of thirty, Franzl Oesterlein, watches Mesmer with evident affection and desire, her features overcome by an expression of unrelievable tenseness.

Slowly the door opens and Frau Mesmer, a woman of fifty, watches the scene, torn between envy and outrage. The bark of her voice throws the younger woman into a paroxysm of hysterics.

In the salon, Mesmer finds a young man in a red velvet coat playing on a glass harmonica, fragments from a Mozart concerto. It is Mozart.

At the piano Mesmer accompanies him in a rapturous improvisation, shifting gradually to a series of discordant sounds that grow into a monstrous cacophony.

Franzl Oesterlein covers her ears and falls to the floor in convulsions. Mesmer motions Mozart to make the cacophony worse, in crescendo, till the girl's convulsions reach a peak and subside.

Frau Mesmer kneels to console the victim, berating her husband for his cruelty. Mesmer holds the girl's hand and gently strokes her forehead till the faintest of smiles appears, and a wide-eyed ingenuous thank you. The girl is relieved. Reluctantly, Frau Mesmer bids her son Franz to help the girl to her bed.

"Place these magnets on her body," says Father Maximilian Hell, S. J., court astronomer to the Empress Maria Theresa. "Each one is designed to the shape of an afflicted organ. They should bring her to a crisis faster."

Franzl Oesterlein, heartsick and suffering from sexual stasis, is alone in her room with Mesmer who hangs a heart-shaped magnet on to the skin above her heart, slightly brushing her nipple, the shock of which makes Franzl complain of a hot piercing pain. Mesmer moves the magnet further down her body, just not touching her, causing the pain to move to her abdomen, then lower, as the girl goes into convulsions. The pain has left through her toes. She feels better.

Frau Mesmer and her son, each in their own way jealous, are horrified at Mesmer's placing magnets on Franzl's naked body.

Mozart asks Mesmer why, if this magnetism is everywhere, in all the universe, it is not also in man. "Why do you have to use magnets?"

Mesmer makes passes over Franzl's body with his hands; the results are the same. He brings her to a climax of relief.

Dr. Ingenhousz, a friend of Mesmer's, and a consultant to Empress Maria Theresa, is struck by the recovery of a happy Franzl Oesterlein. But he is doubtful when Mesmer says to him: "Some cosmic or magnetic power, not metallic but animal, moves through my body by means of which I can heal." From the tea tray Mesmer fills five cups, bidding Franzl turn away while he makes passes with his fingers over just one cup. "Not only am I a vehicle for this magnetism," says Mesmer, "I can transmit it and store it in a vessel from which it can be used as effectively as when I operate directly."

Ingenhousz is told in mime to select one cup at a time and approach Franzl Oesterlein. Three cups have no effect. The magnetized cup powerfully affects her.

Patients flock to Mesmer's house, so many—rich and poor alike—that he magnetizes the fountain in his garden, placing iron rods within it for his patients to touch the afflicted parts of their bodies, which brings them to convulsions. Mesmer explains that the convulsive crisis unblocks the ailment and allows a universal fluid to flow through the patients' bodies, making them well. Duchesses and coachmen hold hands around the fountain making a closed circuit for the power.

At the Academy of Medicine a red-faced man pounds the conference table and accuses Mesmer of being a charlatan, a quack. On the wall hangs a painting of Vesalius performing an anatomical dissection on the cadaver of a naked female. In one corner stands a skeleton.

"How," asks Dr. Ingenhousz, "can you call a Doctor of Divinity and a Doctor of Medicine a quack?"

"I can only assume," says the President of the Academy, Dr. von Stoerck, "that like Dr. Faustus he has sold his soul to the devil. . . . In any case, he has made a mockery of the profession of medicine in Vienna."

Ingenhousz: "He claims to cure only patients suffering from ailments of a psychic origin."

One of the doctors laughs. "Then three-quarters of the patients of Vienna must be suffering from psychic ailments. My patients have dwindled to a trickle. I'm told they've gone to Mesmer."

"What's more," says another doctor, "he appears to cure them."

Von Stoerck: "An illusion. He simply makes them think they're cured."

Ingenhousz is thoughtful. "What if that were so. So long as the patient feels better?"

"A dangerous precedent," says Stoerck.

Mesmer closes the door into a roomful of patients of different ages, sexes, and social positions, all clamoring to be healed and touched. Frau Mesmer holds a folded note with the Imperial seal. "We are summoned to the Palace."

"By the Empress?" Mesmer frowns. Frau Mesmer reads the note. "Tonight at ten. To hear a sonata written by Mozart for the Emperor's protégée Maria Theresa Paradis, and for heaven's sake don't rant about your magnetism. This is Wolfgang's chance to be placed on an imperial stipend."

Though sixty and portly, the Empress is still in command of herself as she speaks to her personal physician von Stoerck. "And he charges nothing for his services? That seems most charitable and Christian."

"On the face of it," replies von Stoerck. "At heart it is dangerous."

The Empress smiles. "To the sick people of Vienna? Or to the organized physicians of Vienna?"

Von Stoerck remains serious. "The matter of consequence to the Empire. You cannot disrupt one branch of organized authority without endangering the entire structure of the state. Already as a result of Mesmer's practice, the scum of Vienna mixes freely in his clinic with the finest of the aristocracy. I received a report only yesterday that the Duchess of Braganza was holding hands with her brother's coachman watching the Marquis of Dipplesdorf having convulsions. Some democratic tendencies lead straight to revolution."

Empress: "You mean there is no discrimination of any kind in Mesmer's clinic?"

"Mesmer says that disease shows no discrimination in the classes."

In a book-lined room, mysterious in the flickering firelight, with steaming retorts, microscopes, mathematical and astronomical symbols, a terrestrial sphere, and a dark blue vault charted with major constellations, Dr. Barthe addresses Mesmer.

"I have heard such tales of your cures I could no longer stay away ... in duty to our profession."

"My clinic," says Mesmer, "is open to the world."

"Your theories," says Barthe, "are in conflict with the entire world of medicine. The causes of disease are plethora and obstruction. You let blood for one, and purge for the other."

"Half the people who consult us are only ill," says Mesmer, "because they imagine it. With leisure enough and money enough, they fall sick the moment they are bored. People refuse to live a natural life, take too little exercise, eat deadly food. We have become divorced from nature. If every man and woman would open himself to the ebb and flow of what I call the Universal Fluid ... "

Barthe: "Is this fluid scientifically demonstrable? Does it have weight? Can you see it? Smell it? Analyze it?"

"No," says Mesmer. "No more than microbes and the nebulae could be seen before the invention of this microscope, that telescope. But the Greeks had indications of a microcosm and a macrocosm long before we saw them with our eyes.

"The universe is not an empty soulless place, an inert unspirited void, indifferent to the lives of those who inhabit it. It is permeated by invisible rays, as yet undiscovered and unnamed by science, through which all beings are communicant, through which they can affect and aid each other at a distance. Our so-called normal senses do not present things as they are. Yet man is not restricted to his senses, or even to the mechanical extensions of them. During their crises, my patients see through solid objects, describe—without benefit of lenses—what I see on a slide through a microscope, view the interior of muscles and inner organs, see the invisible poles on which all human bodies are dependent, read each other's thoughts at a distance."

Dr. Barthe: "And you have performed these experiments along scientific lines, with solid evidence?"

Mesmer: "I have. With the result that I have made one of the most startling scientific discoveries of the century. Paracelsus, the father of modern chemistry, perhaps the greatest physician of them all, knew quite well that all bodies in this universe affect each other at a distance. So he enlarged the concept to include all creatures on this planet, and recommended the lodestone for its therapeutic value. I used these magnets on my patients."

Dr. Barthe withdraws. "But that is witchcraft!"

Mesmer: "No more than the sulfur baths you recommend for sterile women. Fear not. The lodestone is only effective on those who desire it."

He discards the magnet which Barthe makes an involuntary gesture to retrieve as if it were a relic.

"Its use is over," says Mesmer, "I need no magnet. Anything can be magnetized: this lamp, that piece of paper, Bello the dog. All organisms can attract and repel healthy and unhealthy currents." He places his hand over a potted plant.

"This plant I have treated every day."

Kirlian photography shows rays emanating from Mesmer's hands to effect the aura of the plant. "It has grown three times as fast as this one I neglect. How does the transference of energy take place? By spiritual or animistic means? By chemical radiations? By the pulverization of infinitesimal particles? Is the energy derived from the terrestrial globe? Or is it divine in origin? Does it issue from the stars? Our star? Is it physical or mental? Is it the product of the human will? I do not know. But of all the bodies I have studied, none is so powerful in drawing on this mysterious force as the human body itself."

His fingers ripple over the delicately flowering blossoms.

The delicate hands of a girl move from the bass of a piano towards the treble in a cascade of shimmering Mozartian harmonies. The girl, in her teens, very pretty in a décolleté dress, is reaching the climax of a piece by Mozart.

Mozart leans against a baroque column following the music with evident approval, his eyes attentive to the beauty of the girl whose fingers run like animate entities across the keyboard.

On a low throne, the Empress listens with a maternal proprietory expression—after all she owns the palace, the furniture, the piano, the player, even the composer—though the music, from the inappropriate movements of her fan, escapes her. Leaning toward von Stoerck, she whispers: "The child looks pretty tonight, but the music . . . it is superficial!"

The girl comes to the finale with abandon. The candlelight is reflected on the piano, in the mirrors, in the chandeliers, in her eyes, which are sparkling as she looks off into space.

There is general applause, patronizingly led by the Empress. All eyes turn to the doorway as a footman announces Dr. Franz Anton Mesmer. The girl, with a strange faraway expression, blinks, then closes her eyes as if about to faint.

Mozart steadies her. "What a strange sensation," says the girl. "Who is this Dr. Mesmer?"

Mesmer makes his excuses to the Empress, who replies: "I understand that half of Vienna is at your doorstep."

"It was a doctor," says Mesmer, "who detained me. It seems the Academy of Medicine is taking an interest in my methods!"

Empress: "I am told they are quite revolutionary." She looks across the room at the girl. "Verging on the miraculous. Or should I say satanic?"

"The devil," says Mesmer, "and the saint derive their power from the selfsame source."

Von Stoerck: "Your Majesty is getting tired."

The Empress puts a hand to her head. "You're right. What would I do without you." She starts for the door, much older, much less energetic.

A middle-aged courtier, unsure of himself, approaches Mesmer. "I am Paradis, secretary to Her Imperial Majesty. Is it true you can cure the blind?"

"In certain cases," says Mesmer.

The pianist moves across the room bumping into a table. It crashes. Everyone turns.

"My daughter," says the Imperial Secretary, "is blind, quite blind."

In Mesmer's sitting room Maria Theresa Paradis stands between her mother and father, her head swathed in veils.

Mesmer moves his hand back and forth across her veiled face.

"What was that?" asks the girl. "It felt as if a feather were probing at my brain."

Her father interrupts. "She cannot be touched. She goes into convulsions if touched by a physician."

Mesmer asks the girl why, if she cannot see him, she moves.

"I can feel you," says the girl.

Gradually Mesmer induces her to remove her veil and reveal her eyes which show only the whites.

Mesmer touches her temples, her cheeks, her throat, her shoulders. The girl gives a shiver. "It feels as if the sun were shining on me."

Her breath comes in short, panting gasps. Mesmer's hands encircle her brow. She is seized by a fit of trembling; her head jerks back in a series of convulsive movements. Her eyes twitch and roll as her parents anxiously watch.

The girl is clearly in a trance as Mesmer raises her eyelid with a fingertip to study the pupil.

"How long has the girl been blind?"

"Since she was three."

"An accident?"

"No. One night she started to scream. She was addicted to nightmares. She was sleeping in our room. I had to use all my authority to control her. In the morning she was blind."

"What treatment was she given?"

"For sixty days her eyes were sealed with a plaster cast while leeches sucked her temples."

"With what result?"

"It brought on convulsions. Then the Empress took her as her godchild and the most modern techniques were employed. A thousand electric shocks were administered to the optic nerve with needles by Dr. Stoerck and by our own physician Dr. Barthe."

"In that case," says Mesmer, "there is little I can do for her." He looks from one to the other. "Except on one condition. That you leave your daughter in my house at my complete disposal."

Von Stoerck and Dr. Barthe are strolling in the Academy of Medicine, past niches with the portraits of classic physicians from Galen to Harvey on to which are cast the shadows of the cloistered arches.

"Quackery," says Barthe. "He admits himself that most of his patients aren't ill at all. With a lot of hocuspocus he befuddles the ignorant, and with thaumaturgical nonsense about the influence of the sun and moon upon the earth, about invisible rays by which people can communicate at a distance, he confounds the rational."

"Yet he did cure that Oesterlein girl of hysteria."

"Pha," says Dr. Barthe. "By laying his hands on her crotch! What man could not perform such a cure with a girl near thirty, unmarried. Now he wants to try his hand in the Paradis case."

Mesmer and Mozart talk against a background of pictures, statues, bannisters, drapes.

"I'm sure now," says Mesmer, "that the optic nerve is not defective. It's been paralyzed by some sort of shock, something the girl did not want to see. The poultice, the leech, the electric needle, merely compounded the trouble, strengthening her desire to seek security in blindness."

"What sort of shock," asks Mozart, "could make a girl choose to be blind?"

"If I knew that," says Mesmer, "I could cure her. Something in the behavior of her parents has me puzzled."

"So you think there is hope?"

"There is always hope. There is nothing the spirit cannot do, especially with animal magnetism. It can even revivify the flesh. The problem is to revivify the spirit. Get the girl to *wish* to be well."

Dr. Barthe is sipping coffee in a bourgeois drawing room with Paradis and his fat corseted wife.

"Does it seem strange," asked Barthe, "that this Mesmer should refuse the child the company of those it loves best? What reason could he have? Unless he is holding the girl for some purpose of his own."

The Imperial Secretary puts a hand on his sword. "If I thought for a moment . . ."

Barthe raises his hand. "Purely a supposition. With your delegation I might ascertain the truth."

Mesmer issues from a room dressed in black, donning a pair of black gloves, calling through the door, "Dear child, put on your clothes and meet me in the music room."

Bumping into Mozart, he puts a finger to his lips with the expression of one who only feigns to keep a secret. "My boy, the simplest cure for any maid." He moves two or three steps and pirouettes. "Desire! Desire to love and be loved, to look upon life as a game."

Spreading wide the drapes of the music room he reveals the sunlit garden full of flowers, singing birds, gently waving trees, clouds drifting in a clear blue sky. With a bolder gesture he draws the drapes except for the lighted candelabrum on the piano.

"This is now her world. Let us see if we can spirit back that curtain."

At the piano, Mozart makes a brilliant arpeggio.

Theresa Paradis enters, startlingly beautiful in a simple, well-cut gown, her hair loose to her shoulders, a chiffon bandage round her eyes. She too pirouettes and bows in the direction of the piano.

Holding the seven-pronged candelabrum, Mesmer raises a hand, demoniacal in the flickering light, his face suspended in an endless void. Taking the girl's hand, he sits her facing a large gilt mirror, saying to Mozart, "It reflects and intensifies the magnetism, just as it doubles the light of the candles. The force within me must have some of the properties of light."

The girl puts her hand to her head. "I have a pain. It's moving forward. It's as if my head were being split. Now it's behind my eyes. Sharp needles pricking at my eyeballs. Stop! Stop! I cannot bear it."

Mesmer makes one more pass, then ceases. Maneuvering the girl by her shoulders, he faces her towards the black velvet drapes, his hand moving to and fro to ascertain that it is invisible against the backdrop. Throughout the séance Mozart plays quietly.

Mesmer: "Now I shall remove your bandage." The girl says nothing, is apprehensive. "Do not open your eyes until I say so."

As he removes the bandage, the girl's full features are revealed, eyelids closed, tremulous.

Mesmer takes a piece of paper from the desk, holds it before the girl's face so that it reflects the light strongly.

"Open your eyes," orders Mesmer.

The girl's eyes open, blink, then screw up as she puts her fists to them. "It hurts. It makes my whole body ache."

"Then keep your eyes closed until I tell you."

Mesmer puts down the paper and picks up a soft gray tobacco pouch which he holds before her eyes. "Try now."

The girl's eyes open, blink; but she keeps on looking. "It hurts, but not so badly."

Mesmer turns to Mozart, whose music takes on a suspenseful air, then reaches for a black chamois wallet. "What effect does this have?"

Girl: "None."

Mesmer picked up the paper. "And this?"

"It hurts."

"Excellent," says Mesmer. "The light affects your retina. It means that you are seeing."

The girl's expression is of wonder, like a newborn babe whose eyes and hands are uncoordinated. "Is that seeing?"

Mesmer: "Yes, my beauty. And soon the whole wide world will open up before your eyes. This piece of paper is white. This tobacco pouch is gray. It reflects less light. This wallet is black. It reflects no light."

The girl has a strange expression. "So black is the color of my blindness."

Turning her head she leans against Mesmer's shoulder.

The Empress is talking to von Stoerck. "You don't expect the Jesuits—black as they are—to be involved in magic of the darker sort! Why should I ban magnetism on the grounds of witchcraft, when Father Hell, my court astrologer, is fascinated by the mysteries of magnetism."

Von Stoerck: "Father Hell is a man of God. Mesmer is a mountebank!"

Empress: "His reputation is above reproach. Bring me proof that he has harmed rather than helped a single one of my subjects, and I shall reconsider my opinion."

Theresa is seated at Mesmer's piano, playing with her usual flowing brilliance. Her eyes are bandaged and she is alone in the room except for the dog Bello lying by the fire. Mesmer comes in quietly, stands listening for a moment, then locks the door and tiptoes towards the girl who brings the piece to a close, turning to look at him as if she had known all along he was there.

"Is it true?" she asks.

Mesmer takes her hand and helps her rise, leading her to the couch where he lays her down, head and shoulders propped against a pillow. On the edge of the couch he leans forward till his face is very close to hers. For a moment he studies her features, then reaches for the lamp on the table which he turns down as far as it will go without going out. Their movements are barely distinguishable in the penumbra.

Mesmer: "I wanted to be sure we'd be alone and undisturbed." He takes her hand in his. "You have known me for some time, have come to trust me as a doctor, almost as a father. Yet you have known me only through my voice, my touch." He runs his fingers over her hand. "Not as woman and man. Come closer." Raising his hand to her temple, he gently caresses her cheek. "Try not to be surprised. Try not to cry out."

His face draws nearer and he removes her bandage. With his free hand he reaches for the lamp as if to put it out. Instead he turns it up and floods his features.

The girl gives a gasp and withdraws. Her eyes are open, features contorted with disgust. "It's horrible . . . grotesque!"

Mesmer's face, accented by light, moves with emotion

and inner power. The girl stares as if fascinated by a snake. "It is part black, part white, and none of it is still..."

Mesmer speaks gently, "My child, you are looking at a human face, the first you have seen in fifteen years." He takes her hand and with her fingers touches the various parts of his face, explaining, "Ears, eyes, lips, nose..."

The girl's expression is partly disgust, partly fear. "Is that your nose? That thing which sticks out as if it wished to gouge me. Do all people have such noses?"

"Mostly. Some are large, some smaller, some more or less hooked, but all, I am afraid, are equally revolting."

The girl realizes she may have been offensive. "I did not mean to be rude. It is all so new and strange. Really, I am grateful."

She takes his hand and puts it to her lips, then looks at him once more. "Now what are you doing? Your eyes have grown so small. Your lips are turning up. What are those shining..."

Mesmer shows his teeth. "I am smiling."

From the fireplace the dog barks, interrupting.

"It's Bello," says the girl, "I want to see his face."

At the sound of his name, the dog moves to the couch and lays its head on her lap. Leaning forward, she looks long and earnestly into the dog's happy face. "But dogs are far more beautiful than men!"

Again the dog barks. Someone is rattling the locked door, which bursts open to reveal Dr. Barthe's contorted expression. Mesmer's valet, Antoine, tries to restrain him.

Mesmer: "What is the meaning of this?"

Barthe reacts to the sight of the girl on the couch, the drawn drapes. "It is I who should ask that question."

Mesmer: "Have you no professional ethics to interrupt a doctor with his patient?"

Barthe: "Is it professional ethics to have one's patient on a couch in a locked room with the drapes drawn?"

The girl has risen and approaches Barthe with an expression of wonder. "Are *you* Dr. Barthe? The one I have known since childhood?"

Barthe looks at the girl with equal amazement, not quite

sure if the girl is out of her mind and should be treated accordingly.

The girl reaches out and gives Barthe's vandyke a short sharp pull.

Mesmer laughs as Barthe gives the involuntary yelp of a kicked puppy. "There, Barthe, how is that for progress?" Mesmer turns to Theresa. "That, my dear, is a beard, of a style made famous by a portraitist from Flanders."

The girl looks up at the portrait of a seventeenth-century nobleman wearing a vandyke. "But he's so beautiful. His features are strong and manly." She turns towards Barthe, "Yours are undecided, as if part of you were dead."

Dr. Barthe recovers. "It's all a cheap conspiracy. You have pre-arranged the entire charade." From the table he picks up a small bronze figurine of a devil, complete with pitchfork, cloven hooves and pointed tail. "If you can see . . . what's this? Tell me what this is."

The girl looks unhappy and frightened.

Mesmer sees she is upset. "She cannot answer because she knows not what it is."

Barthe: "Just as I thought. Any more than a parrot can converse."

Mesmer: "Do not undo the work of months." He turns to comfort the sobbing girl.

Barthe: "Months of prestidigitation. It is you who are undone." He strides towards the door. "The Academy will hear of this, and so will the Empress!"

In the shattered atmosphere, Mesmer holds the girl by the shoulders, waiting for her sobbing to subside. "Don't be upset. It's the way of the world. They cannot accept a mystery unveiled. They must destroy and defame, to bolster their own uncertainty. Come let's put a little harmony into the chaos."

The girl wipes a tear and smiles. At the piano she closes her eyes and starts to play a slow, nostalgic tune. Gradually she puts more gaiety into it, more spirit, and her expression changes to suit the music, her head moving from side to side as she looks into space. At a running passage her expression becomes intent, she looks at the keyboard, misses a note, repeats the phrase, misses again, stops, stares at her hands in despair.

Theresa: "These strange white creatures running on the keys!" Slowly she raises her hands. "They are *my* fingers." Turning to Mesmer: "When I see them, I can no longer see the music."

He leans over her, grasping her shoulders. "It is only natural, my child. In a few short weeks you will have to coordinate what for a child takes years."

He looks up towards the drawn drapes. "But when you have done so you will have two worlds to live in: your own private universe, in which, with your inner eye, you can create a million dreams: and another universe, a common one, which you can share with all creation: this miracle we call reality."

Looking up, Theresa moves her fingers over his face, cheeks, eyes, forehead, ears. "What a mask through which to look upon the world!"

A wigged head rises to reveal the features of the Imperial Secretary, Paradis, as the Empress speaks: "I have a new court composer, and I want your girl to play his works."

Paradis mumbles, "I regret, Your Majesty; that will not be possible."

The Empress frowns as if she had not heard correctly, while Paradis stutters: "Dr. Mesmer has her in his house and will not let her out."

"Against your wishes?"

"We have given him authority. He maintains he can restore her sight."

"But I thought she was incurable. All the experts . . ."

Paradis: "At last reports she could distinguish black from white."

Empress: "What a nuisance. I had counted on the child to give a concert for the Elector. Do you believe in this cure?"

Paradis' expression is that of a schoolboy faced with the theory of relativity.

Dr. Barthe has a similar expression. "I do not know. I tell you, I do not know. At the time I was convinced it was a hoax. Now, looking back, how could the girl have known I was coming?" He strokes his beard. "How could she have memorized those lines?"

"A trick," says von Stoerck, "and a subtle one. Hence all the more dangerous. This so-called cure must be stopped. Is there nothing in the files of the Committee for the Defense of Morality?"

"He's been thoroughly investigated. His private life is unimpeachable."

"Not even with this girl? Did you not find them closeted together?" He pauses as a thought strikes him. "But if the girl could see, she would no longer be a prodigy. Just another pianist. She would be unworthy of the 200 gulden she now receives. She would have to give public concerts, private lessons."

"That," says Barthe, "will touch the Imperial Secretary."

Heavy rain obliterates the view of Mesmer's garden. In the distance sad emotive Mozart is played with skill. Mozart has a note in his hand. The music grows louder as Mesmer enters.

Mozart waves the note. "They have turned me down. The court cannot see its way to support me as court composer. The Empress thinks my music is too facile. I shall have to look for work in Paris."

Mesmer listens as the music reaches a passage of great musical complexity, yet crystalline clarity.

Mesmer: "Facile! I tell you when the Empress sees that girl in all her beauty playing your concerto, you will be at court, and with one opera after the other in a splendid theater." The music is suddenly grandiose with full orchestra, then fades to the single piano. Mesmer nods towards the garden. "No more *Bastien ans Bastienne* at the bottom of my garden."

The piano weaves spirals of beauty, then a note is missed, the phrase is interrupted, fists crash onto the keys.

"When fatherland ignores you, you have to move," says Mozart. "Too much is against us. They do not want my music any more than they want your science. What they want is lackeys to their system."

"Go," says Mesmer, "go to Paris. But I promise you the

day will come when this country will depend for its name on the fame of Mozart."

"Your daughter," says Dr. Barthe, "has been a great success in Vienna. She has touched the Empress's heart. But were she to regain her sight, your daughter would no longer be a prodigy. The Empress could no longer grant her 200 gulden. Your position at the court might suffer."

"But the child could see," says Paradis.

Barthe shakes his head. "The public's taste is jaded. They don't come to see a normal child. They come to see a blind girl play. I doubt if she even could make a decent marriage, if Mesmer continues with his plan to publicize her cure. The entire world will know of their affair."

Frau Paradis tries to withhold her husband. "Leave them. What if she does love Mesmer. Is it not better that the child can see!"

Theresa pirouettes before a full-length mirror, dancing, singing, looking at her reflection, mimicking her movements, sticking out her tongue and laughing. "Oh, it's quite miraculous. How can this flat surface reflect so full and round. Truly it is a miracle, your ... our, reality. And I can play again! I played the whole sonata—without a single fault, better than ever before. You were right. With only the inner eye, or only the outer eye, one is blind; but with both ..." She gives Mesmer a radiant sparkling smile. "I want to dance. I want to sing. I want to travel. I want to follow Mozart and see the whole wide world with all its beauties."

Mesmer leads her towards the heavily covered french window and pulls the drape back. The garden is illuminated by torches. The fountain canopies and sparkles. In the hedgerow a shadow moves.

Theresa looks at the sky, and her features are full of life. "Those must be the stars. Why did no one tell me of their beauty in the night. It is as if they were drawing me up. Now I know that my world and theirs are linked."

She turns a pair of strong bright eyes onto Mesmer, as the strings vibrate.

Mesmer looks at his Andromeda, smiling. She looks at her Perseus, raising her lips to be kissed.

From the shadows, the Imperial Secretary leaps out. "So it's true! You're no better than your mother."

Mesmer turns. The girl clings to him, her expression contorted.

Paradis: "The girl is coming with me."

"No! No!" cries Theresa.

"Paradis," says Mesmer, "this sort of scene can cause irreparable damage."

Paradis draws his sword, which flashes in the torchlight.

Theresa covers her face and screams.

Frau Paradis comes running up with Frau Mesmer. "Don't. Not before the child! You'll do it again."

Theresa is on the ground in convulsions.

Frau Paradis clings to Paradis, impeding his sword. "It's all my fault."

Mesmer kneels by the girl. With great intensity he makes passes with his fingers over the girl's features. The girl lies still. Mesmer pulls back her eyelid.

"She is once more blind."

"She could never see," says von Stoerck, "Mesmer obtained control over her. He has forced the child to his will and perpetrated a hoax upon society. The girl is as blind as ever. Mesmer's magnetism is an invention, a figment. I move that he be expelled from the Fraternity of Medicine in Vienna and that all physicians be proscribed from healing in any way with magnetism."

In the window the drapes rustle at the sound of distant thunder.

Mesmer stands with his back to the fire which radiates around him like an aura as he speaks to his wife. In his hand is a note with the Imperial seal. "So, my dear, I shall be obliged to give up my practice. We shall have to leave this lovely house and follow Mozart into exile to the only capital that still accepts and welcomes refugees ... to Paris, *la ville lumiere*."

"*You* may have to leave," says Frau Mesmer, "there is nothing in the decree that indicates that I must go. It is my house. I shall leave it to my son Franz. You brought this on yourself."

Left alone, Mesmer stares at his framed degree as a Doctor of Medicine beside a framed print of the Hippocratic oath, then pulls a volume from the bookshelf entitled *Paracelsus* from which he reads:

> You have built up an artificial system which is good for nothing but to swindle the public and to prey upon the pockets of the sick. Your safety is due to the fact that your gibberish is unintelligible to the public, who fancies that it must have a meaning, and the consequence is that no one can come near you without being cheated. Your art does not consist in curing the sick but in working yourselves into the favor of the rich, in swindling the poor.... You live upon imposture, and the aid and abetment of the legal profession enables you to carry on your impostures, and to evade punishment by the law. You poison the people and ruin their health; you are sworn to use diligence in your art, and all your boasted science is nothing but an invention to cheat and deceive.... Until you understand that the spirit is master, imagination the tool, and the body merely plastic material, you will go on in the future laming, crippling, and killing your patients in Nomine Domini as you have in the past....

He stares at the fire. From the next room comes a series of clashing discords; they affect his features, as if he too were about to crumble.

At the piano, Franzl Oesterlein is pounding discords. Without seeing Mesmer, she addresses Franz von Bosch. "And he made it worse and worse. Suddenly it all caved in and vanished. When I opened my eyes I heard Mozart." She plays the delicate gossamer music of the first scene, her eyes radiant. Seeing Mesmer she jumps up and runs to him, dragging Franz.

"Dear Dr. Mesmer, we are to be married, Franz and I. Now we shall really be a family."

Mesmer smiles and takes a hand from each. "I am happy. But go on playing. Doctors too can use the succor of a fellow spirit."

Franzl plays, as Mesmer slips into the garden where it has begun to snow.

As snow piles into banks, Mesmer leaves Vienna in a horse-drawn sled, driven by his valet Antoine.

The squareness of the city dissolves into a succession of stunning landscapes. The sun appears to cast an aura around Mesmer's massive head. Icicles sparkling in the snow-covered forest draw him from the sled to stomp across the silent, pregnant earth, leaving Antoine enveloped in steam from the horses' nostrils. Mesmer is once more in his element, energized, in harmony with the cosmos.

The Piedmont of the Alps gives way to the rolling country of the Seine-et-Oise. Sunset reddens the highest steeple of eighteenth-century Paris. In a second-hand carriage Mesmer enters *la ville lumiere.*

At night the rue de Rivoli is bright with lamps and candles in the windows. Parisians, freer than the Viennese, are gayer, their cacophony is a stimulant after the quiet of the country.

In the Place Vendôme near the Café Royal (where the Ritz is now) Mesmer rents rooms in the house of the brothers Bornet. The great square, with its Corinthian columned palaces and Girardon's equestrian statue of Louis XIV, is the scene for chariot races applauded by the gentry and the people.

From his window Mesmer sees the Tuileries gardens and the outlines of the Louvre.

At the Café Royal a poster advertises Gluck's *Iphegenie in Tauris* at the Opéra. Mesmer's imposing figure, towering over the smaller Frenchmen, is recognized as foreign by patrons who have read about him in their pamphlets. Indoctrinated by Voltaire, Rousseau, Lavoisier and Laplace they speak more openly of science and philosophy than in Vienna, demanding an explanation from the visitor of his miraculous cures.

A group pursues him to his rooms begging to be admitted for a cure. Irked by this welcome as a wonderworker, Mesmer is still a healer: so he takes them in—rich, poor and bourgeois alike—complaining to Antoine: "These people will

only make it more difficult for me to have my great discovery
accepted by the medical profession of Paris."

In the entr'acte to Gluck's performance of *Iphegenie in
Tauris*, Glück takes Mesmer by the arm and introduces him
to Parisian society: the Duc de Bourbon, the Prince de
Condé, Baron de Montesquieu, the Marquis de Lafayette,
and Madame de Lamballe, a lovely Piedmontese princess
who has accompanied Queen Marie Antoinette, just then entertaining in her box the American Minister to Paris, Benjamin Franklin, a frail old man of seventy-two, wigless, in a
brown jacket contrasting with the pastel rainbow of the other
courtiers, the ladies with the high creped coifs, the men in
brocades and silk. All make witty or curious or ingenuous remarks about Mesmer's animal magnetism. Dr. Charles
LeRoy, president of the French Academy of Science, tells
Mesmer the academicians would like to hear more of his discovery.

At the Austrian Embassy to France, the Ambassador,
Florimund de Mercy-Argenteau, a grave old conservative,
whose main job is to watch over the behavior of Maria Theresa's daughter Marie Antoinette, warns the Abbé Fontaria
of the Academy of Sciences that Mesmer's reputation among
the doctors of Vienna is that of a quack. He also warns him of
Mesmer's practice of treating the poor without charge.

When Mesmer enters to present a letter from the Minister of Foreign Affairs in Vienna, the Ambassador puts it aside
and says sternly: "In France a physician's prestige is not increased by the treatment of the poor. Even the successful
treatment of four middle-class individuals is worth little
against the curing of a marquis or a count. Four marquises
are equal to the successful treatment of one duke. Yet four
dukes restored to health are nothing to the successful treatment of one prince."

In his carriage, Mesmer visits the hospitals of Paris: La
Charité, St. Sulpice, Les Invalides, and the biggest and most
overcrowded of them all, the pestilential Hôtel Dieu, or
House of God, on the Ile de la Cité in the Seine, reserved for
the poorest of the poor. The ventilated stairs are mere shafts

to transmit foul odors to the wards above where the patients, four, five and even six to a verminous straw mattress, are indiscriminately mixed, the dead with the quick—the rate of death being one in four of all who enter.

The windowless women's convalescent ward gives onto the smallpox ward. The mental ward leads to the surgical section: four rows of beds in the passage to the bread room. In the operating room the patients are lined around a central table waiting their turn to be cut up or amputated without benefit of anesthetic or antiseptic. The operating detritus and sewage overflows into the lying-in ward where half the women, three or four to a bed, die regularly of puerperal fever, their blood-stained linen indiscriminately washed with that of the contagious wards in the river to be hung from the windows to dry.

From the hospital Mesmer visits the house of detention with its living dead, the insane, the indigent, the troublemakers, the totally poor and the unwanted.

Unable to find doctors, the poor of Paris turn to faith healers, quacks and purveyors of concocted medicines. Charms and elixirs are everywhere sold by the ounce and the dram. Faith healers parade the streets proclaiming their wares.

The Academy of Sciences, instituted by Colbert at the direction of Louis XIV, is an almost feudal organization subsidized by the government. Its highest ranking members are twelve noblemen with honorary status. A few salaried members are divided among the six disciplines of geometry, astronomy, physics, chemistry, botany and anatomy.

They meet Wednesdays and Saturdays from three to five in the Old Louvre. LeRoy, President of the Academy, both chemist and physician, has arranged a meeting for Mesmer with the members.

Wishing to make a good impression, Mesmer is at the Louvre early enough to watch the arrival of each member, mostly foppishly arrogant nobles with ruffles and laces, though some are authentic scientists such as Lavoisier who is chemist, geologist, cartographer, economist and more.

Mesmer has brought with him a statement on animal

magnetism spelled out in scientific terms, which he tries to read to the academicians proclaiming the discovery of a superfine fluid which he says permeates all bodies like gravity.

The members are too disorderly to listen. With closed minds they remark, "It's outside the realm of science," or "It's a product of the man's imagination."

Some are uncivil to Mesmer and curt with the President for having dragged them to meet an impostor.

After several of the members have left, LeRoy persuades Mesmer to address those remaining; but they too interrupt his speech with: "Give us a demonstration! Cure somebody for us!"

A man with asthma is produced but is so sceptic in his negative asides to the audience that Mesmer cannot establish rapport with him. Most of the remaining scoffers drift off.

Mesmer complains to LeRoy that he's been made a fool. "These people aren't interested in a scientific explanation, they just came for a show."

LeRoy promises to introduce him to a subtler group of scientists.

In the masonic atmosphere of the Lodge of the Nine Sisters, adorned with Pythagorean symbols, Benjamin Franklin is the master. Count de Gebelin, author and philosopher, who believes that man was once master of the universe but lost his power through sinning, is the secretary.

Philippe of Orleans, cousin of King Louis XVI, the future Philippe Egalité, is Grand Master for all France, Voltaire now eighty-five, is an honored member, as is André Chenier. Joseph Ignace Guillotin is there, as are various future revolutionaries such as Lalande de la Meurthe, Jean Sylvain Bailly, the Marquis de Condorcet, Roucher, Camille Desmoulins, George Jacques Danton, the Abbé Siéyès, and, among the lady members, such future Girondists as Madame de Stael, who hopes for a limited monarchy, and such devoted royalists as the Duchesse de Bourbon and the Princesse de Lamballe.

Their illuminist motto is "unity and freedom" (as opposed to the Catholic deity and duty), their philosophy—a pantheistic world unity with man's recovery of his original essence through science and love.

The Marquis de Lafayette, then twenty-eight, hero of the American Revolutionary War, suggests to his devoted friend Franklin that Mesmer's magnetism may be a force allied to the static electricity Franklin has discovered with his kite.

Franklin taps the crabtree stick given him by Madame de Frobach, one of the legion of his female admirers, and answers: "Delusion, in some cases, may be of use while it lasts. There are in every great city a number of persons who are never in health because they are fond of medicines and always taking them, whereby they derange the natural functions and hurt their constitutions. If these people can be persuaded to forbear their drugs in expectation of being cured by only the physician's finger or an iron rod pointed at them, they may possibly find good effects, *though they mistake the cause.*"

Mesmer answers: "It is not as a physician but as a scientist I wish to be accepted. My object is to prove the existence of a physical agent never before observed, not to rouse against my discovery a cabal of medical men whose personal interest leads them to oppose both my cause and myself."

LeRoy suggests that Mesmer first prove his cures to a less conservative body than the Academy of Sciences, that he try the newly founded Royal Society of Medicine.

But Mesmer can no longer remain in the Place Vendôme. The crowds of patients waiting for him have grown unmanageable and the police complain.

Two miles from Paris, in the quiet village of Creteil, in a large house with a lovely park, Mesmer prepares to demonstrate methodically to the members of the Royal Society of Medicine just how he goes about the curing of a patient, using as his examples an epileptic girl and the Chevalier Charles de Hussay, an army officer of forty who arrives with a high fever, dragging a paralyzed leg; his chest is caved in, his eyes protrude, and he's so sick he can hardly speak intelligently, constantly overcome by involuntary fits of manic laughter.

Two doctors from the Royal Society of Medicine, Antoine Mauduit and Charles Andry, are there to check on Mesmer's patients.

They watch as Mesmer sits opposite the epileptic girl. Placing her legs between his knees, he runs his fingertips over her whole body searching for the positive and negative poles along which he claims the Universal Fluid flows. As Mesmer's hands reach the girl's hypochondriac region, she begins to gasp, palpitate, convulse and then improve.

Mesmer explains that cosmic magnetism enters the body through its north pole at the top of the head, and telluric magnetism from the earth through the feet. His object is to get these forces to flow in harmony from point to point throughout the body.

Back in Paris, to the assembled physicians of the Royal Society of Medicine, Dr. Mauduit explains that the girl had previously been his patient and was deliberately sent to Mesmer as a test. She is only pretending to be epileptic. Maudit says he has long since cured her epilepsy with bouts of electro-therapy.

At the Place Vendôme Mozart arrives with his ailing mother only to find Mesmer gone. He is penniless and his mother is desperately ill; no doctor will come to their hovel and Mozart does not have the means to seek out Mesmer in Creteil.

In their squalid quarters Mozart spends the night lying on his bed with a lighted candle waiting for dawn to go in search of help. Every so often he goes to his mother's bed to turn her pillow and fan away the flies.

The heat is terrible, like a fetid fog. At last, in the early morning, an old German doctor agrees to visit them, but several days go by before he arrives, while Mozart watches his mother weaken.

The doctor prescribes rhubarb powder mixed with wine. Mozart protests that wine is heating, that all his mother craves is water.

"By no means," says the quack, "wine does not heat, it strengthens. Water heats." At the door he promises to return; but two more days go by.

When he does return he shakes his head. "If she leaves her bed she will die. Better have her say her confession."

Mozart runs out and comes back with a German-speaking priest who gives his mother the last rites. She becomes delirious, screaming and flailing her arms.

Mozart crouches in the hot dark room, holding her hand till she dies, then falls on his knees and also asks to die. A breath of air rustles the curtain. His mother is gone.

At last Mozart rises, lights a candle, and sits down to write to his father.

The heat becomes oppressive but Mozart has no money to bury his mother. His last sous go for a carriage to visit Baron von Grimm who says to him, "My dear Wolfgang, in a country where all the mediocre and detestable musicians such as Piccini have made great fortune, you cannot possibly succeed. There are only two avenues for you. Give piano lessons, which means chasing about on foot all over Paris, affording you no time to compose, or go back to your father in Mannheim."

Mozart leaves without seeing Mesmer.

In Creteil, as a result of Mesmer's ministrations, the Chevalier de Hussay is totally recovered. He can speak clearly, stand upright, and walk with a spring. For Mesmer's benefit he writes a simple but powerful affidavit. Mesmer turns it over to the Royal Society of Medicine. But the secretary, Vicq-d'Azyr, who is also private physician to Marie Antoinette, returns it unopened.

Dejected, Mesmer is also prepared to leave France, but his mood of depression at Creteil is relieved by the arrival of a graceful, charming and intelligent young man of twenty-eight, Charles Deslon, a doctor from Paris who is amazed by the change in the Chevalier de Hussay.

Ever since childhood, says Deslon, he has suffered from stomach pains and violent headaches that no treatment will alleviate. Will Mesmer magnetize him?

After a careful examination, Mesmer tells him that his organs are too physically degenerated, that he cannot cure him, only alleviate his pain with magnetism. This he successfully accomplishes.

So impressed is young Deslon by Mesmer's candor, and by his own loss of pain, that he reveals to Mesmer that despite his youth he is a professor on the Faculty of the University of Paris and first physician to the Count of Artois, brother of King Louis XVI (who will be Charles X). Deslon says he intends to devote himself to convincing the medical world of the truth of animal magnetism, a gift to humanity too important to be ignored.

He will help Mesmer set up shop in a proper establishment in Paris to demonstrate to the Faculty of Medicine by an overwhelming number of cures that they must abandon their outdated practices and take up animal magnetism.

The Hôtel Bullion on the rue Montmartre is an opulent spacious residence with lofty ceilings, inlaid floors, paneled walls, full-length mirrors and oriel windows, where the *beau monde* of Paris were entertained. The furnishings are in the style of Louis XV as is the art work on the walls.

Everything in the "clinic" is especially designed to tranquilize and put the patient at ease. "I want them to feel as far from a hospital as possible," says Mesmer.

Soft carpets, heavy velvet drapes, dampen the noise and glare from the streets. A more subdued light from the baroque chandeliers and candelabra is reflected and subtly intensified by scores of mirrors.

Mesmer lays out the clinic as meticulously as if he were stage setting a play. Astrological wall decorations add mystery to the atmosphere. A small orchestra of violin, harmonica and piano plays soft music.

Several young and handsome assistants are hired by Antoine and dressed in lilac velvet liveries. There is a German doorman and Swiss guards at the gate to regulate the traffic of hansom cabs and carriages.

As the patients arrive they are announced by the German doorman with three kinds of whistles according to their social standing.

Four large baquets have been prepared. Three for the gentry, adorned with flowers, a fourth is for those who cannot pay. The baquet is a large circular tub of water about two feet high filled with iron filings and magnetized bottles, arranged like the spokes of a wheel. Iron rods protrude through the lid which the patients can apply to their ailing organs.

Among the arrivals are people of all stations: abbés, marquises, prostitutes, soldiers, intellectuals, dandies, statesmen, doctors. Among the members of the lower classes are peasants, tradesmen, cobblers, scullery maids and innkeepers.

As the patients enter—scrofulous, paralytic, deaf, blind, with dropsy, St. Vitus's Dance, or, like one poor girl, covered in disfiguring scabs, they are cursorily examined by Mesmer, given a quick preliminary treatment, then assigned to a place at one or other of the baquets.

A man is carried in on a litter. A woman, Magdelon Prim, a portress, has tumors the size of oranges on her legs and thighs.

At the baquet, the patients draw near to each other, touching hands, or knees, to complete a circuit.

The handsomest of the assistants hold the iron rods to the variously afflicted parts of the patients' bodies. In mounting suspense they await the return of Mesmer, filling the rooms with heavy breathing and heavy sighs, which mix with the subdued music, only to increase in volume and tempo as Mesmer enters dressed in a powdered wig with a purple silk gown, ruffles of lace at the wrists, shining buckled shoes. In his right hand he holds a wand of wrought iron.

Tension grows around the baquets as he moves from patient to patient extending the wand to touch the afflicted or to gaze deeply into their eyes.

Other patients he holds by the hands, with middle finger to middle finger to establish deeper rapport.

In front of some he crosses and uncrosses his arms to generate a flow of fluid which he then directs from a distance, his finger pointed at a patient's specific affliction.

To some he whispers a word of advice; for others he gives instructions to an assistant who, at the right moment, and at his command, will touch the patient with a rod on the directed spot.

As the fluid moves through the patients, their bodies are subjected to spasmodic movements, their limbs jerk, their throats contract, hypochondriac regions tumesce, their eyes dilate. Piercing cries are followed by tears, hiccups, death rattles, piteous moans, and extravagant or sardonic laughter. Some are overcome by vomiting, expectorations, profuse sweating or even incontinence.

Those approaching crisis fall back with catalepsy or convulsion. Assistants help them to special rooms with padded walls and floors. There the women can roll on the floor or beat their heads against the walls till they pass into a state of quiescence.

Those recovering from their crises are in a state of either languor and reverie, or of exhaustion and drowsiness, easily startled by any unexpected noise.

A change in the tempo of the music, signaled by Mesmer, hastens these crises.

Some of these patients rush rapturously into each other's arms, rejoicing and embracing. Others thrust each other away with apparent horror.

To hasten these crises Mesmer looks piercingly into a patient's eyes, points a wand or a finger, touches a female patient in the hypochondriac region. For some patients it is clear that Mesmer recommends more powerful crises, for others milder transports.

The musicians can also help bring on crises or soothe the patient as they shift from one type of music to another at a signal, and the mood of the patients mirrors the changing musical moods.

Recognizing a distraught, sobbing, but very pretty woman—the Princesse de Lamballe—Mesmer follows her into a padded room, closing the door behind him.

Deslon takes over Mesmer's role, mimicking his every move, applying the wand, the hand or the eye, wherever it suits best.

In charge of the fourth baquet, for those who cannot pay, a *valet toucheur* carries on for Mesmer.

From the closed room, Mesmer reappears with the pretty Madame de Lamballe no longer distraught, but radiant and tranquilly smiling. Several patients come up to Mesmer to thank him joyously for the loss of their symptoms. The halt, the blind, the deaf, are evidently cured.

Among the patients is a well-known Parisian lawyer, Nicolas Bergasse, whose unkempt clothing and bushy wig characterize him as a *philosophe*. He bears a fixed fanatical expression of deep melancholia.

To convince the world of Mesmer's remarkable cures, Deslon invites a dozen members of the Faculty of Medicine to dinner at his house. Because he is a fellow member of the faculty, and because of his position as first physician to the Count of Artois, they accept, but the dinner does not go well. Mesmer insists on reading to them in his strong German accent twenty-seven propositions on his Universal Fluid. Heads shake, mouths yawn, and all but three of the guests excuse themselves.

Deslon arranges for their stalwart ones—the doctors Bertrand, Malloet and Solien—to visit Mesmer's establishment, and report to their colleagues on the results of his treatments.

Again the afflicted are cured before their eyes, scales fall from the whole body of a young girl who was suffering from a congenital disease termed leprous, the egg-sized tumors vanishing from the legs and thighs of Magdelon Prim, lumps disappear from the breasts of several women, the Marquis of Rochegarde rises from his paralytic bed, the blind can now see, the deaf can hear, and the doctors report that the facts are amazing; only the results are inconclusive.

Malloet says the cures are due to nature alone. Bertrand admits of a paralytic who can walk, that his hand has improved. Of a blind girl who can see, Solien says he is no longer sure the girl was blind. Of the cure of a scrofulous girl with a hernia who had lost the sight of one eye, the doctors ask wherein is the proof that nature was in any way aided by Mesmer's animal magnetism.

Mesmer is disenchanted. "It is the same as Vienna. There is no place for me or for my discovery in Paris. I must look elsewhere for recognition."

Mesmer closes the gates to the Hôtel Bullion, and has his trunks prepared.

The crowds of patients are frantic, in a panic at the announcement of Mesmer's departure.

Madame de Lamballe, the pretty widow, who Mesmer has cured of a tick which spoiled her beauty, along with her close friend, the Countess de Malmaison (who Mesmer with his hands has cured of paralysis from the waist down brought about by her husband's neglect), decides to approach the Queen and beg for her intercession on the part of Mesmer.

The Queen, in enforced mourning for the death of her mother, Maria Theresa, cannot take action directly, but agrees to speak to the King.

The King, just past thirty, fat and weak-faced, is looking into a chamber pot of Sèvres porcelain, which he has made as a present for the Contesse de Polignac. On the bottom is painted a likeness of her hero, Benjamin Franklin.

The King is listening to his Chief of Police, Lieutenant-General Lenoir, who describes from an agent's report the dangerous practices carried on by Mesmer in his clinic. "He puts the women into an erotic trance. As their crises develop, their faces become flushed by degrees, their eyes become ardent."

The King is breakfasting on his usual meal of four chops, a fat chicken, six eggs with ham, and a bottle and a half of champagne.

In his mind's eye, the King re-creates a scene to match the policeman's words. "This is the signal by which nature announces the arrival of physical desire. The woman lowers her head, covers her eyes, her natural modesty awakening automatically. As the crisis grows, her eyes become disturbed, an unequivocal sign of the total disorder of her senses. The eyelids become moist, respiration is short and spasmodic, the breast rises and falls tumultuously, tremors begin, along with precipitate and brusque movements of the limbs and of the entire body. In this final stage, even with the most balanced and sensible of women, the end is the gentlest of emotions and a body spasm. Languor and quiescence follow; perhaps a short sleep after such extreme agitation."

The Queen is announced, and Louis bids the policeman hide behind an arras. To Marie Antoinette's entreaty that Mesmer be made to stay, that he is of inestimable value to the sick of France, the King replies that there appears to be a serious matter of morals, that Mesmer may be in a position to take advantage of innocent women.

"And so?" says the Queen. "What better cure for a woman whose husband will not perform or cannot perform.

Look at Casanova and the Marquise d'Urfe. He's proved the point, more than once."

Alone with the King, the policeman makes a suggestion: "Set Mesmer up with a clinic, at state expense, but insist on having three or four agents to spy on what he does. That way we will learn his secrets. Then Your Majesty can dispose of him as he sees fit. I have a collection of alchemists, sorcerers and fortune tellers who are trained police informants, even better than priests at getting secret information."

Mesmer and Deslon are summoned to the office at Versailles of the King's Minister, the Comte de Maurepas, a calm, cautious old diplomat of over eighty.

Mesmer is offered over 20,000 livres a year to open a school of animal magnetism, plus 10,000 livres for the rental of a building. The only condition is that Mesmer accept three students designated by the King, and promise not to leave France until granted permission.

Mesmer asks if the government will formally agree to recognize the utility and existence of his discovery of animal magnetism before the school is opened.

Maurepas replies that he does not have that authority.

Outside Versailles, Mesmer explains to Deslon that unless the government publicly recognizes the value of animal magnetism the device is too simply a trap. With three spies, they can steal his secrets for a mere 30,000 livres, and then get rid of him. "On the other hand if the King will deed me some piece of property where he alone has authority but not the commissioners from the Academy of Sciences of the Royal Society of Medicine, then I will agree."

The government refuses. Mesmer addresses a letter to the Queen in which he stipulates: "I am seeking, Madame, a government that will see the necessity of speeding to the world a truth which through its effect on the human body can work changes and direct a proper cure. Since the conditions offered to me in the name of Your Majesty would not achieve this, my fixed principles forbid me to accept them. I have decided to look elsewhere for that which I can no longer reasonably expect here. When public opinion decides to, it will do me justice. If it does not do this in my lifetime, it will honor my tomb."

Mesmer decides to leave France and go to where he can recover his energies. A rich patient, the Marquis de Fleury, gives him the means to travel.

Deslon will not follow. He wishes to continue the battle alone.

In Spa, famous as a watering place, Mesmer is once more tranquilly surrounded by a countryside of broad buttercupped fields, thick woods and clear running rivers.

Bathing in the health-giving springs he discourses on their salutory magnetic qualities, suggesting that the waters of Lourdes must also have magnetic qualities. In this bucolic atmosphere he starts to write *A Short History of Magnetism.*

In Paris Deslon is writing *Observations on Animal Magnetism.* He has challenged the Faculty of Medicine to put him on trial to force a decision as to whether he deserves to remain a member.

The members are delighted by this opportunity to dispose of him once and for all.

Before a plenary meeting of the Medical Faculty Deslon rises to say that "animal magnetism is the most important scientific contribution of the age."

He is greeted with silence. Dr. Roussel de Vauzières rises and shatters the decorum with a violent attack on both Mesmer and Deslon. He accuses Deslon of conduct unworthy of his profession by allying himself with a charlatan. Deslon has insulted the Faculty by propounding principles repugnant to sound medical theory.

Vauzières dredges up all the old tales about Mesmer's Viennese failures, rebuffs and scandals, sprinkling his discourse with the names of Hell, Ingenhousz, Stoerck and Paradis. He scoffs at the notion that animal magnetism ever cured anyone or was in any way a reality. He charges Deslon with promoting a superstition in the guise of science.

Deslon protests at the violence of his opponent, and delivers a moderate reply, the main thrust of which is to insist that the cures obtained by Mesmer be examined with an open mind.

The Faculty is overwhelmingly against him. His voting rights are suspended. He is threatened with erasure of his name from the rolls if he does not disavow his *Observations on Animal Magnetism*. Leaving the premises Deslon remarks that once again so many Aristotelians will not look through Galileo's telescope.

Deslon refuses to retract his *Observations.* He is dropped from the Medical Faculty, loses his professorship, and earns the opprobrium of his fellows.

Yet thirty young doctors vouch for Mesmer's cures. They are told by the Faculty to take an oath of loyalty abjuring Mesmer and Deslon or face expulsion. Like Galileo twenty-eight of them recant. Two follow Deslon.

In Spa, Mesmer has been followed by the young lawyer Nicolas Bergasse, so thoroughly recovered from his patholog-ical depression that Mesmer does not recognize him. Bergasse has given up his practice of law to devote himself to the spread of animal magnetism. Since the academies and the au-thorities will not cooperate, he has found a group of fifty in-dependents ready to put up 400 louis d'or apiece to form a secret society dedicated to mastering Mesmer's wisdom and techniques.

As Mesmer and Bergasse walk through the fields of Flanders bright with poppies, Bergasse gives vent to his dreams of regenerating humanity by applying "Rousseau's" nature to government, society, education and the arts, in or-der to produce a Rousseau paradise in which noble feelings, virtuous acts and political freedom may at last have a chance to flourish.

To launch the Society of Harmony, Bergasse has brought the immediate financial support of an Alsatian financier, Guillaume Korman, whose son Mesmer has cured of partial blindness.

For wider support, Bergasse calls on all of France "to protect a scandalously persecuted man from the blind hatred of his enemies."

He asks that people form groups to practice and teach Mesmer's system. The appeal has enormous success. Notices from interested parties pour into Bergasse's office from all over France. In a short time contributions amount to 240,000 francs.

It is a time of great excitement in Paris. Charlières and Montgolfier have astonished Europe by lifting man into the air in a balloon. On the Champs de Mars Benjamin Franklin and 50,000 spectators see a silk balloon (filled with hydrogen made from oil of vitriol poured on iron filings) slowly rise into the sky to the sound of drumbeats, cannons and martial music. The spectators, shielding themselves from the rain, asked to what use a balloon can be put. Franklin replies: *"Eh, 'a quoi bon l'enfant qui vient de naître?"*

Already children are eating *dragées au ballon*, and the ladies have started the fad of *chapeau au ballon*. When the aeronauts land in a remote field they are greeted by the peasants with "are you men or gods?" followed by a parade through the villages as the workers kiss their clothes.

Newton's "most subtle spirit which pervades and lies hid in all gross bodies" appears to be a reality. The time may be ripe for Mesmer's Universal Fluid.

In Paris, Mesmer sets up luxurious headquarters in the Hôtel de Coigny, rue Coq Heron, where he is mobbed in the street by admirers who wish to see and touch him.

Inside the huge establishment the Secret Society's meeting place is to be a vast room decorated with expensive tapestries and mirrors. Mesmer has agreed to teach the members how to control and apply animal magnetism. Diplomas will be offered to qualified pupils, allowing them to set up as practitioners of animal magnetism in their own establishments.

The list of subscribers includes some of the greatest names in France: aristocrats, professional men and members of the clergy, among them the Marquis of Lafayette, the Marquis of Chastellux, and another veteran of the American campaign, the Comte Maxime de Puysegur.

Bergasse, a lively mind, draws up the statute for the Society of Harmony outlining its organization and the duties of its members.

A good speaker, he delivers the address at the opening session, welcoming new members, who include some of the great aristocrats of France: the Duc de Coigny, the Duc de Lauzun, Baron Talleyrand, the Marquis of Jowrcourt.

The large salon on the first floor has many light fixtures disposed in threes. The seats were artfully arranged around a raised dais for the President and Vice-Presidents of the society who sit at a table covered with a flaming red carpet.

A huge mirror behind the dais is decorated with symbolic scenes depicting animal magnetism. Initiation of new members takes place in this assembly room with typically masonic rituals.

New members recite a religious oath, placing themselves in "Mesmeric rapport" with the Director of the Ceremony who embraces them with the challenging admonition: "Go forth. Touch and cure!"

Mesmer starts a series of lectures, giving instruction about animal magnetism, and how to administer its benefits. "Patients will show you the place of pain, but a good magnetizer by his touch will more easily locate the source of affliction, which is often on the opposite side of the body." The lectures are followed by seminars.

Bergasse gives lectures from the podium, drawing elaborate explanations on a blackboard, pointing out details on large illustrated charts and diagrams.

He arranges models with wax balls to represent the movements of atoms through space, of colliding molecules, and of currents of magnetism which attract, repel, expand or whirl as fluids of light, heat, gravity or electricity.

Bergasse explains Mesmer's three basic principles: "God," the uncreated principle, and "Matter and Movement," the two created principles. Animal magnetism is a pure movement, outside time.

Charts show how magnetism works and flows through the body and its vital organs—charts very similar to Chinese charts of acupuncture points.

He explains that the objective is to mesmerize the sick back to health and to prevent injustice. The dream is to attain a universal physical and a universal justice.

Man, to Bergasse, is a naturally social creature who wishes to create a truly natural society, ruled by harmony like the original cosmos.

Bergasse maintains that conscience is a physical organ united by numerous slender threads to all points in the universe. "It is the organ by which we put ourselves in harmony with nature. Good is harmony. Evil is disharmony. A peaceful flow of the magnetic fluid will produce a blissfully healthy, happy and justly organized society."

The Society of Harmony is thus a combination institute, medical school and philosophical clinic. Like the Hôtel de Bullion, the Hôtel de Coigny has the usual *sales de cure*, with baquets, padded rooms for crises, and rooms for rest. Special rooms are set aside for distinguished patients to live in.

Places at the baquet became so much in demand they had to be booked well in advance, like seats at the opera, and reportedly bring in 300 louis a month. Flowers are placed at the baquet for "ladies of breeding."

Within the society these great names of France behave in an absolutely egalitarian way. Among the new subscribers are the Marquis de Tissart, the Comte D'Avaux, parliamentary counselor Duval d'Epremesnil and Lafayette.

Lafayette's house at 138 rue de Bourbon (now 81 rue de Lille) has become the rendezvous for English and American *philosophes*, such as Franklin, and such successful North American revolutionaries as Hays and the Adamses, who are frequent guests for dinner.

Lafayette speaks English as readily as French, though scattered with plenty of gallicisms. His children have been taught to sing the war songs he learned in America.

A half-breed Indian warrior, Peter Ostriquette, is treated as a member of the household, and young Kayenlaha, dressed in native costume, calls Lafayette "father," serving him as a page.

Conversation is openly liberal and republican, dealing with masonry, visiting and befriending tenants, Negro emancipation, and attacks on the French mercantile and financial privilege through special tariff arrangements for the American traders. Lafayette speaks constantly of Mesmerism and promises to initiate George Washington into the secret of animal magnetism. The half-breed Indian is in no way surprised by the notion of animal magnetism, explaining that American Indians use the same system of laying on of hands which they have passed down from the greatest antiquity.

Court de Gebelin, Director of the Paris Museum of Natural History, and author of *Le Monde Primitif*, tells Franklin that the Phoenicians traveled to America long before the Norse, and that he believes the ancients had a brighter civilization which is lost.

"Man," says Gebelin, "was once master of this universe, and had reached a state of knowledge superior to that of modern man. He has lost this mastery mostly through ignorance and sin."

Gebelin, whose face is yellow as sulfur, has been ill for months showing pronounced symptoms of a loathsome disease which has made his legs swell up so that he cannot move without being carried and has to wear his culottes to his knees. Lafayette suggests that Gebelin see Mesmer for a cure.

As the Society of Harmony has now collected over 350,000 livres, Mesmer can afford to travel in a sumptuous carriage on a highly successful tour of the new chapters of the Society of Harmony in Lyons, Bordeaux, Toulouse, Grenoble, Lausanne, Turin, with members numbering in the thousands.

In Strasbourg Mesmer stays with the head of the local Society of Harmony, the Comte de Puysegur, who has a phenomenon to show him. Victor, a stuttering young peasant of twenty with no education, is able, when put into a trance with Mesmeric passes, to converse in cultured tones, using complex Latin. He can also describe in detail his ailment, pointing out the inner organs of his body which he says he can clearly distinguish, foretelling the day and manner in which he will be cured. Just as easily he can see into the bodies of other patients, diagnose their ailments and the manner of their cures. Incidents in a very remote past are easy for him to re-cover. Awakened, Victor reverts to his peasant stuttering, and remembers nothing of what has occurred.

Puysegur does the same with a young girl whom he makes obey his every command. She can impersonate with equal ease and with frightening verisimilitude, a general, a nun, a bishop or a fish wife. With her eyes bandaged Puysegur directs her out into the park and through the village, where she uncannily avoids all hazards. Back in the castle the girl can describe in detail the movements of persons miles away, following one all the way into the room they occupy.

The girl says she can see a fluid emanating from both Mesmer's and Puysegur's hands, as a brilliant shaft of light. She says iron conducts this current, glass augments it, wax and copper disperse it. Silver reflects it back to the rod. She says the same fluid radiates from trees and other living objects, differing in color and brightness. She describes magnetic rays issuing from both the sun and the earth.

The girl sees the fluid passing into water or milk which appears luminous to her. Puysegur says this magnetized milk can be retained by a stomach which rejects all other forms of nourishment.

Another girl lying with her stomach bared can read, hear, smell and distinguish objects with the skin at the pit of her stomach. By means of a long thin string stretched to a far room she can hear whispered conversations and do the same if a long chain of people hold hands. But if a piece of wax is placed in the circuit she can no longer operate.

Says Puysegur to Mesmer, "The whole secret is to believe and to will."

"There is a force," says Mesmer, "by means of which the soul can work upon a bodily organism," and he quotes Paracelsus about the power of the spirit over matter, concluding that in a trance-like sleep, an individual's outer senses become subservient to an inner sense which appears to be in tune with the cosmos. Thus the somnambulist can see with his eyes closed, the clairvoyant can see events taking place on the other side of the earth, and by breaking the time barrier the prophet can predict the future. "The cosmos itself," says Mesmer, "is timeless. Past, present and future are different vectors in this universe. And God alone, beyond space and time, sees everything."

In the Museum of Natural history, in the office of the Director, behind heavily shaded windows Court de Gebelin is listening to Cagliostro who is seated before a crystal ball. Wearing a turban and an exotic cloak, he is predicting that Louis XVI must beware of dying on the scaffold before his 39th year. Gebelin figures that would be in 1789.

Cagliostro adds that he can see in the ball a Marie Antoinette prematurely wrinkled from grief, going from the prison to be beheaded.

Parting the drapes, Cagliostro lets light into the office as Gebelin agrees that corruption in France has reached the stage that revolution may overwhelm the country if something is not done quickly to put the country back on the track.

Mesmer is announced and introduced to Cagliostro who says he can do no more for Gebelin, and is happy to turn him over to the care of Mesmer.

In a pitiful state Gebelin is carried into the Hôtel de Coigny.

As Mesmer begins to magnetize him, he says "the day will come when the great principle of physical health will be the equal right of all, with independence of wills and opinions."

The policeman Lenoir has prepared for the King a secret report in which he suggests counter-measures: "Mesmerists are mixing radical political ideas in their pseudo-scientific discourses."

Lenoir complains that in the Hôtel de Coigny there is a communist egalitarian society with perfect equality of rank among members who applaud the American Revolution and believe that American principles will one day rule the world. He promises to infiltrate one of his agents into the Hôtel de Coigny before the danger reaches high into establishmental organs.

As Mesmer magnetizes Gebelin, they listen to Louis-Claude de Saint Martin who believes the material world was subordinated to a more spiritual realm over which primitive man once ruled, and into which modern man must be integrated. The German butler announces the arrival of Claude-Louis Berthollet, member of the Academy of Sciences and of the Faculty of Medicine, a well-known chemist.

"What has brought me here?" says Berthollet. "You may well ask. An open mind and an unprejudiced look at the facts."

The effect on Mesmer and his entourage is electric. "With the support of such a member of the Academy of Science," says Gebelin, "your case is made."

The pamphleteers pick up the news and spread it around Paris.

A Dr. Portal arrives and has himself magnetized.

Policeman Lenoir tells the King, "I now have reports of what is going on in Mesmer's Hôtel de Coigny. These secret societies are plotting the end of the monarchy. The place is full of Rosicrucians, Masons, Illuminists, all republicans, and all despite their great names, are anti-royalists, challenging vested interests."

Under Mesmer's intense personal treatment, Court de Gebelin is back on his feet though Mesmer warns him that like Deslon his disease has gone too far to be permanently cured. Gebelin thanks him for the new and painless lease on life he has received and says he believes that animal magnetism can "reestablish the primitive harmony which had once reigned between man and the universe."

He gives Mesmer an attestation announcing his extraordinary restoration to health which is widely spread by pamphleteers.

The physicians unanimously announce that Gebelin was never ill.

Policeman Lenoir, Claude-Louis Berthollet and Dr. Portal are in conference. Berthollet reads a document he is about to publish which he says will make a splash, attacking Mesmerism as a total fraud.

Portal reads a statement in which he says he feigned symptoms, for which Mesmer fell, thus exposing the folly of magnetism.

Lenoir says the time has come. He will release a major attack on Mesmer in a pamphlet by Michel Augustin Thouet, member of the Academy of Science, called *Investigations and Doubts Concerning Magnetism* which details Mesmer's failures in Vienna, and his ouster.

At the Tuileries Theater Maria Theresa Paradis is playing a concerto written for her by Mozart, the "Paradis Concerto" in B flat major which makes no concession to her disability.

Louis XVI and Marie Antoinette are in the Royal Box enjoying the concert, but someone has distributed to the audience pamphlets explaining how the blind artist had been cured by Mesmer of blindness.

When Mesmer is recognized, the concert is disrupted by cat calls, and ridicule is heaped on Mesmer.

To make things worse, on his return to the Hôtel de Coigny, Mesmer finds that Count de Gebelin has had a relapse and died.

The physicians now announce that Mesmer's cures are certain killers.

The King reads to policeman Lenoir a petition he has received from his personal physician Joseph de Lassone, in which Deslon asks that a Royal Commission be established to investigate the claims made for animal magnetism.

"Just what we want," says Lenoir. "Your Majesty can name a commission of eminent men who will squash the subject once and for all."

The King nods. "And we can make that old freak Franklin head of the commission so he can take the blame! He's old and doddery and only thinks of women. We'll have the report written by some reliable member of the Academy of Science such as Bailly and he'll get Franklin to sign it."

Lenoir: "And we'll let them investigate Deslon, which is easy, and thus get rid of Mesmer without running any risks. When Deslon is disposed of we can attack Mesmer on the grounds of his corrupting moves and of taking money; a *lettre de cachet* will do the rest."

Baron de Breteuil, an official of the Royal Household, receives the order to name a commission of members of the

Academy of Science and of the Royal Society of Medicine to investigate animal magnetism.

Antoine-Laurent Lavoisier receives his nomination to the commission in his chemist's laboratory surrounded by retorts and bunsen burners. He is intent upon explaining to Franklin his discovery that air is not an element but is made up of hydrogen and oxygen.

In a greenhouse in the most beautiful botanical gardens, the Jardin des Plantes, Antoine-Laurent Jussieu, thirty-six, is working with a plant when a messenger picks his way through the collection of stunning and exotic plants to hand him his nomination to the commission.

A severed head rolls as the blade of a guillotine decapitates a body. Dr. Joseph-Ignace Guillotin turns from the model of his invention to receive his nomination to the commission. "This is the most humane instrument of execution!" Guillotin explains.

At the Royal Society of Medicine, a group of doctors are standing around a naked corpse searching with their scalpels for what makes it tick when each receives his nomination to the commission.

In the salon of his house, Deslon is preparing a baquet as he speaks with police chief Lenoir.

"Could a man not take advantage of a woman in the crisis room?" asks Lenoir.

"Yes," says Deslon.

"So you and Mesmer might not take advantage, but an unscrupulous person could magnetize a girl and have his will with her?"

Deslon nods.

"Could you teach others to magnetize?" asks Lenoir. "Could you teach me, for instance?"

To Mesmer it is clear from the presence of Lavoisier and Majault that the commission is stacked, and when he hears that the commission is to investigate his discovery through Deslon, he immediately writes to Franklin complaining that he cannot comprehend how animal magnetism can be adequately examined except through him.

Lafayette supports Mesmer saying to Franklin that the

commission should declare Mesmer the "fountainhead to which they must apply. To come to the truth the commission must go to Mesmer just as others do and be led by him into the secrets of his system."

In his residence Deslon is ready with his baquet, assisted by several young men in powdered wigs and lilac jackets in imitation of Mesmer's clinic.

When the commissioners arrive they inform Deslon that if their vote is favorable the government will publish a letter declaring that Mesmer has made a useful discovery. The King will then grant him the necessary property and money with which to spread his discovery to the doctors and people of France.

But it is clear from their laughter and their jokes that they are negatively disposed towards the outcome. They say they feel nothing from Deslon's baquet, or from his magnetic passes. One commissioner complains of a slight migraine.

As Franklin is too old and sick to travel to Paris, the commissioners repair to his house in Passy.

Franklin is in his bathroom in the midst of a chess game with Madame Brillon who reclines in the bath. It is early morning and they have been playing all through the night. Franklin is wearing his newly invented bifocals which enable him correctly to play the pieces and yet clearly admire his opponent.

As an excuse he says: "When one's ears are not well accustomed to the sounds of a language, a sight of the movement of the features of him or her that speaks, helps to explain. So I understand French better by the help of my spectacles."

In Franklin's salon Deslon sets up a portable baquet while Madame Brillon's daughter plays Mozart on Franklin's glass harmonica, making witticisms about the procedure. Some members of the local gentry arrive and join the proceedings.

Franklin and Lenoir the policeman go about the baquet with an electrometer and nonmagnetized needles to see that the baquet hasn't been surreptitiously electrified or magnetized.

The gentry are asked to hold hands around it and have the rod administered to them. But when the commissioners try to examine them and ascertain their maladies, they all feign embarrassment considering the questions quite improper.

Franklin attempts to imitate Deslon by placing his hand on the ladies' crotches, but instead of magnetized crises he only elicits laughter. Deslon complains that the experiment cannot work with subjects who won't answer or who are not actually ill, but he assures the commission he will convince them of the power of magnetism by means of another experiment.

In Franklin's garden is a large apricot tree which Deslon magnetizes with Mesmeric passes of his hands. According to Deslon the tree will now affect with its magnetism any sick person brought to it.

For his experiment he blindfolds a twelve-year-old boy and leads him from tree to tree in the garden. At the first unmagnetized tree the boy begins to cough and sweat profusely. At the second, he feels a pain in his head. At the third he says his headache gets worse as he approaches the tree. At the fourth he has convulsions and faints. None of the trees was the magnetized apricot.

Deslon excuses himself by saying the experiment only works with really ill people. They should get some proper patients.

Several poor patients of the lower class, suffering from a variety of diseases, are offered money to allow themselves to be diagnosed and magnetized. One by one they file in as the commissioners examine them.

The widow Saint-Amand is asthmatic. A woman called Anseaume has a swelling in her thigh. Claude Lenand is six years old, scrofulous and tubercular. Geneviève Leroux, nine, has St. Vitus's dance. All maintain they feel nothing of the stream of Deslon's magnetism.

François Grenet, who has a tumor in his blind eye, says he feels a little pain in his left eyeball as Deslon moves his finger back and forth in front of it. A woman called Charpentier complains of having been kicked by a cow. She feels a tingling sensation when Deslon presses her abdomen. One patient says he can see fluid streaming from the end of Deslon's fingers which makes him feel alternately hot and cold.

The commission withdraws to deliberate and finds that animal magnetism cannot be perceived by any of the senses, that it has no effect on either themselves or the patients. Its use is liable to produce a deplorable effect on the imagination, an imagination which then produces the convulsions. They believe the spectacle of crises is dangerous to observers because it inclines them to imitation. To sum up, Mesmer's cures are most probably attributable to abstinence from the remedies previously taken by the patients.

Bailly reads the commission's report to Franklin for his signature. Franklin agrees with the unanimous opinion of all the commissioners that there is no such thing as Mesmer's animal magnetism. "As there is no Universal Fluid, there can be no cures by it. A thing which does not exist can have no utility."

Only Jussieu holds a differing opinion. He finds the commissioner's findings insufficient to account for the facts observed. In his opinion the principle of vitality appears to be intensified by the human will. "The commission," says Jussieu, "has neglected the most important evidence of the Fluid's power: the hundreds of cures it has performed. If Mesmer's cures are due to imagination, then why not use imagination in the treatment of patients. It is the duty of the physician to cure disease. If imagination can be proved to be effective, why not investigate how an agency that is beneficial can best be directed. The commission may have discovered that a thing which does not exist may yet possess utility."

Jussieu recommends suspending judgment until conclusive evidence be accumulated, adding: "Nothing can be more certain than the lethal character of conventional medicine."

The report, signed August 11, 1784, is presented to the King, along with a secret report on the moral dangers involved in magnetism, intended for the King's eyes only.

Bailly tells the King that most of the women who come

to Mesmer are not really ill; they come out of idleness and to be amused.

"The magnetizer," Bailly explains to the King, "touches their hypochondriac region and sometimes the ovaries and the most sensitive parts of a female's body. After thus applying his left hand, the experimenter passes his right hand behind the woman's body and they bend towards each other and encourage this two-fold contact. Their breath is intermingled, physical impressions are mutually felt and the reciprocal attraction of the sexes is greatly excited. No wonder the senses are influenced."

As a result of the commission's report the Faculty of Medicine formally outlaws the employment of magnetism in medical practice. Any physician practicing animal magnetism will be dropped from its rolls.

Deslon, at the end of his rope, smarting from ridicule, gives up and dies though only thirty-five.

Mesmer points out that the same medical profession refused to accept proof of the circulation of the blood, treated quinine as rubbish and refused inoculation. "I venture to flatter myself that the discovery I have made lies beyond our present knowledge of physical, just as the microscope and the telescope lay beyond it."

The government prints and distributes 12,000 copies of the commissioner's report followed by long attacks on Mesmerism by Thouret of the Royal Society of Medicine.

Lenoir's police suppress works in favor of Mesmerism.

Expecting an edict to outlaw him, Mesmer prepares to avoid a *lettre de cachet* by flight to England. But Bergasse holds firm: he denounces the commission's report "for violating the basic rules of justice and morality" as well as "the first principles of natural law."

Jean-Jacques Duval d'Epremesnil, a leader of resistance to the government, and a strong supporter of Mesmer, suggests to Mesmer that he petition the Third Estate to stand up against this royally commissioned lawlessness by placing Mesmerism under the protection of Parliament.

Bergasse requests Parliament to sponsor an honest investigation of Mesmerism and calls for "the destruction of that fatal science, the oldest superstition in the universe, that tyrannical medicine, which, first seizing man in his cradle, weighs on him like a religious prejudice."

Mesmer writes a letter to the Procurer-General describing his struggle against official persecution.

The anti-Mesmerists under the influence of the Faculty of Medicine and the Academy of Science launch a violent campaign to ridicule Mesmer.

During a carnival floats are built at great expense showing Mesmer with a magic wand mesmerizing women into convulsive crises under a huge banner "Harmonica."

A doctor riding backwards on an ass magnetizes its rear, followed by all kinds of patients with masks showing a variety of horrible diseases also simulating convulsive crises.

A flood of anti-Mesmer pamphlets is dispersed among the crowd. Containing salacious cartoons about what goes on in the *salle de crises*, asking why did only men mesmerize women and only on the hypochondria?

Dozens of songs lampooning animal magnetism make the rounds. Two burlesques entitled *Modern Doctors* and the *Baquet of Health* put Mesmerism on the stage for the public to laugh at.

Deslon and Mesmer are portrayed as a couple of rascals injecting incredulous patients with animal magnetism and laughing behind their backs while they count up piles of money.

Outraged by the performance of *Modern Doctors* Duval d'Epremesnil tosses into the audience copies of a manifesto comparing Mesmer to Socrates ridiculed by Aristophanes: "If my personal position as a magistrate does not permit me to extend to Mesmer the aid of the law, at least I owe him in the name of humanity a public testimonial of my admiration and gratitude for his great discovery."

By this time half the parliamentarians had been won over to Mesmerism. Parliament accepts Mesmer's petition, and appoints its own investigating commission.

Mesmer and Mesmerism are no longer subject to government persecution.

Mesmer's success in challenging the commission inspires

others to attack the order of society. "Science," they declare, "must become free from despotism against the human spirit."

Jacques-Pierre Brissot, the thirteenth child of a provincial tavern keeper, a devotee of Marat, a strong supporter of Rousseau, and a journalist with a wide knowledge of Europe and America, comes out from two months in the Bastille for pamphleteering against the government. Joining Mesmer, he declares that "Mesmerism offers a new scientific explanation of the invisible forces of nature."

He accuses doctors of keeping people sick in order to maintain them in a state of exploitation. "Richelieu and his despotic successors," says Brissot, "founded academies and stuffed them with men of great wealth, breeding an ignorance in order to use them to stifle new truths of science and philosophy."

Brissot's friend Antoine Servan attacks the Faculty of Medicine. "You maintain ceaselessly the most complete despotism of which man is capable. You have become absolute sovereigns over the sick common people. You are the first supporters of despotism."

Bergasse adds: "The corps of doctors is a political body whose destiny is linked with that of the state. Thus, in the social order, we must have diseases, drugs and laws, and the distribution of drugs and diseases influence the habits of the nation perhaps as much as do the guardians of the law. Doctors use every means of enervating the human race, of reducing it to the point of having only enough strength to bear docily the yoke of social institutions."

At the same time, Bergasse accuses the more civilized classes of living in such an advanced state of depravity that their children cannot regain health and virtue as the peasants did, merely by being exposed to nature.

Bergasse claims that luxury, gluttony, debauchery and the whole gamut of sensations offered by the modern French way of life produced disharmony in men and corrupted their morals. He accuses political institutions of buttressing this way of life.

"We owe almost all the physical ailments that consume us to our institutions." And he vows that in a new regenerated

Mesmerized France these protected institutions will collapse, while better bodies will then lead to better politics.

First to go, says Bergasse, must be the doctors. This would set natural laws at work to root out social abuses. "It is the despotism of doctors," says Bergasse, "and of their academic allies, that represent the last attempt of the old order to preserve itself against the forces of the true science of nature and society." The fight against the "despotism of the academies" has become a fight against "political despotism."

Bergasse now calls for revolution, but says it will be doomed if done in the open. "We must wrap ourselves in mystery. We must write under the pretext of experiments in physics but actually to overcome despotism. We must call on the people to write to the King in order to make all citizens noble and all nobles citizens."

Bergasse is joined by Adrien Duport, Jean-Louis Carra, the Rolands, Brissot and Lafayette. Together they form the Gallo-American Society, and *Les Amis des Noirs*, a French society to promote friendship with the blacks.

Thomas Jefferson, who replaced Franklin as Minister to France, hailed the symbol of the victory in the American Revolution of Rousseau's principles of popular sovereignty.

Bergasse wants a king and two chambers, a constitutional monarchy, under the rule of Parliament. He began to draft a plan which he said must be rigorously executed.

In August 1788, at the Café of the Palais Royal, Bergasse directs letters to the Ministers who are attempting to crush Parliament, and to prevent the calling of the Estates Général. In an open letter to the King, he demands the dismissal of the Brienne ministry—then flees the country. D'Epremesh insists on a de-Bourbonized France.

The King and the Queen are now in trouble over the famous diamond necklace, and over Marie Antoinette's extravagent spending. As Madame de la Motte leaves Cardinal Rohan's chambers assuring him that all is well, that Marie Antoinette will meet him in disguise in the gardens of Versailles, that she longs for the diamond necklace, Cagliostro warns Rohan not to become involved, that Marie Antoinette does not want the necklace, that she has twice turned it down when it was offered her, once by Louis XV who wanted to seduce her with it, and once again when Louis XV simply wanted to make her happy with it though he could not afford it. Cagliostro warns the Cardinal that the de la Motte woman is a phony who will get him into trouble. But the Cardinal is obdurate.

The result is disaster for all concerned. Rohan is arrested and sent to the Bastille, and Cagliostro as his friend must follow him. When the courts vindicate Rohan and Cagliostro, convicting Madame de la Motte to be stripped and publicly whipped and branded, the plot backfires on Louis XVI: the people are aroused against *l'autrichienne* Marie Antoinette whom they now believe to be culpable. Their mood is nasty.

With the fall of the Brienne ministry Bergasse returns a hero. He is elected to the Estates Général along with Bailly. They are with the deputies who take the oath in the tennis court to give France a constitution.

In the Constitutional Committee of the National Assembly, Bergasse and Bailly find themselves together trying to prepare a constitution for revolutionary France. But they argue because Bergasse insists on the necessity for going back to the "rule of nature." Bergasse wants to use Mesmerism as the basis for the new society he wishes to build, a "natural" society whose guiding rule is harmony. He says that in order to live according to nature "we must make a clean sweep of the unnatural institutions of France, including or especially the absolute monarchy."

Mesmer stands apart from this political offshoot of his theories. He will not repudiate Bergasse's argument that Mesmerism can propagate mental health which will bring better institutions, run by saner people especially when governed by saner institutions. But he refused to take part in the mêlée. He has run his clinic for all classes. Let the government be run by all classes. He will observe the results.

July 14 the people rise in arms and seize the Bastille, handing the keys to Brissot. The people then call for Lafayette to command the revolutionary militia of Paris and for Bailly (who is having lunch with the Duc d'Orléans and his mistress) to be mayor.

The King, though determined to retain his absolute powers, is forced to comply and grant certain freedoms to the country.

Lafayette and Bailly are now responsible for bringing the King from Versailles to Paris. In the course of the day the King consumes three hundred pounds of peaches. Arriving at the city, a virtual prisoner, Louis XVI remarks to Bailly: "It is sad that having given liberty to the nation, I shall now be deprived of it myself."

But the King still gets an ovation when Bailly gets him to put on the tricolor cockade.

In the Tuileries Palace while the King consumes his usual repasts, the flour for the bread which he has brought from Versailles to feed the people of Paris is exhausted, giving rise to Marie Antoinette's "Let them eat cake!" The starving populace starts to hang bakers.

To put a stop to this anarchy, Bailly hangs out a red flag and proclaims martial law, which only incenses the people.

As Lafayette and Bailly ride out to the Champs de Mars on horseback, the people start to throw stones at them. Bailly orders Lafayette's men to fire on the people, and a dozen civilians are killed.

The terror is at hand. The Royal Family is in the Temple under arrest. In his cramped quarters the King continues to indulge in his normal repasts of four entrées, two roasts, four puddings, three kinds of stewed fruits, a bottle of Bordeaux, and a bottle of Madeira.

Madame de Lambelle of her own free will goes with the Royal Family to act as a messenger and courier to the outside world. As Madame de Polignac puts it: "The good Lamballe seems only to wait for danger to show her worth."

Lambelle is seized and judged. Ruffians kill her, rape her dead body and cut out her genitals. With her pubic hair one of the ruffians makes a moustache and then sets off towards the Queen's apartment with Lamballe's head on a pike, its lovely long golden hair streaming in the wind. At the Temple the crowd shouts for the Queen who is playing tric-trac with the King. Approaching the window, the King is warned not to look. They wish to show him the head of Lamballe. At which the Queen faints.

Disaster avalanches. The King, caught negotiating with the enemies of France, is condemned to death, and his severed head is displayed to the crowd. The Committee of Public Safety is formed.

For the French National Convention, Mesmer composes a manuscript in which he advances notions worthy of the severest Jacobin: sovereignty belongs solely to the people; law is the expression of the general will; taxation shall be used to create the greatest possible equality.

Mingling with the crowds, Mesmer compares their tidal movements to the tide of magnetism, to which he is himself attracted. From the crowd he witnesses, one by one, the execution of the protagonists of his dreams.

Heads begin to fall at the rate of two or three dozen a day. Lavoisier is tried. The judge says: "The republic has no need for men of science." His head rolls.

Mesmer's supporters follow each other to the scaffold.

Brissot's head falls. So does d'Epremesnil's.

Bailly, long-faced and long-nosed, is arrested and called as a witness to the trial of the Queen. The Queen is executed.

To revenge themselves for Bailly's raising the red flag of martial law and for shooting into the crowd at the Champs de Mars, he is dragged back to the spot where a special guillotine is raised for him.

Mesmer is among the onlookers. As Bailly stands shivering in the cold, one of the crowd shouts to him: "So you tremble, Bailly!" To which Bailly replies: "It is cold, my friend."

When Bailly's head rolls, Mesmer doffs his hat in respect. Someone sees the gesture and incites the crowd to anger. Mesmer only narrowly escapes. In disguise, hiding from his pursuers, he makes his way to the Swiss border, leaving behind his property, his money, all of his manuscripts.

Bergasse and Guillotin are about to be guillotined, but Robespierre is overthrown, on the Ninth of Thermidor, and is executed in their stead.

In Vienna, Mesmer finds his wife has died. Mozart and Gluck are dead. The music he hears is the Eroica of Beethoven whose powerful revolutionary strains dominate the musical scene of Vienna.

Part of Mesmer's house is rented to the Princess Gonzaga. As her landlord, Mesmer pays her a courtesy visit. The conversation turns to the French Revolution. The princess abominates regicides. Mesmer suggests that the French had long been overexploited, trying to convince her of the difference between the excesses of the Sans Culottes and the justified struggle for freedom of the Girondins. The princess becomes strident and orders Mesmer from her quarters.

In Vienna there are circles who sympathize with the Jacobins and want to spread the revolution. Denounced as a dangerous radical and as sympathizer with the Terror in France which has guillotined the daughter of Maria Theresa, Mesmer is arrested and jailed.

As the weather turns from fall to winter, Mesmer is in prison being investigated, listening to second-hand reports of Napoleon's victories.

When nothing sufficiently incriminating is found against Mesmer he is ordered out of the country as an undesirable partisan of the French Revolution.

Back at Meersburg on Lake Constance near where he was born Mesmer can once more commune with nature in his familiar woods and streams, with their beautiful mountain backdrop. At home he devotes himself to his harmonica and to occult interests, curing those who come to him in need, such as the parish priest, Father Schreiber, and rewriting the manuscripts he lost in Paris. He is cheerful and talkative, enjoying wine and conversation, ready to be persuaded to read from his latest manuscript, or to perform a solo on his glass harmonica. He now believes that animal magnetism may also be an emanation from ourselves, guided by the will.

In Prussia, at the Academy of Berlin, serious professors are discussing the subject. When a subtle point eludes them, one of the professors, Dr. Karl Christian Wolfart, suggests they address themselves to Mesmer. The others are astounded. "Is he still alive?"

On a trip across Lake Constance to the island of Mainau where a bird fancier has settled a flock of canaries, Mesmer, now seventy-eight, is surrounded by the birds as if he were Saint Francis. One canary follows him back to the boat and all the way home, perched on his hand.

With his finger Mesmer can stroke his new companion into a deep trance or wake it up easily. Every morning the bird wakes Mesmer with a song, and a lump of sugar in his breakfast coffee.

A deputation led by Dr. Wolfart arrives from Berlin with a commission from King Frederick Wilhelm III to offer Mesmer a position in Berlin and a subsidy for his research which is now highly appreciated.

Mesmer is grateful, but declines. He says he is too old and will soon die. Instead he hands his latest manuscript, the summation of his life's work, to Wolfart who promises to have it published in Berlin under the title of *Magnetismos.*

Wolfart returns to Berlin where he is named Professor of Mesmerism in the Academy of Berlin, with a special hospital of 300 beds for the practice of Mesmer's principles.

Alone in the sunset, Mesmer calls for a young seminarist devotee of Father Schreiber to whom he bequeaths his glass harmonica on condition he plays for him as the sun goes down.

Upstairs, stretched out on his bed, Mesmer watches the last of the sun's rays reflected from the lake onto the ceiling. Slowly the life goes out of his eyes. His pet canary, fluttering round the bedstead, gently lowers the master's eyelids with its beak. With an added trill to the fading melody of the harmonica, the canary flies out the window towards a band of red and purple clouds, powerfully magnetic in their voluptuous embrace, from which a shaft of lightning illumines the great vault of sky, followed by a peel of thunder rumbling into silence.

Nostradamus

In 1939 occupied Europe was not only enduring the on-slaught of Hitler's armies but a barrage of prophecies flutter-ing down from German planes. They announced to the conquered people that submission was inevitable. It had al-ready been prophesied in 1568 by Nostradamus. The British took this psychological warfare seriously enough to spend a considerable sum on counter propaganda.

Were these prophecies made so long ago actually au-thentic? In one of Nostradamus's most amazing predictions he even calls Hitler by name (if we will accept the anagrama-tic "Hister" for the Führer.* In the 16th century the "s" re-

---

*Nostradamus and the Nazis, by Ellie Howe.

sembled an "f," making the anagram even closer). If others were in doubt, Hitler recognized himself in this and other quatrains:

> Wild beasts for hunger shall swim over the rivers,
> The greater part of the battlefield shall be against
>   Hister.
> He will drag the leader in a cage of iron,
> When the child of Germany observes no law.
>   Centuries II, quatrain 24.

Certainly the Nazis crossed many rivers to gain their victories in the first part of World War II. Could the cage have meant a tank? Or imprisonment of the mind? Hitler had his own astrologer, a man named Krafft, to keep him abreast of astrological developments. Perhaps he sought to reinterpret the dire end Nostradamus predicted for him.

The first question one asks oneself is: can there be any credibility in prophecy? Are the eternal mysteries—where do we come from?—where do we go?—what will the future bring?—beyond the penetration of any man who ever lived or ever will? Whatever the answer, the question lives on from age to age, century to century. And always some self-proclaimed mystic has sought to penetrate the veil, peer into the darkness and report the generally gloomy outlook that lies ahead. Indeed, it would seem that any news worth reporting must always be bad. Prophecy was the eternal warning that if ways were not mended, deities properly served, the future would become the grave of the world.

Such moral finger-shaking, such gloom-and-doom storm warnings always found ready audiences and attentive scribes. The Bible is full of them, from Isaiah to Revelation. The heights of Delphi housed an oracle always good for a quick forecast. Rome, Egypt, Babylon had their soothsayers. No place, people, or age has not been similarly served. And if the methods of prophecy differed, the purposes seem generally the same.

Seers, prophets, visionaries. Men—and women—recording lunar tides in a cup of tea, foretelling man's destiny

with the turn of a Tarot card, unveiling the future by inter-
preting the position of the stars, scrutinizing the hazy images
in a crystal ball or a bowl of vibrating water, deciphering
messages from a Ouija board, conjuring a spectral voice or
raising a spirit in the confines of a magic circle drawn in the
prescribed manner. Such persons claim to offer a glimpse into
the galaxy of infinity, a step beyond man's everyday knowledge, a key to all our tomorrows.

Of these "mystics" much is told and little is known.
Myths accumulate like heat waves blending into mirage,
blurring the edges of truth, making proven fact seem fanciful
and the eternal mysteries logical. Often their writings draw
the flies of contention, their life patterns leave gaps of lost
years. Seers, prophets, visionaries? Or frauds, deceivers, and
con artists? Only scientific proof can convince the skeptical—and no proof has ever been necessary for the true believer.

But perhaps of them all none has recorded with more
specific and factual accuracy the events that were to come.
Nostradamus's books, however deliberately laden with
enigma, name names, dates and places centuries ahead. Obviously, much that we know of him has been embellished by
legend and shaped by speculation and interpretation. Yet
there are recorded facts of his life and from these we may
form a composite portrait, far from complete yet finally re-
vealing enough to stand as an image of one who may have
been the most fascinating and mysterious seer of all.

In foreseeing the future of his own time—and beyond to
the end of time (if future predictions prove correct), he set
down his forecasts in the form of quatrains and he called his
work *The Centuries*, because each book contained 100 prophecies in verse form. They were not written in order. He never
completed the Seventh Century, but went on to produce 12 in
all. Some have been lost. It is probable that the numbering of
the quatrains follows a secret code and plan. Predictions were
set down in a deliberately obscure mixture of languages. With
the French of his period, he mixed Provençal patois, Italian,
Greek, Latin, and interspersed anagrams to further confuse
any hostile reader. But why, one wonders, if he had a mes-

sage to deliver about the fate of the world, was it so necessary to make that message so difficult to decipher? To understand, we must know a bit more about the man and the time in which he lived.

The Middle Ages were a time of paradoxes. Small and large kingdoms battled for supremacy in the kindergartens of Empires. Intrigue was a way of life. Machiavelli was the voice of the true sentiment of princes. Nobles confined their scholastic interests to the arts of war and the chase, leaving the Church to guard the feeble flame of learning. In the peace of monastic cells, monks could laboriously transcribe Plato, Seneca, St. Augustine or Socrates, but few men outside the church or universities could read. Fewer still could write. Local histories, folk medicine, skills and crafts, were stored in the memory banks of village elders and handed down by word of mouth.

Michel de Nostradam was born at midnight, December 23, 1503, according to the Gregorian calendar. (In *The Prophecies of Nostradamus* by Erika Cheetham* the time is given as noon, December 14, according to the Julian calendar.) He was born into an age of discovery. Magellan and Columbus offered vistas of other continents, new worlds to explore—and alas, to conquer. New vistas of religious freedom—and alas, contention—were emerging in the teachings of Martin Luther and John Calvin—both comtemporaries in Germany and Switzerland. In Nostradamus's France their followers were called Free Thinkers and Huguenots. But protest against the established Church and the Pope was bringing violent counterreaction. Torquemada, the First Inquisitor of Spain, launched the Church upon a trail of bloody vengeance that led directly to France.

Into this inflammable political and religious landscape a would-be visionary who could foretell when his king would die, and by whose hand, walked the tightrope of his own utterances across a veritable Grand Canyon of the Holy In-

---

*Published by Neville Spearman.

quisition. One slip of the tongue could have plunged Nostradamus into an *auto-da-fé,* that human bonfire with the victim as *plat du jour.* But Michel de Nostradam's position was far more precarious than any mere Huguenot. He was a "Converso"—a converted Jew. In 1480 when Ferdinand and Isabella drove Spain's Jewry into extremely low profile, many of them fled into Provence.

The attraction across the border was Good King René of Anjou, who had sworn himself an advocate of religious freedom. This enlightened ruler even appointed a Jew, Jean de St. Rémy, as Court Physician-Astrologer (the two sciences being of equal importance). Not to be outdone, King René's son imported his own Jewish physician, Pierre de Nostra Donna. These two scholars found much in common besides their antecedents. In the course of time St. Rémy had a daughter and Nostra Donna a son. Inevitably a marriage was arranged.

By 1488, the climate of religious tolerance was clouding over. Charles VIII ordered all Jews in Provence to convert to Catholicism, or suffer confiscation of their property. A few, including the two physicians, felt sufficiently protected by position to keep their religion. But in 1501 when Louis XII added the death penalty for the obstinate, the two Court Physicians were among the first to the baptismal font. Since the French have a natural aversion to all foreigners, the son gallicized his name to Nostradam. Two years later when his own son Michel was born, the child went to his own baptism uncircumcised, a fact which must secretly have chilled the hearts of his grandfathers. The child was judiciously named for the Archangel Michael, acceptable to both religions.

A man may change his religion but the habits of the scholar are less easily broken. Michel's maternal grandfather undertook the lad's education to prepare him for the University of Montpellier. Michel was taught Hebrew, Latin, Greek, mathematics, and the art of the apothecary—for which he showed unusual talent. He developed a love of astronomy, hardly distinct from astrology in his day. He pursued it with the same dedication as a present day atomic scientist delving into higher physics. Michel was also tutored by Grandfather

Nostra Donna. One of these venerables introduced him into the mysteries of the Schalscheleth hakabbalah—the Chain of Tradition of the Cabala, a mystical science rooted in the earliest Jewish writings. James Laver in his scholarly book* points out that this knowledge stretches back to first-century Alexandria, but in fact its origins are so lost that the truth will probably never be known. Most religious authorities state that God gave the wisdom to Abraham, but nobody knows when Abraham lived, and a case has even been made for the knowledge having reached man from other worlds.

Rabbi Moses C. Luzzatto* says the Cabala offers conclusive proof via cause and effect—that there is a motivating cause behind everything and that the effect must inevitably follow. "True cause must be able to withstand tomorrow's events. For who can be so bold as to make predictions when one has not tasted or experienced the events of the future?" The Cabala teaches that the creator exhibits his light to his seers through the images of prophecy. The Cabala is in effect the Tree of Life, and the Tarot card deck is an integral part of the pattern of the knowledge. The esoteric philosophy combines the occult teachings of East and West in the ancient Tree of Life. It is the basis of all religions. Because the Cabala is written in symbols as well as Hebrew, it has been universally understood, transcending the barrier of language. Yet the meaning of its formalized rituals is obscured by time. Like "the great work," alchemy, it combines scientific, philosophical, and religious concepts. Its teachings incorporate many of the mysteries of all occult knowledge. It offers a technique by which the human mind can be put into contact with the elemental universal forces, transcending time and space, past and future. This knowledge was possessed by Nostradamus.

It must be remembered that he lived in an age steeped in superstition, fear and legend. Doctors of his day warded off the Black Death by magical means. Next to their skins they wore rough cotton shirts soaked in seven magical liquids and

---

*Nostradamus, the Future Foretold, published by Collins, 1942.
*General Principles of the Kabbalah, published by S. Weiser, N.Y.

stained with seven symbolic colors. Over this went a heavy leather jerkin to keep out foul air. It was believed that the plague was caused by miasmic conditions. A vinegar-soaked sponge was tied over the physician's nose, a pair of spectacles shielded his eyes, and a clove of garlic was tucked under his tongue. Such standard gear bred a healthy respect for the medical profession, and no doubt promoted an aromatic bed-side manner. Like other citizens, the doctor covered himself with amulets and charms. A bone from the head of a toad was considered beneficial. A pregnant patient was advised to wear as many precious stones as she could afford on neck and hand, and to touch the left breast with them as often as pos-sible. As apothecary and medical student, Nostradamus ob-served quacks doing a roaring trade in elixirs compounded from unicorn horn (more obtainable then than now). They were said to revive the heart and corporal spirits and to pre-serve against the pestilence. Other liquid remedies included red wine mulled with a heated new steel blade. If it failed to ward off the plague, at least the patient felt less pain. Balsa-mum dissolved with pearls, gold and ground philosopher's stone (as difficult to obtain as unicorn horn) was available to the affluent. Ground red coral was cheaper, and no doubt tasted no worse. Grave diggers had a more earthy remedy. In a glazed pot they boiled and evaporated their own urine blended with cuckoldwart, wormwood, and ironwart. A pinch of the above on bread dipped in sweet oil was taken in the morning on an empty stomach with a glass of herb wine. The Old Corpse Washer of Leipzig, a man of simpler tastes, merely knocked back a draft of his urine upon waking—in the name of the Father, Son, and Holy Ghost.

During the years that Nostradamus worked towards his doctorate at the university, he travelled extensively through the worst of the plague epidemics. He absorbed all accumu-lated knowledge practiced by the physicians of the day. Though he did not always follow his prescriptions, which may have accounted for his survival and successful cures, he read the advice of Paracelsus—to wear the venomous "tongues" of snakes. Pope Hadrian VI had worn an amulet containing ar-senic. Lesser folk contented themselves with a hazel nut filled with live mercury, arsenic, or tragacanth made into a paste and wound with silk thread, worn next to the heart. Paracelsus's magic therapeutics were derived from such sources as the Cabala. They were based on the concept that a common original force, "Magnale Magnum" or "Universal Soul," connected all living beings to each other. The philosophy that every body possesses an individual spirit which influences those related to it, and can affect the state of their health, is based on the mathematical equation of the Tree of Life—which brings us right back to the Cabala.

Nostradamus had studied the teachings of Gentile of Foligno; witchcraft joined with herbalism. Gentile recommended drinking powdered emerald, which was so potent, said he, that if a toad took it his eyes would crack. One wonders what effect it had on people. He also advised wearing an amethyst etched with the figure of a man girded with a serpent. The head is held in his right hand and the tail in his left, forming the sign of the Ouroboros—alchemical symbol of the eternal cyclic nature of the universe—from the One to the One.

Nostradamus's astrologer-teachers quoted him the advice of Hermes Trismegistus, the Greek deity: "When the Sun is in the sign of the Lion and the Moon does not turn towards Saturn don a belt of lionskin with a buckle of pure gold in the shape of a lion." But such plague protections were not as easily available as a stick of charcoal. In almost every village of Southern France Nostradamus saw the word "Abracadabra" scratched in a triangle on a wall. A plea to the Gnostic god, Abraxas.

Medical practice still followed the advice of the University of Paris first set down in 1348: "The constellations with the aid of nature strive to protect and heal the human race." They suggested avoiding night air, that bathing was injurious, and that men should preserve their chastity if they valued their lives especially those living by the seaside.*

---

*The Black Death: 1347, by George Deaux, published by Hamish Hamilton.

In Nostradamus's day most doctors still blamed the stars. They were certain that Sirius, the Dog Star, caused the pestilential forces in the atmosphere to increase. And if astrological conditions were responsible, the plague could only be fought by astrological means.

Nostradamus's preventative measures seem strangely modern. It is known that he used a secret disinfectant on his person. Perhaps he had created a kind of insect repellent, for the plague-bearing lice and fleas who acted as flying delegates between rat and human seem to have left him alone. He used remedies based on the principle of fumigation—effective even today in those parts of the world where the plague still exists. By 1525 his reputation as a fearless healer was widely known. Though no one was aware that the plague was being imported on rat-infested trading vessels to ports like Marseilles, Nostradamus seems to have stumbled on a connection. He ordered rat-infested areas to be burned, and flea-ridden bedding destroyed.

His travels carried him through most of Southern France, and while treating the poor with remarkable success, he did not neglect the Bishop of Carcassone. This worthy was treated with a miraculous pomade containing lapis lazuli, coral and leaf gold which Nostradamus called "an elixir of life." If he was a man of the future, he was also a man of the present. Among its numerous attributes was the guarantee "to preserve from headache and constipation and augment the sperm in such abundance that a man can do whatever he wishes without damaging his health." One wonders to what use the Bishop put this stimulating preparation.

Nostradamus drifted on to Toulouse and Narbonne, which had a large "Converso" community, a Talmudic school, and a plethora of alchemists. In this congenial habitat he increased his store of knowledge, developing a side line in beauty preparations and preserves, especially quince jelly. It later ingratiated him with Queen Catherine de Medici.

In 1529 he finally sat for his examinations. The Faculty of Montpellier were less than elated with his unorthodoxy, but his remedies succeeded in curing the sick and so he was

admitted to the doctorate. Now he could settle down to a lu-
crative practice, but his insatiable curiosity drove him once
more to wandering. In the town of Agen he met and married
a beautiful young heiress. Little is known of this lady, except
that she bore him two children. Then in 1534 an ironic stroke
of fate brought the plague to his wife and children, sparing
only him. His wife's father blamed the physician; sued him
for return of dowry, and to compound these troubles Nostradamus fell foul of the Inquisition. Seeing a craftsman at work
on a bronze Virgin for the local church, the physician reminded him of God's Commandment against the making of
graven images. This rash remark caused Nostradamus to be
sent for by the Inquisitor. Happily for the history of prophecy, the Dominican escort arrived too late.

Nostradamus had flown the coop, this time out of France
and into one of those periods of wandering that set most mystics apart from their fellow men. Little is known of the eight
years he spent in Italy and Sicily, but it was during this
sojourn that he became fully aware of his gift of second sight.
He met a swineherd monk near the village of Ancona and felt
suddenly compelled to fall to his knees before the youthful
Franciscan, hailing him as a future Pope. Felix Peretti was
amused, but remembered the prediction when he became
Cardinal Montalto and, in 1585, Pope Sixtus V.

Passing through Lorraine on his return to France, the
prophet was invited by the skeptical Seigneur de Florinville
to stay at his château. Stories were circulating about buried
treasure unearthed through Nostradamus's divining. One
may imagine the elegant nobleman, a clove-stuck orange po-
mander held to his nose, leading his guest through the pig-
gery to exhibit a pair of piglets—one black, the other white.

"Tonight," he informed the prophet, "we shall dine on
one of these. Unless of course—you have religious objec-
tions?"

Such inquisitorial traps would have hardly phased the
prophet. "Washed away by baptismal waters a generation
ago, sire."

"Then, perhaps, you will predict which piglet will grace
our board tonight?"

"The black one, sire. For sad to say, the white piglet will be devoured by a wolf."

The ludicrous suggestion amused de Florinville. "What would you stake on your prophecy, Nostradamus?"

"The divine powers that make me their instrument forbid me to wager money."

"And yet you wager your reputation with every prediction." De Florinville promptly ordered the white pig killed for dinner.

That night beneath the heavy tapestries, in the raucous atmosphere of gastronomic vulgarity, dwarf jesters jousted on dogback with long loaves of bread. A bagpiper led in the chief steward bearing the dressed suckling pig, apple in mouth. De Florinville tasted his victory.

"Superb white suckling pig, is it not, Nostradamus?"

"We are dining on the black piglet," the prophet assured him.

De Florinville's eyes fixed the steward. "Did you not kill the white piglet as I commanded?"

"That I did, sire," replied the nervous steward. "It was dressed and waiting for the ovens when a tame wolf cub belonging to your huntsman made off with it. So I was forced to butcher the black pig, or you'd have had no banquet tonight."

Such stories, true or false, were making a reputation for Nostradamus which was not long in reaching the ears of Catherine de Medici. On his first command appearance at Court, Nostradamus took the precaution of presenting the Queen with his finest cosmetics and quince jellies. For her part, Catherine tested the prophet, bringing him into the presence of three men identically dressed. Nostradamus had no difficulty recognizing his King, Henry II. But there were some in France who accused Nostradamus of employing magic for his prophecies and his miraculous cures. Again he found it expedient to stay in motion.

But in Salon he met a young widow, Anne Ponsart Gemelle, who anchored him. They were married in 1547 and bought a house in the Ferreiraux quarter which still remains. Relieved of financial considerations by this substantial marriage, and approaching his 50th year, he could now devote himself to writing. In 1552 he published his first book, *Traite des Fardemens*, a collection of remedies, cures, recipes. It even contained a recipe for a love philter. He took for his "sorcerer's apprentice" a student from Beaune, Jean Aymes de Chavigny. Most of what we know of the life of Nostradamus has come from three sources. Chavingy's *La Vie et le Testament de Michel Nostradamus*; a book by the prophet's son César, *Histoire et Chronique de Provence* published in 1614, and another by the prophet's brother, Jean de Nostradame. Recent historians have questioned the accuracy of these three sources, but since they agreed at the time they may be assumed to be reliable witnesses. Chavigny tells us Nostradamus had been working for years on the prophecies, which were finally published in 1555. The first edition contained three complete Centuries, but only 53 quatrains of the fourth. They brought him overnight fame throughout Western Europe.

The preface, dedicated to his son César, makes it clear that the prophecies were deliberately obscured. "Consider also the words of the true Savior, 'cast not your pearls before swine,'" he wrote, insuring that only those armed with the key of wisdom would clearly understand. It is possible that a real key existed and that he gave it to Catherine de Medici and Henry II. This theory was elaborated by P.V. Piobb,* who suggested that in the second edition of the Centuries, the dedication to Henry II contained Biblical references. Their chronological calculations offered "two series of numbers ... constituting a key which, by a series of additions permits us to link up the verses and the date and extract a meaning ..." This key applies up to 1792. It would be interesting in our computer age, if someone were to feed in the proper data and perhaps unlock the key to the prophecies!

Nostradamus was also protecting himself from the In-

Le Secret de Nostradamus, 1927.

quisitor, but he was prophesying for future generations. There can scarcely be doubt that he foresaw the French Revolution 200 years before it happened. Time has deciphered many of the mysteries. Names, places, and dates have become history. In this chapter we can touch only on a few. Perhaps it would be fair to start with Henry II and Catherine. The King's death was predicted in Centuries I, quatrain 35:

> Le Lion jeune le vieux surmontera,
> En champ bellique par singulier duelle
> Dans caige d'or les yeux lui crevera,
> Deux classes une, puis mourir, mort cruelle.

Of the four translations we have read, wording differs only slightly.

> The young lion shall overcome the old,
> In martial field by single combat,
> In a cage of gold he will pierce his eyes,
> Two wounds from one, then he dies a cruel death.

The facts were incredibly accurate. On June 28, 1559, four years after the publishing of the quatrain, Henry jousted in tournament with Montgomery, young Scottish Captain of his Guard. Proud of his athletic abilities, Henry had been on the go all day. Towards evening he demanded one last bout. Montgomery tried to avoid it, but the King insisted. In the third exchange, Montgomery's lance splintered. The haft pierced the grill of Henry's visor, which was formed like a golden cage. It entered the King's eye. Another splinter entered the King's throat. Henry lingered on for ten days; indeed a cruel death.

Most who had read the Centuries recalled the quatrain. The prophet was burned in effigy in Paris. Indeed it seemed probable that the Church would follow suit with an *auto-da-fe* for both Nostradamus and Montgomery. But the King had declared it an accident, and forbade vengeance against Montgomery. Not wishing to press his luck, the Scotsman fled to England. The prophet had also predicted Mongomery's fate:

> He who in fight on martial field shall
> Have carried off the prize from one greater than he,
> He shall be surprised by six men at night,
> Suddenly, naked, and without harness.
> Centuries III, quatrain 30.

In England Montgomery joined the Huguenots and led a Protestant invasion of Normandy. He had surrendered and so was technically "without arms—or harness." Catherine sent six men of the Royal Guard to seize him in the night. They entered his bedroom and dragged him naked from his bed—on May 27, 1574—as Nostradamus had predicted 19 years earlier.

After Henry's death, Catherine had sent for Nostradamus. To the Court's amazement she placed him under Royal Protection. Any man who could predict so accurately was more useful alive than dead. She built him a laboratory in her château at Chaumont-sur-Loire. Here she consulted him on the fate of her seven children who were destined to rule and die young. His predictions were completely accurate. He also foretold that on the death of her last son, Charles IX, the kingdom would fall to Henry of Navarre, her cousin. Catherine took the precaution of marrying her daughter Margot to this prince. The prophet foresaw the bloody massacre she engineered on the night of St. Bartholomew, and was brave enough to put it in writing.

Napoleon recognized himself in the prophecies, although he was not mentioned by name. Others were.

> The lost thing is discovered, hidden for many centuries,
> Pasteur as a demi-God will be honored,
> It is when the moon completes her great cycle,
> But by idle talk he shall be dishonored.
> Centuries I, quatrain 25.

This quatrain actually supplies a date for Pasteur. His Institute Pasteur was founded November 14, 1889. The "cycle of the moon" referred to ran from 1535 to 1889. The word *vent*, translated as rumors, idle talk, etc., no doubt refers to the opposition of the medical establishment of the day.

One quatrain would seem to us to apply to John Law and the Mississippi Bubble, a neglected episode of French history. John Law had invented paper money and in 1715 became Finance Minister of France. He sold shares in the Mississippi with the blessing of Philip, Duke of Orleans, Regent of France. Wild gambling with the stocks and shares led to inflation and the bursting of the Mississippi Bubble.

> The copies of gold and silver inflated,
> Which after the rape were thrown into the lake,
> At the discovery that all is exhausted
>   and dissipated by debt,
> All scripts and bonds will be wiped out.
>   Centuries VIII, quatrain 28.

Nostradamus did not overlook the Spanish Civil War:

> Franco will drive the parliament from Castile.
> The Ambassador, displeased, will cause a schism,
> The supporters of Ribiere [Rivera] will be in the fight
> And will prevent entry into the great gulf.
>   Centuries IX, quatrain 16.

The Dictator Primo de Rivera was deposed by Francisco Franco. Perhaps the great gulf refers to Communism which Spain avoided by Franco's seizure of power. It is certainly striking that Nostradamus mentioned both men in the same quatrain.

Again he envisions the air age between World Wars I and II:

> Pestilences being past, the world becomes smaller.
> Peace for a long time inhabits the land,
> People will travel safely through the sky
>   over land and seas.
> Then wars shall begin anew.
>   Centuries I, quatrain 63.

Several of the quatrains have been suggested to apply to the Kennedys since they refer to three brothers:

> The world put in trouble by three brothers,
> The great man will be struck down in the day by a thunderbolt.
> The successor will avenge his handsome brother
> And will occupy the realm under the shadow of vengeance.
> Centuries I, quatrain 26.

Centuries VIII, quatrain 46, links them in time to a Pope Paul, mentioned by name.

Modern warfare is presaged complete with oxygen masks, searchlights, tanks, whistling bombs and radio communication:

> They shall think to have seen the sun in the night
> When they see the half pig man -
> Noise, screams, battles seen fought in the skies,
> The brute beasts shall be heard to speak.
> Centuries I, quatrain 64.

The description of this vision seems to indicate that Nostradamus saw and heard the future, although he could not necessarily understand what exactly he was seeing. What actual means did Nostradamus employ to visualize events to come? He tells us in Centuries I, quatrains 1 and 2:

> Seated at night in my secret study alone, it reposes on a brass tripod, a slender flame leaps out of the solitude and makes me pronounce that which is not to be believed in vain. With divining rod in hand, in the middle of "Branches" [either the legs of the tripod or the oracle of Branchus—who gave the gift of prophecy] I moisten the hem of my garment and foot. A voice—my arms tremble with fear. Divine splendor! The divine sits nearby.

It would seem that Nostradamus used the method of a bowl of water set on a tripod, the same used by the prophetess of Branchus. A similar description is given in *De Mysteriis Egyptioru*, a fourth-century work by Iamblichus.*

He sees three "antichrist" figures in history: perhaps Napoleon, Hitler, and one yet to come, which leads into the end of the world.

> The third antichrist will be soon annihilated,
> His war of blood will last 27 years
> Heretics will be slain, enslaved, exiled.
> Blood, human bodies, crimson water, hail upon the earth.
> > Centuries VIII, quatrain 77.

Nostradamus predicts the end of the world:

> In the year 1999 and seven months,
> There will come from heaven the great King of Terror,
> To raise again the great King of the Mongols,
> Before and after, Mars shall reign at will.
> > Centuries X, quatrain 72.

And finally, Nostradamus predicted his own death:

> On returning from his embassy [the prophet had traveled to Arles representing Salon]
> The King's gift safely put away,
> He will do no more, for he will have gone to God
> By his near relations, friends and brothers
> He will be found, dead near the bed and the bench.

And so he was found, having fallen during the night of July 2, 1566—the Feast of the Visitation of Notre-Dame.

He had left instructions for his burial. Not wishing even

---

*In the 19th century this technique of divining was reintroduced in England by Francis Barrett. It was known as "scrying."

when dead to be trodden underfoot, he asked to be placed upright in the wall of the Church of Cordeliers in Salon. He left a curse on anyone who might disturb the tomb, which he also seems to have predicted. During the French Revolution his tomb was violated and the church destroyed. His bones were later removed to the chapel of Notre-Dame in the Church of St. Laurent. He also predicted his works would be more widely read after his death. Certainly of all his predictions, this one is beyond doubt.

CRIMINALLY INSANE

REIGN IN blood

SLAYER

JESUS
SAVES

NECROPHOBIC